Books which have been published in connection with the Centre for Cross-Cultural Research on Women, Queen Elizabeth House, Oxford include:

PERCEIVING WOMEN
Edited by Sheila Ardener

DEFINING FEMALES
Edited by Sheila Ardener

FIT WORK FOR WOMEN
Edited by S. Burman

WOMEN AND SPACE: GROUND RULES AND SOCIAL MAPS
Edited by Sheila Ardener

WOMEN'S RELIGIOUS EXPERIENCE
Edited by Pat Holden

THE INCORPORATED WIFE
Edited by H. Callan and Sheila Ardener

IMAGES OF WOMEN IN PEACE AND WAR
Edited by S. Macdonald, P. Holden and S. Ardener

GENDER, CULTURE AND EMPIRE
Edited by H. Callaway

NARROWING THE GENDER GAP
Edited by G. Somjee

THE PERFECT WIFE
Edited by J. Leslie

ANTHROPOLOGY AND NURSING

EDITED BY

PAT HOLDEN

AND

JENNY LITTLEWOOD

London and New York

First published in 1991
by Routledge
11 New Fetter Lane, London EC4P 4EE

Simultaneously published in the USA and Canada
by Routledge
a division of Routledge, Chapman and Hall, Inc.
29 West 35th Street, New York, NY 10001

© 1991 the collection as whole, Pat Holden and Jenny Littlewood;
each chapter, the individual contributors
© 1991 Chapter 5, Longman Group UK Limited.

Typeset by NWL Editorial Services, Langport, Somerset TA10 9DG

Printed and bound in Great Britain by
Biddles Ltd, Guildford and King's Lynn

British Library Cataloguing in Publication Data

Anthropology and nursing.
1. Medicine. Applications of anthropology
I. Holden, Pat
II. Littlewood, Jenny
610

Library of Congress Cataloging in Publication Data

also available

ISBN 0–415–00612–0
ISBN 0–415–04881–8 (pbk)

CONTENTS

Contributors   vii

Preface   x

Introduction   1

1 USING THE PAST: NURSING AND THE
  MEDICAL PROFESSION IN ANCIENT GREECE   7
  Helen King

2 THE DOCTOR'S ASSISTANT: NURSING IN
  ANCIENT INDIAN MEDICAL TEXTS   25
  Julia Leslie and Dominik Wujastyk

3 SOCIAL CHANGE IN THE NURSING
  PROFESSION IN INDIA   31
  Geeta Somjee

4 NURSING IN JAPAN   56
  Joy Hendry and Lola Martinez

5 COLONIAL SISTERS: NURSES IN UGANDA   67
  Pat Holden

CONTENTS

6 A WARD OF MY OWN: SOCIAL ORGANISATION AND IDENTITY AMONG HOSPITAL DOMESTICS 84
Liz Hart

7 NURSE OR WOMAN: GENDER AND PROFESSIONALISM IN REFORMED NURSING 1860–1923 110
Eva Gamarnikow

8 HUMAN ABUSE AND NURSING'S RESPONSE 130
Lee Ann Hoff

9 GENDER, ROLE, AND SICKNESS: THE RITUAL PSYCHOPATHOLOGIES OF THE NURSE 148
Roland Littlewood

10 CARE AND AMBIGUITY: TOWARDS A CONCEPT OF NURSING 170
Jenny Littlewood

11 NURSES BETWEEN DISEASE AND ILLNESS 190
Helle Samuelson

Bibliography 202

Name index 220

Subject index 224

CONTRIBUTORS

Eva Gamarnikow teaches Women's Studies and Sociology at the Institute of Education in Human Rights and Education. Her PhD thesis was concerned with gender and the nurse–doctor relationship in nursing reform. She is now researching struggles between nursing and medicine over the 'ownership' of anaesthesia.

Liz Hart is Lecturer in Social and Industrial Anthropology at the University of Keele. She has studied at the Universities of Keele, Cambridge, and London and at the present time is carrying out research into the work and home lives of hospital nurses.

Joy Hendry is Senior Lecturer in Social Anthropology and Japanese Society, Oxford Polytechnic; she is author of *Marriage in Changing Japan*, *Becoming Japanese*, and *Understanding Japanese Society*, and co-editor of *Interpreting Japanese Society*. Fieldwork was carried out in Fukuoka and Chiba prefectures, Japan, including association with Tateyama City Hospital.

Lee Ann Hoff is Associate Professor of Nursing and directs the Life Crisis Institute at Northeastern University in Boston. She holds graduate degrees in nursing and in social anthropology and does research on women's health issues and violence. Her teaching includes contemporary issues in nursing; women's health; social and cultural issues in health; life crises; and nursing research. Major publications include *People in Crisis* (1989) and *Battered Women as Survivors* (1990).

Pat Holden is Social Development Adviser with the Overseas Development Administration. She was previously a Research Associate at the Centre for Cross-Cultural Research on Women,

Queen Elizabeth House, Oxford. She has carried out extensive research on health in developing countries and has taught Health Studies at Sheffield City Polytechnic. Her publications include *Women's Religious Experience* (Croom Helm, 1983) and *Images of Women in Peace and War* (1987) co-edited with Shirley Ardener and Maryon McDonald.

Helen King is a Lecturer in History at St Katharine's College, Liverpool Institute of Higher Education. Her first degree was in Ancient History and Social Anthropology, and she has held research fellowships in Cambridge and Newcastle. Her work investigates the relationship between ancient Greek myth and medical writing, with particular reference to women.

Julia Leslie is a Senior Member of the Centre for Cross-Cultural Research on Women and a Research Associate of Queen Elizabeth House at Oxford University. In 1987/8 she was Visiting Lecturer and Research Associate in the Women's Studies in Religion Program at Harvard Divinity School. Her publications include *The Perfect Wife* (Oxford University Press, 1989) and a novel *Perahera* (Gollancz, 1983; Arrow, 1984; Heywood Books, 1989).

Jenny Littlewood is Senior Lecturer in Community Health in a Research Centre funded by the North East Thames Regional Health Authority, and Polytechnic of the South Bank. Her work involves carrying out applied research in general practice and community nursing. Her publications include *Community Nursing* (Churchill Livingstone, 1987), *A model for nursing using anthropological literature* (International Journal of Nursing Studies 1989).

Roland Littlewood is Reader in Psychiatry and Anthropology at University College, London, and a consultant psychiatrist at the Middlesex Hospital. His DPhil (Oxford) was based on fieldwork with a new religious movement in Trinidad. With Maurice Lipsedge he has written *Aliens and Alienists* (new edition 1989, Unwin Hyman) and with Jafar Kareem *The Theory and Practice of Intercultural Theraphy* (Blackwell – to be published 1990).

Lola Martinez is Lecturer in Anthropology at S.O.A.S. Her area is Japan, and specifically, popular culture in the media, the anthropology of tourism, ritualism and gender relations.

Helle Samuelson has worked as Assistant Programme Officer in UNICEF Quetta, Pakistan since 1987. She has a PhD in Anthropology from University of Copenhagen, Denmark (1987).

From 1985–7 she did medical anthropological research study for the Danish Cancer Society.

Geeta Somjee is a full-time researcher and international development consultant. She attended the London School of Economics and took her PhD at Baroda University. She has been a Visiting Fellow at Queen Elizabeth House, Oxford, and at Wellesley College Center for Research on Women, and has spent several years doing longitudinal field research in rural and urban India. Her published works include *Narrowing the Gender Gap* (1988) and *Reaching Out to the Poor*, with A. H. Somjee (1989, both London, Macmillan).

Dominik Wujastyk is on the staff of the Wellcome Institute for the History of Medicine in London, with responsibility for cataloguing the Institute's large Sanskrit manuscript collection. His publications include the first volume of a Handlist of this collection and an edited volume, with G. Jan Meulenbeld, *Studies on Indian Medical History with Egbert Forsten* (1987).

PREFACE

This book arose out of a workshop convened by Pat Holden and held by the Centre for Cross-Cultural Research on Women, Queen Elizabeth House, in April 1986. The Centre consists of a group of women researchers with mainly anthropological research interests. The workshop was attended by anthropologists, sociologists, historians and representatives of the medical and nursing professions. The aim was to develop new insights into nursing as a topic of anthropological study. The workshop demonstrated what a rich and interesting field the profession presents. Jenny Littlewood has subsequently convened three further workshops on the anthropology of nursing including one on disability and one looking at anthropology in nurse education, at the Centre for Primary Care, London. These workshops have provided academic researchers and nurses with an opportunity to share insights and for nurses to consider the relevance of these to their everyday work. As a result, an anthropology of nursing group has been formed with plans for future workshops. The idea for this book owes much to the late Edwin Ardener whose influential writings on women as 'muted' groups enabled female anthropologists in the 1970s and 1980s to explore the ways in which women experience the world as a separate reality from that of men and to evaluate positively that experience.

P. Holden and J. Littlewood
February 1990

INTRODUCTION

This book deliberately sets out to be an anthropology of nursing rather than an anthropology for nurses. The importance of drawing this distinction was particularly emphasised at a recent gathering of nurses and anthropologists in London.

For the anthropologist who is not a nurse by training, nursing provides an ethnographic field to be studied like any other. It has its own esoteric language, symbolic systems, and collective identity–features which define the traditional anthropological areas of study. The social anthropologist is concerned with documenting and analysing the rites and practices of this group as s(he) might any other. Most of the contributors in this book – anthropologists, sociologists, or historians, some of whom have a background in health care – adopt this approach.

For nurses anthropology has recently assumed a new dimension. It has begun to appear as a subject in health courses and in schools of nursing. The implications of this are that it is being seen increasingly as a 'tool' to be used by nurses in their everyday working lives and not just as an academic subject. This can loosely be referred to as anthropology for nurses.

The reasons for this incorporation of the subject into syllabuses is not difficult to ascertain. Most western societies are now what is referred to as 'multicultural'. Nurses, usually defined for this purpose as predominantly white and middle class, increasingly encounter people from ethnic minorities whose perceptions of the body, notions of the self, of illness, and of social attitudes towards illness and disease can differ radically from their own. As a number of contributors in this book point out, the western scientific medical paradigm remains in the ascendancy and the nurse is

1

placed at the interface between western medical values and the values of patients. Social anthropology is thus seen as providing the nurse with the means for better understanding her/his patient.

This approach, however, is not without pitfalls. North America now has a large transcultural nursing 'movement' established as a sub-discipline in universities and nursing schools. The aim of the 'movement' is to increase the knowledge of specific cultures amongst nurses in order to develop their understanding of other peoples. It involves the development of what are referred to as 'transcultural' theories and the movement has become the body which defines what constitutes specific cultures and the implications of this for treatment.

Herein lies the problem. It is by now a truism of social anthropology that cultural identity and the world culture itself are infinitely manipulable concepts. The question needs to be seriously addressed within schools of nursing, both in America and Europe, as to whether such checklists of cultural attributes help the nurse to provide a better service or provide her/him unwittingly with the power to label and socially control the patient.

This book argues that it may be desirable to see the nurse as an ethnographic fieldworker. This method requires the interplay between the instrument – the researcher – and the field through observation and the language of informants (verbal and symbolic). The end product is the creation of a coherent world view based on intimate observation, but acceptable only if it is recognised by those observed. A good ethnography enlarges people's understanding of themselves. Like the anthropologist, the nurse must be immersed in understanding the patient's world and see patterns and relationships in behaviour and ideas that are intelligible.

The study of anthropology does indeed appear to have provided some nurses with new perspectives on their own profession. As a speaker noted at the anthropology of nursing workshop, with the advent of new technology and changes in medical care anthropology may in the end be most useful to the nurse in addressing the problem for her or him of 'who am I or what is my role?'. The emphasis in the medical profession on scientific 'objectivity' and conformity to scientific paradigms has indeed resulted in a movement within nursing research into the more qualitative methods of anthropology. Samuelson's paper on cancer patients in Denmark makes the point that the nurse acting as ethnographer among her/his patients can provide them with insights which can be positive aids in the treatment and healing process.

Davies (1980) in the influential *Rewriting Nursing History* challenges the 'largely congratulatory' view that the history of nursing as it is conventionally presented is 'an advance...progress out of the dark ages to the present modern times'. Davies' work and that of her contributors is informed by a feminist perspective which sees modern nursing as located 'unambiguously within patriarchally constructed femininity' (Gamarnikow) because it is the professional embodiment of traditional female attributes such as passivity, self-sacrifice devotion and subordination. This book continues the process of historical deconstruction but also shows that nursing, while essentially a Western professional construct which developed within particular historical circumstances, has been variously understood and interpreted in different societies. As Somjee, writing about nursing in India says 'the term nurse evokes different reactions in different cultures, despite the fact they all probably begin with an image of someone who handles socially less desirable things such as the bedpan'. Many of these different perceptions are illustrated in this book for countries such as Japan, India and Uganda. Nevertheless, there are many common themes which cut across history and culture.

SYNOPSIS OF THE CHAPTERS

Helen King's work is an analysis of early Greek texts. She looks for the description of a 'nurse' which is not apparent. The *iatros* or Greek doctor, she suggests, keeps an intimate supervisory role in respect of all his care 'lest those tasks which we call nursing receive the credit for the cure'. Further, her analysis of fourth and fifth century Greek texts found most women seen as 'natural patients as even in health she cannot exercise full control' (a theme seen later in Roland Littlewood's paper on UK nurses). It was seen as 'unnatural' for women to look after men as they might take advantage of man's state of being out of control.

Julia Leslie and Dominik Wujastyk explore Indian textual material, contemporaneous with Helen King's material from Greek history, on nursing. 'Nurses' are given mention 'though brief and general'. The term nurse in its current form suggests an independent vocation so Helen King and Dominik Wujastyk explore rather the term 'helper' – the doctor's assistant. Cleanliness and dexterity are common to doctor and assistant. Knowledge and experience are essential doctor qualities, whereas ability to wait on someone and loyalty to the doctor are the qualities of the helper. The sex of the helper is determined by the sex of the patient. 'One who stands nearby ready to serve' is one of the four factors necessary for alleviation of disease.

The notion of cleanliness, obedience, and loyalty is followed through to modern-day India, Japan, and Uganda, where class association with the nurse is important, and where the uniform is explored as a symbol of authority and cleanliness. Geeta Somjee's chapter on 'Nursing in India' shows how changes in the nursing profession reflected the changes in Indian society as a whole.

Joy Hendry and Lola Martinez explore illness in Japan at a time when family and relatives can express the closeness of their relationships non-verbally. Cleanliness and hygiene are very important. They distinguish the Japanese ideas of 'inside' and 'outside'. 'Inside' are people close to you with whom one would 'share one's germs' (shown in the sharing of drinking cups). This contrasts with 'outside', non-relatives or close family who are 'dirty'. This applies to hospitals which are peopled with 'outsiders'. Joy and Lola suggest that close relatives contain and care for their sick relative in hospital, and preserve an unpolluted space around their relative's bed by surrounding the bed by relatives and friends. Japanese ideas on healing incorporate a 'holistic' approach. The patient is affected by the environment, physical and social, and the focal point is therefore not the doctor–patient relationship but the family and community in which the patient lives. Like nurses in India, nurses in Japan are perceived as being concerned with pollution and so the profession has difficulty attracting women from other than lower social classes.

Pat Holden, in her exploration of Ugandan nurses, shows how nurses inherited the colonial ideas of the selection of nurses from 'the right type of woman' and class. The control of sexuality, the use of the uniform as a symbol of order and cleanliness changed with the crisis within the hospital. This in turn reflected, as in Geeta Somjee's chapter, wider social changes. The outstanding feature in Pat Holden's observations was, at a time of economic crisis and general disorder and breakdown of the hospital service, the continued use of a perfectly laundered uniform worn by the nurse. As society disintegrated, so did order and discipline within the hospital change. The separation of 'hands-on care' from technical care has removed an essential part of their role. Relatives now carry out the hands-on care. The introduction of the eastern style of relatives caring for patients disrupted the western notion of order and control. In Uganda, relatives' care was a part of an integral symbolic system and understanding of what constituted illness, as in Japan. This was in conflict with the Ugandan nurses' colonial ideas, as in the western healing system relatives have no place in the hospital, since it is a symbolically different system.

Much of contemporary nursing in the UK is concerned with the role of 'helper' and the acknowledgement of much of the care for the patient being carried out by relatives and unskilled helpers. Within the ward there is dissension over control order and what might constitute dirt – the theme of Liz Hart's chapter on ward domestics. She explores the ward as the symbolic home and how integral a part of it is the cleaning. Cleaning, however, is traditionally a woman's role. Ward domestics and nurses are women and the boundary between the two is fluid. The domestics take pride in their work and build up a caring relationship and network with the patient's relatives, an aspect of care destroyed in the privatisation of this sector of women's work.

The first chapters introduce the sexual division of labour debate and the development of what might constitute 'a nurse'. Eva Gamarnikow's chapter looks at the debate about the profession-alisation of nursing. This was perceived, on the one hand, by doctors who saw gender difference as the ultimate way of selecting and controlling their helpers, and that 'women are peculiarly suited to this', and, on the other hand, by women as the recognition that women's work was professional work. Nurses were therefore advised to use gender not as an adjunct to professional subordination, but to mitigate its effects.

Lee Ann Hoff looks at women as victims and suggests that nurses as women are victims of a dominant, essentially male profession. Rather than take this model further, she uses as the model physical violence, which she equates with the increasing oppression of women/nurses in hospital.

Roland Littlewood's chapter explores earlier themes of gender relations in nursing and medicine, and suggests that the patient has essentially female characteristics and the doctor male characteristics. The nurse–doctor dyad is similar to the female (patient)–male (doctor) relations. In a similar theme to that of Helen King's chapter, Roland suggests that women are medicalised in everyday life in a way that is not so for men. He examines the everyday contexts from which the sick role is derived. He points to the fact that the common measure of nursing 'morale' on a ward is the extent of sick leave. Its relevance in this chapter is to thinking about high absenteeism, high drop-out rates, and high levels of sickness in nursing – still predominantly a female profession. In order to understand it, he suggests, we need to examine the symbolism of the nurse and medicalisation of women.

Jenny Littlewood's chapter explores further the theme of women as carers. The chapter examines the position of the nurse as the manager of ambiguity. She is seen to straddle the classificatory divide. Bodily excretions are part of and not part of self; she mediates between doctor and patient; and she helps maintain the sick person in the social world by restating tempero-spatial relations.

In the final chapter Helle Samuelson looks at one aspect of the theme in Jenny Littlewood's chapter, that of the nurse being a mediator between doctors and patients in relation to cancer. As in the chapter by Joy Hendry and Lola Martinez, Helle Samuelson explores the nurse's role in respect of the biological, social, and psychological components of healing rather than the strict search for pathology.

The world of the nurse as explored in this book is not that of facts and figures and controlled experiments or of the prestige associated with the wielding of the knife but, as this book shows, that of cleanliness, control of excreta, blood, urine, birth, and death. It relates to her symbolic role in healing and shows how the doctor–patient relationship and hospitals as healing institutions are symbolic of wider social structures. It also shows that, while the content of the nurse's work may differ in different societies, her universal role, that of caring, is restating that particular society's cultural values. Each culture has its own special risks and problems and in that it does, and that nurses articulate these systems by ritually protecting the person from reduced marginality, her role will differ in different societies.

NOTE

1. Frankenberg R. (1988) *Medical Anthropological Quarterly* 2: 458.

Chapter One

USING THE PAST: NURSING AND THE MEDICAL PROFESSION IN ANCIENT GREECE

HELEN KING

> Ancient and modern medicine are far removed from one
> another. And the difference is one not only of detail, but of
> fundamental outlook.
>
> (Edelstein 1931: 110)

Since the publication in 1980 of Celia Davies's volume, *Rewriting
Nursing History*, the development has continued of a new
anthropology and history of nursing to replace the traditional
model of 'progress out of the dark ages to the present, modern
times' (Davies 1980: 11): the Sarah Gamp to Florence Nightingale
model questioned by one of the contributors to Davies's collection,
Katherine Williams. Modern nursing is usually thought to have
emerged from its 'dark ages' only in the mid-nineteenth century,
and in view of this it may seem that the study of classical Greek
medicine has little to contribute. In this chapter, however, I want
not only to look at the limited role played by the ancient Greeks
in the construction of the nursing past used by traditional histories
of nursing and medicine, but also to suggest a much wider range
of contributions which this particular historical period could make
to the new anthropology and history of nursing.

The argument falls into three parts. It is first necessary to make
some introductory remarks about healing in the ancient world, in
order to provide a background from which to approach the very
different picture given by the highly schematic, 'broadbrush'
(Davies 1980: 11) histories used by the medical and nursing
professions. The second part considers nursing and the ancient
world in more detail, using the social position of medicine in

ancient Greece to suggest why it is institutionally inappropriate for the nursing profession to try to find precursors in the classical Greek world. The final part uses the limited sources available in a more controversial way, trying to uncover wider ideologies of male and female, and suggesting the range of cultural material affecting the position of nursing in any society.

HEALERS AND ACTORS

In contrast to what generations of medical men and women writing to convince us of the antiquity of their professions would have us believe, the professional position of medical practitioners in the ancient world was most unlike that with which we are familiar today. The needs of a professional history have combined with the traditionally high valuation of classical Greek civilisation to produce a very selective picture of rational, empirical medicine in which, as Joly puts it, Hippocratic medicine is seen as 'very close to contemporary medicine', if not in some ways superior to it (1983: 29).

Recent work by classical scholars, however, allows us to reassess the position of the medical practitioners whose writings, dating from the fifth century BC onwards, survive in the texts known as the Hippocratic corpus.[1] These are the *iatroi*, usually translated as 'doctors' or 'physicians', but which simply means 'healers' (Van Brock 1961). We cannot know how far their type of healing differed from the therapies offered by other healers in the society, but what is significantly different is the way in which they try to set themselves apart from other groups concerned with health (Lloyd 1979: 37–49). Briefly, the *iatroi* are all male; they have an image of their own craft which makes it into a coherent system of cause and effect rather than an *ad hoc* combination of unexplained remedies; and although they place their work in the context of the divinely established order of the universe,[2] they do not regard any particular deity as responsible for the cures which they effect.

Their main claim for the sort of medicine which they practise covers all of these points, and has even wider implications. They claim that what they do is a *techne*, and it is important to understand what this means, since it is directly comparable to claims made by medical groups in other periods and societies. In the fifth century BC, the definition of what was and what was not a *techne* occupied drama as well as philosophy. In Aeschylus' play

Prometheus, the culture hero describes medicine as the greatest of all the *technai*. In the distant past, if someone suffered from a disease, he could not be cured; but Prometheus has shown men 'how to drive away diseases' (478–83). Many Hippocratic medical texts are attempts to demonstrate that medicine is a *techne*; *Regimen* 1.12–24 (Jones 1923: 4.250–62) places it in a long list of all the *technai*. But why does it matter so much to have this status? A *techne* has been defined as a 'practical activity that required intellectual competence as well as manual dexterity, was based on scientific knowledge, produced results that it was possible to verify, and was governed by well-defined rules that could be transmitted by teaching' (Ferrari and Vegetti 1983: 202; cf. Edelstein 1931: 106). This definition does not go far enough, for a *techne* also has a particular place in Greek culture and thought. It concerns man's ability to rise above the level of the beasts and to approach the status of a god. One view of the development from past to present current in classical Greece held that, by acquiring the skills of the *technai*, man gradually climbed from a bestial past to the present level of civilisation (cf. Cole 1967). In a way, the *technai* thus define what it is to be human; they are thought to be at the core of civilised Greek life.

The *iatroi* produce written texts describing their cases and remedies and discussing the nature of disease, thus demonstrating their intellectual as well as manual skills. Prose-writing is, however, at a very early stage in the fifth century (Lonie 1981; Lloyd 1983: 115–19), and the way in which they write and argue shows that they are also adept in the art of speaking (Jouanna 1984); of presenting an argument verbally in order to defeat a rival in public debate (Lloyd 1979: 96–8) or to persuade the client or potential client of the value of their therapies. Many of these therapies are in themselves highly dramatic forms of display. In a famous text, a writer condemns those who practise the spectacular therapy of succussion on a ladder, in which the patient is tied to a ladder and violently shaken. This could be done for many reasons; for example, to reduce fractures (*On Joints* 42–4/Withington 3.282–8), for prolapse of the womb (*Diseases of Women* 3.248/L 8.462), or to induce labour (*Diseases of Women* 1.68/L 8.142–4). It is known to be dangerous (*Epidemics* 5.103/L 5.258), but is continued because of its power to impress 'the crowds'; even the writer who condemns it admits that sometimes it is very useful (*On Joints* 42–4/Withington

9

3.282–8; Edelstein 1931: 94). Another writer advises his fellow *iatroi* not to use 'theatrical' bandages, because they imply quackery (*The Doctor* 4/L 9.208–10).

The element of theatre in medical presentation of self is explicit in some of these texts. Healers who deceive the crowds are described as being easily recognised by their extravagant clothing, elaborate perfume, and habit of quoting the poets (*Decorum* 2/Jones 2.280; *Precepts* 10, 12/Jones 1.326; Lloyd 1979: 89–90). Another writer compares those who have only 'the appearance, dress and mask' of doctors with non-speaking parts in tragedy, played by people unable to act, but masked and costumed in character (*Law* 1/Jones 2.262). However, the simple undecorated clothes and pleasant perfumes recommended by the writers of the same texts (*Decorum* 3/Jones 2.280; *The Doctor* 1/Jones 2.310) could themselves be regarded as the costume necessary in order to assume a role.[3]

The Hippocratic healer is thus orator and actor as much as writer and scholar. He accepts the 'well-defined rules' of his *techne* and certain basic principles – perhaps some version of the four humours, or the principles of hot, cold, wet, and dry – but feels free to innovate within these and to disagree in public with other practitioners in order to attract a clientele, while claiming all the time that he is part of a fully developed craft established in the past (e.g. *Places in man* 46/L 6.342). Others professing the same craft may disagree on how far one can go in playing to the crowds, but there is nobody to enforce standards, and no system of training which hands out diplomas to the successful; anyone can claim to be a *iatros*. The *iatros* is thus much closer to what we would class as a travelling quack than to the members of the British Medical Association.

BLAME AND GLORY

What of nursing within this? Wet nurses and children's nurses certainly existed in the ancient world (cf. Herfst 1922; on the Roman world, Joshel 1986); hospital nurses did not exist, because there were no hospitals. My remarks here will be restricted to the field of nursing the sick at home. In his article on doctors in the ancient world for the Daremberg and Saglio encyclopaedia of antiquity, Reinach devotes one sentence to nursing in the ancient world: 'It goes without saying that women, being so to speak born sick-bed attendants and nurses, have at all times carried out these functions' (1904: s.v. Medicus 1682–3). Jones writes more cautiously: 'The conclusion we are tempted to draw ... is that the task of nursing fell to the women, whether slaves or free, of the household' (1923: xxx). Deloughery too assumes that, in the ancient Greek world, nursing was 'an incidental household duty' (1977: 8–9). The assumptions behind such statements, and the cultural differences which they hide, need to be examined further.

The medical profession in later historical periods has made much of its Hippocratic origins, seeing the great Hippocrates as a superb doctor (according to whatever criteria of superb doctors are currently in fashion); rational, positivist, empirical. Histories of nursing have an obvious debt to the errors of traditional medical history. In particular, they praise Hippocrates for his powers of careful observation of the course of a disease – which, for nursing history, is translated as his discovery of 'patient-centred medicine' (Dolan 1978: 34, based on a 1958 rewriting of Goodnow 1919; but see Edelstein 1931: 88 n.3) – and they repeat the idea that he led medicine out of the sphere of religion into that of science. To quote from a standard history of nursing: 'Hippocrates ... stands out as a real person. The chief contribution of his school was to render the magic of medicine into a science' (Jensen 1943: 35; repeated in the 8th edition of Deloughery 1977: 8–9). This is entirely a medical myth; although Plato's *Phaedrus* 270b-c and *Protagoras* 311b-c show that Hippocrates existed as a healer, writer, and instructor famous in his own time, it is difficult to use the Platonic description of the 'Hippocratic method' to show beyond any doubt that any particular text of the Hippocratic corpus was by this writer (Smith 1979; cf. Joly 1983; Mansfield 1983). The rational parts of Hippocratic medicine have historically been over-emphasised at the expense of the sections where remedies are, in our terms, purely magical – the rat droppings and stag's penis school of medicine (Lloyd 1983: 132) – and the idea of the move from religious to scientific healing under the auspices of Hippocrates and his followers is historically inaccurate, since the temple medicine of Asklepios flourishes with and after Hippocratic medicine (Lloyd 1979: 40–6).

In its overviews of ancient medicine, the nursing profession thus follows the historically inaccurate picture of classical Greek medicine propounded by the medical profession and by positivist

11

histories of science, under which medicine in the Hippocratic period is misrepresented as an established and carefully regulated profession, bringing rationality where there was superstition and empirical observation where there was blind dogma. Like medical history, nursing history uses Hippocratic medicine as a precursor, so that histories of nursing invariably have a section on 'Greece'; even if they preface it with perfectly accurate remarks such as that of Guthrie, who writes that 'Hippocrates does not refer to nurses as such' (1953: xi), they invariably find some aspect of Hippocratic medicine which can be used to provide an origin for the profession. Dock and Stewart, for example, suggest that Hippocrates detailed the technique of 'what we now call nursing' (4th edition 1938: 32). In a more recent work we read that the Greeks were:

> the first Western group to become conscious of the need for a
> trained nurse. Though they met this need with apprentices
> and attendants rather than a separate occupational group,
> merely that the need was recognised is extremely important
> in the history of nursing.
> (Bullough and Bullough 1979: 19; cf. Dolan 1978: 33–4)

I would now like to look at what such histories include in these sections, and at their implicit assumptions.

One view found in histories of nursing is that there must have been nurses of some sort in the ancient world; who else could have performed the tasks which we now associate with the nurse? A doctor would not have time to bandage, bathe, mix drugs, sponge the patient and apply poultices (Robinson 1946: 20; cf. Jones 1931: xxx). 'Women doubtless did much noble, if unnoticed work among the sick' (Pavey 1938: 61). In the ancient world, care of the sick was ideally performed by other members of the household or, as in Thucydides' description of the plague, by one's friends (2.51). In some cases, the carer would thus be female; but is there anything to suggest a *preference* for women in this role? In the classical Greek period, the age of Hippocratic medicine, one source which merits mention in the histories of nursing is the advice of Ischomachos to his young wife on household management, which includes the assumption that it is the duty of the wife to ensure that sick slaves are cared for (Xenophon *Oikonomikos* 7.37). It should however be noted that she is apparently not expected to care for them herself.

Another famous example of women in a 'nursing' role comes from a legal case of the mid-fourth century BC in which a sick man, Phrastor, who has quarrelled with his own family and has no children, is eventually cared for by his estranged wife and her mother. They come to his home bringing 'things suitable for the illness',[4] and they 'watch over' him. There is no mention of a healer being summoned,[5] although the patient is so ill that 'his sickness, his childlessness, the care [*therapeia*] of the women and his enmity towards his own kin' persuade him to recognise as legitimate his son by his estranged wife. The important phrase for the history of nursing can be translated as: 'You yourselves know how valuable a woman is in illness, being there to help a sick person' ([Demosthenes], *Against Neaira* 59. 55–60).

To an extent, the presence of any member of the family or friend is better than being ill alone; this comes across clearly in many texts (e.g. Thucydides 2.51; Isocrates 19). This passage should not, however, be read out of context. It is said in order to explain to the audience – the jury – how the sick man comes to agree to recognise the child; the verb used to describe how the women achieved this is *psychagogeo*, literally 'to lead the soul' and thus meaning 'to persuade' or 'to delude'. The reference to women helping the sick is not therefore straightforward praise of their nursing abilities; on the contrary, it points out that when a man is weakened by illness, even a woman can prevail over him.[6]

Nursing histories often refer to the tradition, in both Greek and Roman culture, associating drugs with women; for example, in Homer, Agamede, the daughter of King Augeas, knows 'all the *pharmaka* of the earth' (*Iliad* 11.739–41; cf. Seymer 1932: 13), while Helen of Troy has a *pharmakon* which dispels grief (*Odyssey* 4.220–32). However, as the second passage goes on to make clear, the Greek *pharmakon* means both healing drug and poison.[7] Such a tradition may therefore tell us more about fear of death from a woman's hand than about healing's division of labour in the Greek household. In the Roman world, the emperor Claudius is alleged to have been poisoned by his wife Agrippina, aided by the famous female poisoner, Locusta, and the doctor, Xenophon. After an unsuccessful attempt is made on her life, Agrippina shows another side of 'knowledge of *pharmaka*'; not only has she already taken antidotes to stop poison affecting her, but she also treats herself for her wounds (Tacitus *Annals* 12.66–7; 14.5–6).

13

Two points emerge from this. First, the connection of women with nursing and drugs does not necessarily stem from gentle and caring qualities thought to be 'feminine'; instead, it may owe more to the idea of woman as dangerous outsider taking advantage of illness to further her schemes. Second, the tendency to imagine that there must have been women attendants by the patient's bed, which presents as natural a division of labour between busy male doctor and noble, unnoticed female nurse, is no more than a reading of the past in the image of the present.

As I have already indicated, Hippocratic doctors are not modern doctors. Writing of the pre-seventeenth-century period in general, Connor Versluysen suggests that there was 'little formal distinction between what were thought of as "doctoring" and "nursing" tasks' (1980: 187–8). Another way of using the Greek evidence is thus to show that the distinction between 'doctoring' and 'nursing' was not made. This approach is more helpful than that which assumes there were female 'nurses' but that we cannot see them. It is true that not just diagnosis, prescription, and complex medical procedures, but also the application of the treatment and the monitoring of the patient's environment, formed essential parts of the process of building up a reputation and impressing the patient and the other members of the household. It is useful here to quote at some length from the translation given by Jones of sections of the text called *Decorum*:

> You must practise these things with all reserve, in the matter of palpation, anointing, washing, to ensure elegance in moving the hands, in the matter of lint, compresses, bandages, ventilation and purges ... bear in mind your manner of sitting, reserve, arrangement of dress, decisive utterance, brevity of speech, composure, bedside manners, care, replies to objections, calm self-control to meet the troubles that occur, rebuke of disturbance, readiness to do what has to be done.... The bed also must be considered.... Consider also noises and smells.... Perform all this calmly and adroitly, concealing most things from the patient while you are attending to him. Give necessary orders with cheerfulness and serenity, turning his attention away from what is being done to him; sometimes reprove sharply and emphatically, and sometimes comfort with solicitude and attention.
>
> (8, 12, 15, 16/Jones 2.290–8)

14

By the definitions familiar to us today, much of this creation of an environment conducive to recovery is covered by what we call *nursing*. However, the point that much of Hippocratic medicine was, in our terms, 'nursing' should not prevent us from noting that such tasks were seen very differently in the ancient Greek medical context. Rather than being associated with a caring and submissive female assistant, they are part of the world of the male *iatros* who performs as much as possible of his recommended treatment himself, in order to impress the patient and the patient's family, and to receive the glory when the patient recovers. As *Decorum* 17 (Jones 2.298) puts it: 'Let there be no doubt about the points which will secure the success of your plan, and no blame will attach to you, but achievement will bring you pride [*ganos*, lit. "brightness"].' *Iatroi* performed 'nursing' tasks at least partly to ensure that they were credited with the cure.

The question of blame and glory influences other aspects of the behaviour of the *iatros*. He is careful not to take on hopeless cases (e.g. *The Art* 3/Jones 2.192; *Prognostic* 1/Jones 2.6–8; Edelstein 1931: 93–4); he often blames the patient; and he makes only limited use of any type of assistant. These last two points should be examined in more detail.

The Hippocratic *iatros* may present a model of *iatros*–patient interaction in which the patient is expected to ask questions and the *iatros* to respond (e.g. *Diseases* 1.1/L 6.140–2), but he may have a very low opinion of the competence of the patient: Edelstein (1913: 99) summarises this by saying, 'The patient is believed to be credulous, devoid of real judgement, and a liar'. *Decorum* 14 reads:

> Keep a watch also on the faults of the patient, which often make them lie about the taking of things prescribed. For through not taking disagreeable drinks, purgative or other, they sometimes die. What they have done never results in a confession, but the blame is thrown upon the physician.
>
> (Jones 2.296)

The point that patients do not always obey orders is also made by *The Art* 7 (Jones 2.200–2). Some *iatroi* associate these characteristics with female patients in particular. In the case histories of the *Epidemics*, reports from female patients are sometimes modified by the *iatros* adding, 'if this was true, I do not know' (*Epidemics* 4.6/L

15

5.146) or 'so she said' (*Epidemics* 4.20/L 5.160; 4.22/5.162). Of a woman in *Epidemics* 3.2.14 (Jones 1.280), we are told 'she would not obey orders' (cf. Lloyd 1983: 68 and n.38).

The *iatros* is right; the patient is wrong. However, there is a further possibility which should be taken into account; the patient may be using the wrong healer. Bearing in mind the competitive nature of medicine in the ancient world, it is perhaps not surprising that the *iatroi* often criticise other groups of healers; for example, the famous treatise *On the Sacred Disease* condemns magicians, purifiers, wandering beggars, and quacks, who offer purification, chanting, food taboos, and divine intervention (Jones 2.138 ff.). We also meet diviners, priests, midwives, and root-cutters (Lloyd 1979: 15–29; 1983: 208–9), and drugs (*pharmaka*) are sold in the market by 'drug-sellers' ([Aristotle] *Oikonomikos* 134b22; Aristophanes *Clouds* 766–8). The root-cutters, like the *iatroi*, wrote books; fragments survive of the *Roots* by Crateuas, a root-cutter of the first century BC. Members of such informal groupings are not seen as being within the medical *techne*, and so are usually criticised by others as 'deceivers', but the knowledge that they exist must strengthen the *iatros* in his determination to keep the patient by impressing the household with his demeanour and skills.

The spirit of competition, however, also extends to other acknowledged *iatroi*; although all are supposed to belong to the same *techne*, one *iatros* may be better than the others. Some *iatroi* are too keen on impressing the crowds; others have manual skills, but no intelligence (*On Joints* 33/Withington 3.262). Sometimes the fault lies with those who call in a good *iatros* when it is too late; a case history of a woman who aborts either deliberately or spontaneously says, 'I saw her on the fourth day' (*Epidemics* 5.53/L 5.238). Is this because another *iatros*, or another type of healer, was previously employed? In this case, the patient dies on the fourth night. Another case history describes 'the man struck in the groin by an arrow, whom we ourselves saw' (*Epidemics* 5.46/L 5.234); does this mean that the writer sometimes describes cases he has only heard about from others? In the case of Tychon, wounded in the chest, 'it seemed to me that the *iatros* who took out the wood left part of the spear-point in the diaphragm'. After treatment Tychon 'seemed to the *iatros* and the others to be better', but on the third day he died (*Epidemics* 5.95/L 5.254–6). What is the status of the writer here? Did he himself ever see the patient?

Such texts as these, problematic as they are in terms of the relationship between the writer and the case (cf. King 1989), at least show that the wish to keep the case to oneself could extend to criticism of other *iatroi*. Sometimes, in contrast, it is considered beneficial to summon other *iatroi* to discuss the patient and to help; the writer recommending this, however, also feels that it is necessary to point out that such *iatroi* must not argue among themselves, because this could be seen as a sign of weakness (*Precepts* 8/Jones 1.322). Competition did not necessarily cease at the bedside.

Patients, and other healers of all types, were therefore regarded with a certain unease; they could lead to the *iatros* being blamed when his orders, had they been followed properly, would have led to a cure. What, however, of those working directly under the healer's instructions? The evidence on assistants in Hippocratic medicine is meagre, but it can be supplemented from other sources. There is no special word for a 'medical assistant'; instead, the verb *pareimi*, 'to be present, to stand by', is used in a number of passages. For example, when the 'wife of Theodoros' had a fit of madness in the course of her illness, she 'railed at the assistants' or more literally 'railed at those present' (*Epidemics* 7.25/L 5.394–8). In a discussion of the *oikonomia*, 'household management', of the sick person, 'things concerning the attendants' – or 'things concerning the others present' – are mentioned as something which the doctor should try to take into account (*Epidemics* 6.2.24/L 5.290; cf. *Aphorisms* 1.2/Jones 4.98). If the translation 'assistants' is used, such passages imply people in a specific role, although not necessarily one for which they are formally trained; if, on the other hand, we translate as 'the other people present', then we are suggesting that these are merely other members of the household who may or may not be of assistance to the *iatros*.

In the treatise *Regimen in Acute Diseases* 65 (Jones 2.120), the writer, while recommending baths, notes that few houses have the equipment or the *therapeusontes* for this. Jones translates as 'attendants', and the connection of the Greek word with our 'therapy' may encourage us to see these as medical attendants in a specific role. However, the verb from which it is derived means 'to do service to' (Van Brock 1961: 138) and the most likely translation here may be 'household members', including both kin

17

and slaves. It is while Phrastor is without anyone to *therapeuein* his disease that his estranged wife and her mother arrive, and in another law court speech of the early fourth century BC the male speaker tells the court how he *etherapeusa* ('cared for') a patient for many months with the aid of a male slave, losing much sleep and suffering greatly (Isocrates 19.24–8). 'Nursing' is thus not exclusively a female role; it does not require training and, in the absence of a *iatros* who has economic reasons for assuming control over all aspects of the case, the resources of the household are used rather than any other professional groups.

In the gynaecological texts, another role can be discovered; that of the 'other woman' who assists in the examination of some patients. Is she another member of the household, an assistant of the *iatros*, or a healer in her own right? In most cases the term used translates as simply 'a woman' or 'another woman' (e.g. *Diseases of Women* 1.21/L 8.60; 3.213/L 8.408, 410), and I would suggest that this is simply any experienced woman who happens to be present. In *Excision of the Foetus* 4 (L8.514–6) 'two women' take the legs of a patient who is to be shaken to speed up labour and 'another two women' take her arms. In *Diseases of Women* 1.68 (L 8.144) a similar shaking is used to remove a dead foetus; here 'two men' help to shake the patient, and a 'female healer', designated by *iatreousa* (from the same root as *iatros*), removes the foetus and the umbilical cord.

These gynaecological examples show how 'the other people present' can be enlisted to help the *iatros*; they support the suggestion that these are mostly untrained members of the household, used as required to supplement the resources of the *iatros*. Where a *iatros* is not employed, they watch over the patient and provide what is necessary. Where a *iatros* is called in, they help in procedures requiring more than one person to perform them (baths, succussion) or where they have a particular quality or skill needed by the *iatros*; for example, a boy or a woman can help reshape a broken nose, because they have soft hands (*On Joints* 37/Jones 3.270).

A further passage which occurs frequently in histories of nursing is *Decorum* 17 (Jones 2.298; cf. Jones 1923: xxxi; Robinson 1946: 21; Bullough and Bullough 1979: 17), which mentions 'apprentices' (literally, 'those learning') who can be left in charge of the patient to carry out the instructions of the *iatros*, to administer treatment, and to watch for any change. As medicine is a *techne*, a craft, one way to enter it is through working under a good practitioner (Edelstein 1931: 90), although this is not the only way, since an individual could always impress the crowds by less formal means. The success of an 'apprentice' only increases the reputation of his master, provided that the latter makes it clear who is giving the instructions and to whom any changes should be reported.

It is thus possible to show that, in the ancient world, 'doctors' performed 'nursing' tasks for culturally specific, institutional reasons. Rather than leaving such tasks to invisible but noble women, the *iatros* had a strong incentive for carrying them out himself, since it was through successful and impressive treatment that he established his own authority and gained further cases. With the exception of the apprentices, who were already dependent on their master, assistants of either sex would have no fixed role and would not always be trained, but would be brought in as needed and as available, in order to further the doctor's glory.

POWER AND CONTROL

There is, however, a further objection to the proposal that the tasks we call 'nursing' must have been carried out by a person – particularly a female person – other than the *iatros*, and this takes us into the realms of Greek philosophy of the person and of gender difference. The male–female relationship is central to the anthropology of nursing; nursing has been described as 'an excellent case study of males exploiting females' (Hoekelman 1975: 1150–2, cited in Fitzpatrick 1977: 831). Also important is the role of authority, since nurses have traditionally been seen as 'submissive and dependent on physicians for whatever authority they exercised' (Fitzpatrick 1977: 822). The definition of a 'good nurse' in a given society can be seen to reproduce that of the 'good woman' in general (Gamarnikow 1978: 98 and 114–16).

Foucault's work brings together these themes of sexual difference and authority (1984). Several chapters in Davies use his studies of madness and of the prison system to provide a theoretical framework. The recently published volumes 2 and 3 of his *History of Sexuality* concentrate on the ancient world, and discuss the conception of moral behaviour in the period under consideration here. To summarise Foucault's argument, the Greeks defined moral behaviour in relation to self rather than in

19

relation to an overriding code of action. Whereas a moral code lists what is permitted or forbidden, Greek morality is about weighing up all the variables – one's sex, age, individual nature – and the current conditions, such as the time of year, the location, the winds, and the environment, and only then assessing what would be the best course of behaviour (*Regimen* 1.2/Jones 4.226–30). The important virtues are moderation and self-control; it is primarily for the individual to assess his condition and correct his diet, exercise, and so on. The most important text here is Aristotle's *Nicomachean Ethics*, which discusses the principle of 'the mean', and the dangers of excess and defect (*NE* 1104a25 ff.); it is following the mean which is the route to moral excellence, and this involves exercising the powers of choice and reason in all aspects of life (*NE* 1106b37–1107a8). In the *Ethics* and *De anima*, Aristotle contrasts the uncontrolled man (*akrates*) with the self-sufficient man (*enkrates*), in whom the intellect exercises power over the appetites (e.g. *De anima* 433a1–8; *NE* 1095a4–12, 1111b14–16, 1151a20 ff.).

What is applicable to moral health can also be used to achieve physical health; Aristotle explicitly argues from physical consequences of ignoring 'the mean' to moral consequences (e.g. *NE* 1104a11–17; Jaeger 1957). In this context I would suggest that disease shows the patient is unable to control himself properly, and has made the wrong decisions. The doctor must therefore take over and assess the patient's condition. Indeed, *The Doctor* 1 (Jones 2.310–2) explicitly states that it is by his own exercise of self-control (*enkrates*) that the *iatros* proves himself qualified to assume control over another; he must have a well-ordered life, and look healthy, or no one will believe him capable of healing others.[8] This recalls the 'self-possession' exhibited in *Decorum* 12 (Jones 2.294) and recommended in Aristotle's moral philosophy. The same vocabulary is used in *Regimen* 1, where the author claims that he is able to recognise when a disease is about to start, because it is possible to detect the signs which precede the overpowering (*krateesthai*) of health by disease (1.1/Jones 4.230). Health may thus be seen as a matter of power and control: the power of the individual versus the power of the disease; self-control versus control from outside the self. Sick people, if left to themselves, give up and die (*Precepts* 9/Jones 1.324), so it is essential that control is exerted on their behalf by the *iatros*.

I have been referring here to a male patient, and this is deliberate. A further important point is that, in classical Greek thought, it is only the male who has the responsibility and the right of determining his actions according to the principles of moderation and self-control.[9] Moral excellence is shown by a man in commanding, but by a woman in obeying (Aristotle *Politics* 1260a20–23). The right of the male to exercise control in all other social spheres derives from his ability to control himself. The patient is thought to be unreliable, unable to follow instructions and in need of constant surveillance, precisely because he is no longer fully in control. The doctor, his healthy appearance demonstrating his orderly way of life and ability to control himself, must comfort and cajole the patient back into a position from which he can again resume control over his own life. Phrastor is so ill that the women caring for him are able to control him, persuading him to do what they want; such is the vulnerability of a sick man. A woman, in contrast, is a natural patient, since even in health she cannot exercise full self-control.

Where does this leave women as healers? In a few passages of the Hippocratic corpus it is possible to glimpse women in a healing role; it should however be noted that they apparently attend only other women. A 'cord-cutter' (*omphaletomos*) appears in *Diseases of Women* 1.46 (L 8.106); female 'healers' (*akestrides*) who help women in labour are mentioned in *Flesh* 19 (L 8.614); another female 'healer' (*iatreousa*) has already been mentioned as assisting the *iatros* in *Diseases of Women* 1.68 (L 8.145). The *iatreousa* could be linked to other compounds of the root *iatr-* which are attested in the Greek language after the classical period; for example, *iatreine* or *iatrine,* and *iatromaia* which translates literally as 'healer-midwife'. None of these terms, with the possible exception of the 'cord-cutter', should be restricted in scope to midwifery and childbirth; they all appear to be interested in 'diseases of women' in general (Van Brock 1961: 66–7; Robert 1964: 175–8). This does not make them 'gynaecologists' in our sense, because women's disorders were thought to affect the whole body. In the absence of human dissection, classical Greek writers developed a complex anatomy and physiology of the female, according to which female difference extended throughout the body, since female flesh was of a wetter and more spongy texture than male flesh (King 1987). The womb was also thought to travel around the body causing illness;

bad breath, headaches, pain in the limbs or side could all stem from menstrual suppression and womb displacement. These are therefore 'women who treat women'; should one successfully treat a male patient, she would become invisible in terms of the prevailing ideology in which only a man can prove his self-control in order to take control over a sick person.

In a famous case in Galen's *On Prognosis* (8.1–21; ed. Nutton) the wife of Boethus is ashamed to consult the *iatroi* about her menstrual problems; instead, she calls in the *maiai* (midwives). When there is no improvement, her husband calls in *iatroi*, of whom Galen eventually takes over the case. Control thus passes to the male head of household and the male *iatros*. Several female attendants are also present throughout; one is commended by Galen as 'an excellent woman', but when the patient faints he dismissively describes them as being 'no use' because they 'simply stood around screaming' (tr. Nutton).

At this point the sources on child-nurses provide a useful parallel. Joshel has shown that the 'good' child-nurse is portrayed in Roman culture as someone whose 'activities and physical routine must be carefully controlled and monitored'; she is 'either firmly under the control of her employer or she has a disposition that makes control of her unnecessary' (1986: 8). Like the doctor, she should be capable of self-control; but, as a woman, she should simultaneously be under the control of the male head of household.

The sources for ancient Greek medicine can thus be used to suggest two important areas of cross-cultural comparison to which further studies should be addressed. First, nursing cannot be understood except in relation to the general social and institutional position of medicine. The Greek *iatros* had reason to supervise as many stages of treatment as possible, and would perform those tasks we classify as 'nursing' in order to prevent anyone else from receiving the credit for a cure. Second, the dominant ideology of sexual difference must be taken into account. Far from supporting the claim that a woman's natural fitness for the nursing role 'goes without saying' (Reinach 1904), the texts suggest that the woman caring for the sick man may take advantage of her *unnatural* position of control over a male. The woman who prepares healing drugs for her husband's household may also prepare poisons. The 'natural' position, as the Greeks of the fifth and fourth centuries BC saw it, is that women are 'patients', unable to control themselves even in health; naturally liable to illness as a result of being dominated by excess blood and a moving womb. By becoming ill, a man ceases to have the right to control his own life; a *iatros*, whose own health and ordered life are testimony to his self-control, must take over. According to this ideology of the sexes, a woman healer should not treat a male patient, but can exert the limited control of which she is capable only over another, sick, woman.

The 'fundamental outlook' of the Greeks is thus sufficiently different from our own to make them an inappropriate source for those seeking precursors for the modern nursing profession; but it is precisely this difference which makes their medical world so valuable for any reassessment of the history and anthropology of nursing.

NOTES

1. The earliest texts in the Hippocratic collection probably date to the mid-fifth century BC, the classical age of Greece. In this chapter, I am using much material from those texts which discuss medical etiquette, thought to be among the latest in the collection, perhaps after the third century BC; I am also using sources from Roman medicine when this provides a good illustration or comparison. The danger is therefore always present that, by using examples from the earliest and latest texts, I am conflating the views of entirely different groups of medical practitioners. The reader is warned: the author has little choice. In referring to the Hippocratic texts, I am where possible using the Loeb Classical Library edition of Jones and Withington, because it includes an English translation and is relatively easy to find. The translation is not always reliable since it tends to use inappropriate terms from current medicine; I have therefore indicated where I would prefer a different interpretation. Where a text is not included in the Loeb edition, 'L' refers the reader to the complete French edition of Emile Littré (10 volumes, 1839–61, Paris; reprinted 1962, Hakkert, Amsterdam). For other ancient texts, author and title are given in full, and no specific edition is recommended. Greek is kept to a minimum.
2. See, for example, *On the Sacred Disease* (Jones 2), where it is suggested that the 'sacred disease' (usually identified with epilepsy) is no more sacred than any other; but, it should be noted, this is not the same as saying that no disease is sacred. *Decorum* 6/Jones 2.288 says that all cures come ultimately from the gods.

23

3. See also *Epidemics* (6.4.7; L 6.308) on the ideal doctor, discussed at length by Deichgraeber (1970). In the second century AD, Galen's *On Prognosis* (1.1–4) also discusses those who only appear to be good doctors, who impress by the way they dress and by their 'flashy silver equipment' (tr. V. Nutton). Hippocratic texts were still being used in the fourteenth century to show how a doctor should dress, speak, and act; see Bullough 1966: 94–8.

4. Jones translates 'medicines suited to his case'; this is used by Lloyd (1983: 120 n.19) as evidence that 'laymen sometimes brought medicines and administered them for themselves'. The Greek *ta prosphora* is not this specific.

5. Although Lloyd (1983: 79 n.78) suggests 'no doctor is available'.

6. For evidence of how much the Athenians, in the period in which such speeches were delivered, feared women who persuaded men to act, see Vial (1985: 53–4). The speech cited in the text should be read in conjunction with another, Isocrates 19, from the early fourth century BC. The speaker describes how he cared for the deceased, none of whose relatives came to help (with the exception of his mother and sister who were ill themselves). During this last illness, the deceased adopted the speaker as his son, made him his heir and gave him his sister to be his wife. In [Demosthenes] 59 the care of the attendants persuades the sick man to recognise his son as his heir, but in Isocrates 19 carer and eventual heir are the same person, and as it is the heir who is speaking he makes his adoption appear as a natural action.

7. cf. Euripides *Medea*, where *pharmaka* is used for a cure for sterility (718) and for poison (385, 789, 806).

8. cf. the fable of Babrios, of the frog who claimed to be a *iatros* (120). The fox mocks him saying, 'How can you claim to heal others, when you can't even stop yourself from being so green?'

9. In the military context, it is appropriate for the commander to care for the army. One of the features of the ideal Roman general was thus that he looked after his men when they were ill; cf. Velleius 2.114.1–2. I owe this reference to Tony Woodman.

Chapter Two

THE DOCTOR'S ASSISTANT: NURSING IN ANCIENT INDIAN MEDICAL TEXTS*

JULIA LESLIE AND DOMINIK WUJASTYK

Sources[1]

For this brief survey of ancient Indian textual material on nursing, we have restricted our attention to the two earliest and most famous medical treatises of ancient India: the *Carakasamhita* and the *Susrutasamhita*. These two classical works, the Indian equivalent of the Hippocratic and Galenic texts, enjoy a contemporary relevance far exceeding that of the Greek corpus, for they are still the basis of the *ayurvedic* system of medical care widely practised in India today. Second, we have made no mention of the healing and nursing done by women in the domestic sphere. Finally, all the usual caveats about evidence relating to women based upon texts written by men must be borne in mind.

THE EVIDENCE OF THE *CARAKASAMHITA*

The older of these two texts is the *Carakasamhita*. While the antiquity of this work is not in doubt, scholars have yet to agree on its precise date. According to Ray (1909: I (xiii)), it was composed in the period before the Buddha, before 600 BC. Jean Filliozat (1949: 17–19) prefers the second or first centuries BC. The Chronology Committee of the National Institute of Sciences of India (*Proceedings* 1952) follows Winternitz's choice of AD 100 (1972: I).

For the purposes of our present description, we shall not engage in this debate about chronology, but instead make a few relevant points of a general nature. First, the extant text entitled *Carakasamhita* is a ninth-century edition by Drdhabala of Caraka's original work, together with comments and a whole section added by Drdhabala himself. The core text by Caraka, perhaps composed around the turn of the Christian era, is itself based on a considerably older work by Agnivesa. According to the opening verses of the *Carakasamhita* itself, Agnivesa was one of six disciples of the sage Atreya who attended a great medical conference in the Himalayas, the purpose of which was to alleviate human suffering and prolong human life. All six disciples were asked to compile the teachings of Atreya and Agnivesa's version was deemed the best. According to Indian tradition, Agnivesa himself was a famous teacher at the ancient seat of learning at Taksasila (Gk: Taxila), east of the Khyber Pass, during the time of the Buddha.

It is therefore often said that the medical knowledge and practices described in the text may be compared with those of Hippocrates in contemporary Greece. Some scholars go further still, suggesting that some of the ideas in the Indian text indicate a knowledge at that time of the work of Hippocrates himself (although modern scholarship would not accept that the Hippocratic corpus had a single author). Those who wish to follow up these ideas may begin by reading Jean Filliozat's *La Doctrine Classique de la Médicine Indienne, ses origines et ses paralleles grecs* (1949). But even this excellent work does little more than point out the evident similarities between the medical theories and practices of these two ancient civilisations. Ultimately, this may be all that is possible.

Caraka's references to nurses or nursing are brief and of a fairly general nature. For example, Car.Su.9.3[1] tells us that 'four factors are necessary for the alleviation of disease: the doctor (*bhisak*), drugs or medicaments (*dravyani*), the helper (*upasthatr*), and the patient (*rogi*)'. The word we have translated here as 'helper' (*upasthatr*) means literally 'one who stands nearby' ready to serve. Since this means, in effect, no more than the doctor's assistant, and is so glossed by the commentator Cakrapanidatta, we have preferred not to use the term 'nurse' which carries with it our own associations of independent vocation, choice, and indeed prestige.

Car.Su.9.6 and 8 explain the crucial differences between the 'doctor' and his 'helper' or 'assistant'. 'The four qualities of the doctor (*vaidya*) are excellence in theoretical knowledge (*srute paryavadatatvam*), extensive practical experience (*bahuso drstakarmata*), dexterity (*daksyam*), and cleanliness (*saucam*).' 'The four qualities of the assistant (*paricare jane*) are knowing how to attend to or wait upon someone (*upacarajnata*), dexterity (*daksyam*), loyalty to the doctor (*anuragas ca bhartari*), and cleanliness (*saucam*).' The commentator Cakrapanidatta adds that knowing how to wait upon someone means knowing how to prepare soups and juices, how to massage, how to soothe a person to sleep, and so on.

As we might expect, the requirements of learning and practical experience made of the doctor are not made of his assistant. Again, the words used to describe the 'assistant' are more commonly used in contexts of service. For example, *paricara* means 'one who follows after' in order to serve. This aspect of his function is stressed in the definition itself. Apart from 'dexterity' (or 'efficiency') and 'cleanliness', qualities required of both doctor and assistant, the latter must also be well trained in 'service' (*upcara*), knowing exactly what is involved in tending or attending to a patient. The assistant's first allegiance, however, is not to the patient but to the doctor, for the crucial fourth requirement is that he should be loyal or, more accurately, 'devoted' to 'the one who supports or maintains' him, that is, to his master, the doctor. The word *bhartr*, used to denote the doctor, is commonly used in other contexts to mean both 'master' (in relation to the servant) and 'husband' (in relation to the wife). The associations and implications of such a word are clear.

Car.Su.15.7 lists at some length the arrangements that a doctor should make before he practises medicine. These include making sure that he has at his disposal an unspecified number of assistants (*paricarakan*) capable of variety of tasks. For example, they should be able to prepare pulses or soups, to cook rice, to give baths (*snapaka*) and massages (*samvahaka*), to lift patients (*utthapaka*) and help them lie down again (*samvesaka*), and to grind the necessary herbs for drugs (*ausadhapesakams ca*). All such assistants should have the requisite qualities of good moral conduct (*sila*), cleanliness (*sauca*), a devoted nature (*anuraga*), dexterity (*daksya*), and respectful behaviour (*pradaksinya*, literally, 'keeping one's right side towards objects that demand respect'). They should be skilled in attending the sick (*upacarakusalan*), trained in all the necessary duties (*sarvakarmasu paryavadatan*), and not averse to any kind of work (*sarvakarmasv apratikulan*).

It is clear from rulings like these that the doctor had to organise his own practice or dispensary, from the physical aspects of the house or room and the instruments and facilities within it to the nursing staff or attendants who helped him care for the sick. It is also clear that, while these attendants had a specialised function within the doctor's entourage, they were in fact his personal servants or employees, and that they were dependent on the doctor for their board as well as for their training.

THE EVIDENCE OF THE *SUSRUTASAMHITA*

The date of the *Susrutasamhita* is also much discussed. There is some evidence to suggest that the original text was composed between the time of the Buddha (sixth century BC) and 350 BC. The extant text, however, is a recension of Susruta's work by one Nagarjuna who may or may not be the same as the Buddhist philosopher of that name, or the famous alchemist, or any of several Nagarjunas known to Indian tradition. The Chronology Committee of the National Institute of Sciences of India (*Proceedings* 1952) has opted for the third or fourth century as the date of Nagarjuna's recension, but it is generally agreed that far more research needs to be done on this point. Nagarjuna's work formed in its turn the basis of a commentary by Dalhana in the twelfth century AD.

Susruta discusses at some length the selection and training of the medical student proper (Sus.Su.2.3–4). Such a student was chosen on the basis of age, family background, physical fitness, and intelligence. His entry into the medical profession was marked by an initiation ceremony performed by a brahmin priest on an auspicious occasion and involving Vedic texts, the sacred fire, various offerings, oblations, and so on. Clearly, none of this applies to the nursing assistant. Once again, directives concerning the 'assistant' indicate that the individual concerned is, in effect, the doctor's employee, albeit often a trusted and experienced one.

According to Sus.Su.34.15 and 24, assistants (*paricara*) should be trained to help the doctor or surgeon in treating the patient, and they should tend the patient throughout his illness, remaining always by his bedside. Such an assistant should be friendly (*snigdhah*), non-critical (*ajugupsur*), physically strong (*balavan*), good at caring for the sick (*yukto vyadhitaraksane*), obedient to the doctor's orders (*vaidyavakyakrd*), and tireless (*asrantah*).

Although no explicit statement on this issue is made by Susruta, it becomes apparent that, while the doctor is invariably male, the sex of the assistant is determined by the sex of the patient. Since most of the directives in medical treatises refer to the patient in the masculine form, it is not surprising that the assistant too is assumed to be a man. Where a female patient is specified, however, the nursing assistant is always female.

Thus, the midwife is assumed to be a woman; indeed her primary qualification is the personal experience of having given birth to a child. As Sus.Sa.10.8 explains, 'there should be four female attendants (*catasrah striyah*) at the bedside who are mature (*parinatavayasah*), not easily upset (*asankaniyah*), good at giving birth (*prajananakusalah*), and whose nails are cut short (*kartitanakhah*)'.

The wet nurse is of necessity female. Both Caraka (Car.Sa.8.52) and Susruta (Sus.Sa.10.25–28) describe her in some detail. Among other things, she should be of the same caste as the baby's mother (*yathavarnam*); still young, strong, and healthy; and of a generous, kind, and submissive nature (*silavatim, acapalam, alolupam*). She should be neither too thin nor too fat. Her breasts should be neither too high nor too low: a high-breasted woman makes the child ugly; while pendulous breasts may suffocate him. Her milk should be abundant and clear. She should have no bodily defects, no diseases, and no bad habits; and she should like children. She should be the mother of boys (*pumvatsam*), and none of her own children should have died (*jivadvatsam*).

On battlefields and in army camps, the doctors' assistants were assumed to be men, but women had an auxiliary role. This is described briefly by the *Arthasastra*, an early work on statecraft and government. 'Physicians, with surgical instruments, apparatus, medicines, oils and bandages, and women in charge of food and drink and capable of filling men with enthusiasm, should be stationed in the rear' (Kangle 1986: ii, 441 [10.3.47]).

We may conclude that nursing attendance was deemed a necessity by the early medical treatises, that it was done not by doctors themselves but by those in the service of doctors; that men tended men while women tended women; and that there was a degree of autonomy in their attendance on the sick.

EDITORS' NOTE *

The Sanskrit terminology in this chapter has been reproduced without the usual diacritical marks.

NOTE

1. Abbreviations used:

Car.Su.	*Carakasamhita, sutrasthana*
Car.Sa.	*Carakasamhita, sarirasthana*
Gk.	Greek
Sus.Su.	*Susrutasamhita, sutrasthana*
Sus.Sa.	*Susrutasamhita, sarirasthana*

Chapter Three

SOCIAL CHANGE IN THE NURSING PROFESSION IN INDIA

GEETA SOMJEE

Over the years, and particularly in the last two decades, the profession of nursing in India and the social background of those involved in it have undergone tremendous changes. Such changes appear to be radical when considered against the background of a traditional social organisation which demarcated occupations on hereditary lines and also provided a rigid pollution index indicating what one could or could not do, eat, or touch.

Changes in the nursing profession, as we shall see, involved an open or implied defiance of such occupational directions and taboos, for different castes and of the observance of the norms of pollution. The carrying out of these acts was greatly assisted by the broader social changes which have been occurring in society since the turn of the century. Equally helpful was the restoration (by the colonial administration) of the public health system which had disappeared from India after the tenth century. In the absence of a public health system, nursing had become very much a part of family and caste undertaking. The restoration of the public health system in the nineteenth century created a need for personnel to serve it, who, sooner or later, had to be drawn from a wider and more composite segment of society. Along with that, there were changes in gender relations, notions of pollution, social policy towards health, and vastly expanded opportunities for employment, both at home and abroad, which together changed social attitudes towards nursing as a profession and also towards those who were engaged in it.

TRADITIONAL AND COLONIAL NURSING

The classical civilisation of India witnessed the beginning of the profession of nursing and it survived there as long as there was the public health system. References to ancient Indian nursing are to be found in some of the classical works on health, such as *Ayurveda* (science of life). *Ayurveda*, with its detailed medical and surgical references to various kinds of human ailments and preventive medicine, was equally rich in its references to the importance of nursing of the sick. To the well-known surgeon of ancient India, Susruta, nurse, doctor, medicine, and patient constituted the four *padas* (feet) or integral parts of the curative exercise (Pavey 1959).

Roughly around the same time, the well-known physician Charaka spelt out in detail what a nurse was expected to do, emphasising above everything else patience and skill in waiting upon the ailing (Wilkinson 1958).

The practice of medicine, as an integral part of the public health system, and within it the importance of nursing, came to acquire great importance during the period of Buddhist influence in India (500 BC to AD 300). This was also the period which saw the establishment of hospitals not only for humans but also for animals. During that period Taxila and Nalanda became great centres of learning with their own medical schools. Their graduates were then absorbed by the state medical system, which sought to provide a doctor in every village and also at important crossroads (Wilkinson 1958: 5).

With the decline of Buddhism, the resurgent Hinduism began tearing deep into the fabric of society which had been established on the principles of compassion, castelessness, and a broader responsibility of political institutions towards its subjects, including for public health. The revival of Hinduism saw an extraordinary emphasis on the norms of hierarchy and conformity, in addition to a detailed pollution index indicating what could or could not be touched or eaten. In the post-Buddhist period, therefore, the practice of medicine and the personnel needed to practise it, had to work within the rigidly defined notions of what could or could not be touched or consumed.

Some of these notions referred to the touching of human body and its excretions as highly polluting. Such characterisations were a setback to the continued development of the medical profession, patient care, and, above all, to the nursing profession in India. From then on the various kinds of services previously performed by one composite nurse had to be rendered by specific castes.

Nursing was thus 'chopped up' into several caste functions, as it were, and usually the lower castes were asked to perform those functions within the overall traditional *jajmani* system, a system which had arranged an exchange of goods for services rendered.

The relegation of nursing to caste functions also downgraded it socially as a profession. It then became an occupation for the lower castes and untouchables. The effect of such a social demotion of nursing on Indian society as a whole was long lasting and even today in educated circles unmistakable vestiges of it remain.

By AD 1000 some of the last of the public hospitals, around which the nursing profession had flourished, disappeared. From the eleventh century onwards India was a victim of continuous invasions, conquests, and social destabilisation in general. Within such conditions neither the science nor the art of medicine, nor indeed the profession of nursing in the broader casteless sense of the term, could flourish. Until around the nineteenth century, and the re-emergence of public medical institutions, nursing of the sick remained, almost exclusively, the responsibility of the members of the family, of the *dais* (midwives), and of various castes offering specific services to the sick.

The dissolution of public hospitals and the domestication of medical services, with various castes offering specific services relating to nursing at one's residence, supplementing whatever health care and assistance one's relatives could give, also split such services on the line of gender. Gender differences began to appear within the service castes such as barbers, masseurs, and washer-men. Among them men attended to men and women, almost always from the same families, attended to women. Such a gender division, however, did not affect the top practitioners of medicine who were always men. So far as women, i.e. *dais*, were concerned, their medical jurisdiction did not go beyond gynaecology and midwifery.

For the women patients, therefore, there was little or no medical recourse beyond the *dais*, and the auxiliary medical services provided by various castes. For women to have access to male doctors was considered to be undesirable. And there again, the higher the caste the greater the insulation of women from services provided by males. The worst sufferers in that respect were the women in purdah. In emergencies or desperate situations men, usually the husbands, had to act as intermediaries between the female patients and doctors, with *chaddars* (sheets) with many holes hanging between them.

Such a social situation, which lasted for a long time in India, was a great setback for the nursing profession. In order to stage a comeback, it had to wait for the development of public medical institutions and within them the need for medical personnel who could transcend the deeply rooted barriers of caste and gender. Such an opportunity was provided by the colonial administration, and also by the various developments within the nursing profession in Britain, with far-reaching effects on medical institutions in India.

The British colonial administration had its own health priorities. First of all came the responsibility for the health of the people in the army, then that of the civilians who served in it, and, finally, if resources were still left, that of the civilian population in general. For the civilian population, it often encouraged munici-palities to look after that function. Moreover, it also encouraged wealthy Indian merchants to donate funds for their own people. Nevertheless, in all this it sought to revive medical institutions as public bodies, albeit with differentiated access to facilities within them. It was around such medical institutions that the practice of medicine and the profession of nursing once again flourished.

The figure of Nightingale, depicted as a female nurse who courageously went into the battlefield and nursed the wounded soldiers, together with her interest in the condition of army hospitals in India, led to the exploration of the role of women nurses in India. In 1888, Britain sent a group of ten qualified nursing sisters to organise nursing in military hospitals. Over the years this led to the establishment of several other nursing services.

Women of Indian origin, however, had difficulty in getting into the various nursing corps associated with the army until around 1914 when the army needed many more nurses than it could possibly recruit from Britain. There again, important positions within the profession, including those concerned with instruction, remained the preserve of the personnel imported from Britain.

Thus, the women of Indian origin had two disadvantages: the one imposed by their own social organisation with its rigid notions of pollution restraining women of higher castes from getting into the profession; and the other arising out of colonial rule in India with its fear of Indians picking up too many skills too quickly and then demanding adequate jobs and compensations. Initially, only Anglo-Indians, Parsees, and Christians could enter the profession. It was not until the Second World War that a relatively large number of women were able to enter nursing units which were attached to the army.

Relatively speaking, women of Indian origin had easier access to institutions which were attached to civilian and missionary medical institutions. The missionaries, in particular, given the paucity of their financial resources, began recruiting women from lower social strata, including untouchables, and specially those who were in orphanages, and gave them status and economic independence.

On the eve of independence, the Bhore Committee Report in 1946 for the first time emphasised the need to establish a universal health care system which could be extended to rural communities with the help of sufficient numbers of nurses, health workers, and paramedics. Then in 1961 came the Mudaliar Committee Report, and successive five-year plans which feebly emphasised the need for rural health care. Finally, the Srivastava Committee Report of 1975, and the sixth five-year plan (1979–84) in particular, emphasised the need to devise rural health programmes and, above all, recruit an adequate number of service personnel to be able to implement them (Pyle 1981). That opened up, as it were, a good many opportunities for urban as well as rural women to enter the profession. As one perceptive scholar of the development of health services in India wrote: 'One of the very significant features of health services in India is that a very large number of auxiliary personnel have found a place in it. This represents a very conscious effort at demystification of medical practice'.

Together with such programmes and a large number of principal and auxiliary health personnel, there also sprang up an equally large number of voluntary organisations devoting their efforts to rural health. In the subsequent sections we shall examine the kind of social change in the profession of nursing which such developments induced.

After a prolonged period of trial-and-error, it was also realised that, given the nature of Indian society and the limitation of resources, the auxiliary nurse midwife or the female health worker would be able to play an important role in the future. These would then link their efforts with those of the *dai*, the traditional health resource, who is already there, throughout the length and breadth of India, waiting to be retrained and updated in skills. We shall take up these and other points in detail in subsequent sections.

THE CHANGING IMAGE OF THE NURSES

The term 'nurse' evokes different reactions in different cultures, despite the fact that they all probably begin with an image of a person who handles socially less desirable things such as the bedpan. The term 'nurse', derived from its Latin source which means nourishing people back to health, also has a wider reference, especially in western societies, of 'nurturing, caring, comforting, the laying on of hands, and other maternal types of behaviour', in short mothering (Fagin and Diers 1983).

But those are not the images which nurses evoke within a culturally different situation such as the Indian. To begin with, the nurse comes into the picture only when someone is 'very ill' or 'too ill' to get by without medical attention involving a doctor and a nurse. Consequently, within the Indian situation, it is medical dependence which brings in the nurse in the first place. From then on patients may want more than medical attention. They may want gentleness, kindness, someone to take interest in them, and someone to reassure them that everything will be all right.

Unlike the western linkage between the patient and the nurse, interpreted as 'mothering' (Odlum, 1954) because of the overt expression of caring, the Indian variant of such a linkage may not go beyond sympathetic listening or encouraging. One never hears the term mamata or mother's love used to characterise the patient–nurse relationship in India.

A nurse may do that to a child, but with adults assurances of recovery, encouragement, and talking like an elderly, knowledgeable person, discounting fears, is rather more in evidence than 'mothering'. Such behaviour on the part of the nurse, and the nature of the relationship between her and her patients, is directly or indirectly influenced by the norms which govern social relationships in general.

A nurse then, given the cultural constraints of Indian society, may not be 'mothering' her patients, she may at best be 'eldering' them, or acting as an experienced and knowledgeable guide, and by and large 'nourishing' them back to health, in the true Latin sense of the term, by means of therapy, care, personal interest, and, above all, boosting their morale, so that they (the patients) may, as it were, join in the process of recovery set in motion by the doctor and the nurse.

In terms of the wider philosophical heritage of the various health systems of India, this also means that the patients themselves are an integral part of their recovery process. Over and above therapy and care, they must also 'will' themselves back to health.

Willing or doing things by means of self-determination, deep conviction, and the summoning of the various layers of one's consciousness and personality, for recovery from the present problem of health, is very much a part of Indian social, religious, and medical culture. Under the circumstances, the task before the nurse is more than 'mothering' and of making the patient dependent on herself; it is, on the contrary, one of putting him/her back on his/her own feet through doctor's, nurse's, and above all the patient's own resources of recovery. Her goal then is the speediest possible independence rather than cultivating a mother-dependence of her patients on herself.

While willing oneself to health is very much a part of the indigenous medical systems, such as Ayurveda, along with the necessary herbal and nursing supports, this system is also openly or tacitly subscribed to by practitioners of western medicine in India. For while they practise western medicine, the milieu within which it is practised and the norms governing the conduct of doctors, nurses, and their patients are very much conditioned by the cultural values of the wider society.

Under these circumstances, stereotypes of nurses and the responses they evoke differ in the Indian situation. People in India hold culturally conditioned stereotypes about nurses, as they do about other professions, each of which are influenced and shaped by the pace of social change within the society.

To begin with, perspectives on nursing are very much influenced by the caste and religion of the nurses and what they do openly and behind the scene. During the last decade or so the background of nurses and what they do has altered extensively so that some of the stereotypes about them are now considered, by and large, irrelevant.

As stated earlier, in the past, a rigid pollution index governing what one could or could not eat or touch, relegating nearly 8 per cent of the population to untouchability, determined who could go into the nursing profession and the various auxiliary services associated with it. Conversely, there was also a rule of thumb indicating that, if you were in the nursing profession, you could not possibly be of a high enough caste.

Such rigid stereotyping did not apply to doctors who did very nearly all the same things as nurses did in terms of handling the human body. But so far as the doctors were concerned, they fitted well into the old Brahmanical mould of teaching and healing. Such healers in the past did not touch everyone. Lower-caste individuals did not have direct access to them, though if the healers wished they could practise non-tactile, distance medicine with them. As physicians practising western medicine, the tactile requirement came back for them, but as physicians they were also considered socially high enough to have some kind of a non-stick, non-polluting armour round themselves.

Such an armour of protection did not extend to nurses. This was so despite the fact that most nurses had the help of ayahs, sweepers, and bedpan handlers to do the socially undesirable work for them. Susceptibility to pollution was thus more than a matter of gender. This is because even male nurses were stereotyped as doing undesirable work. What gave protection to the doctors was their antecedent status. Doctors, in the past mostly Brahmins and also learned men, were seen as pursuing a noble profession of healing others. However, nursing involved handling the human body and its excretions; it was meant to be for lower-caste women. Even the non-stick armour of the higher-caste women who happened to be there was, until recently, considered to be precarious.

Moreover, for a long time women who came into the nursing profession in the colonial and post-colonial period, barring some Anglo-Indians and Parsees, were Christian converts from the lower social strata. They therefore could not effectively fight back against the social indignities heaped on them. Such a characterisation of nurses continued long after Indian independence. Even as late as 1975, nearly three decades after independence,

64.8 per cent of nurses were of the Christian faith.[2] And there is no record of how many of them were of untouchable background.

There was a further socially unacceptable aspect of the life of nurses, namely their movement among males who were not related to them: the doctors, auxiliaries, and patients. By traditional definition a 'good' woman would not circulate among males who were not, directly or indirectly, related to her or from the same kin group or neighbourhood or village. If they did, then, regardless of their justification for it, they were considered to be out of the control of their menfolk and were therefore loose women or prostitutes.

Earlier, the first generation of women in the teaching profession, office work, and the professions generally had to fight similar battles. But in the case of nurses where body touching and intimate caring in general are involved, such stereotypes were hard to shake off. What finally did help was the arrival of women from higher castes, and among them a high proportion of those who were married and had families of their own. Since they were a part of the mainstream society, as opposed to the widows, deserted or single women of the nursing profession in the past, talk about their looseness gradually decreased.

The economic dimension also helped in weakening the old stereotype about nurses. Such a dimension could work in a variety of ways, such as in the case of the nurses from Kerala in South India. A large number of Syrian Christian women from that state had joined the nursing profession because of a high rate of dowry for marriage which most parents could not afford. They therefore chose the nursing profession so that they would not be a burden to their parents and brothers. In course of time, however, when better employment opportunities, both nationally and internationally, opened up for them, they were suddenly in great demand as brides. For they could now not only add to the income of the family but also help their spouses to go abroad. Such a turn-around in the fortunes of Kerala nurses has been appropriately described as a new type of hypergamous marriage which gave them access to a class which was traditionally above their own (Dommen 1978).

Similarly, of late, higher-caste Patidar girls in Gujarat, often from upper-middle-class homes, have begun joining the nursing profession, with encouragement from their parents, so that they might be able to get a doctor for a husband, either at home or abroad, preferably in the US.

Moreover, there is also a growing realization among middle-class families that to be able to enjoy a better standard of living and to educate the children – something which is very important to them – both the spouses will have to work, and nursing is as good a profession as any, with little or no unemployment.

The dissolution of the traditional stereotypes about women nurses, as we shall see, has also occurred in relation to health workers in rural communities.

The profession of nursing, with all its expansions, additions, and adaptations, has not remained what it was barely two decades ago. Moreover, the new perceptions of public health, with differing requirements at different levels, have brought the profession closer to the community and thereby facilitated the entry of a much wider range of women into it. Such an expansion has brought into the profession individuals who are integral parts of mainstream society. Within the nursing profession itself you no longer see the exceptional women, whose career has been a struggle, but the kind of women that you might find in any other profession. Most of them are either married and have families of their own or look forward to having them in the future. Like women in any other profession, they are thus engaged in the difficult task of balancing the demands of the profession of nursing with those of their own family life.

Some of the senior instructors at the Trivandrum School of Nursing in Kerala, which has sent out so many trained nurses all over India and abroad, vividly remembered how the nursing students of the past had no hope of getting married and having families of their own. Consequently, that factor alone weighed very heavily on the minds of students barely twenty years ago. Even before completing their courses, they were often depressed by the thought of being denied the normal life of married women with families of their own and the fact that, what is more, the bulk of men would look upon them as women who were less than respectable.

Over the last two decades those instructors have seen a change in the condition and perception of their students. Most of them now look at the profession of nursing as a means of doing better not only economically but also in terms of their marriage. As earning nurses they are now sought after not only by men but also by their parents, who want nurses as daughters-in-law for the economic prosperity and also a possible career abroad for their sons.

A similar trend was reported by the school of nursing in Karamsad near Anand in the state of Gujarat, in western India. There too the Patidar girls have started going to nursing school with the intention of finding a doctor for a husband and possibly settling in America where, they claimed, there were plenty of jobs for nurses. Unlike the girls in Trivandrum, those at Karamsad came from economically secure backgrounds. And, what is more, their own parents were actively involved in planning their careers and in reaching the ultimate goal of finding a doctor with a green card in America, for a son-in-law.

For such parents, the nursing diploma solved the problem of dowry. Moreover, a practising Patidar doctor, settled in the US, wanting to marry a Patidar girl with training in nursing, did not always raise the issue of *gol* or strictly demarcated endogamous circles of villages to which daughters are given in marriage and others from which girls are brought in as brides. A doctor, could transcend those matrimonial constraints with impunity. So great was the craze for going abroad that, during 1980–6, the newly started school of nursing at Karamsad sent literally thousands of transcripts on behalf of their aspiring students.

The realisation that a diploma in nursing could become a means not only of economic advancement but of matrimony as well had begun to attract girls from all segments of society, especially from the upper classes. In the nursing schools around the country there has been a major shift in the social background of those who seek admission. Until recently, in Trivandrum, girls from the Christian community had predominated. But of late a new trend, as the following chart suggests, has been evident:

Social background	1984	1985	1986 *
Christians	12	7	8
Hindus (higher castes)	5	3	8
Scheduled castes	2	3	5
Ezavas	3	8	6
Backward castes	2	–	2
Muslims	1	5	1

* Taken from the register of admissions from Trivandrum Nursing School.

The cost of education in nursing, over the years, has escalated considerably. Moreover, there was an oversupply of nurses, especially in Kerala, resulting in unemployment. This gave the state government an excuse to stop the long-established stipend for students going into nursing. Only girls from scheduled castes and tribes continued to receive it. Ironically, one consequence of this was that, along with them, only the girls from relatively well-off backgrounds could now afford to enter nursing schools.

A similar trend was noticeable at Karamsad. The school of nursing there, officially known as Goverdhanbahi Hathibhai Patel School of Nursing, which was started in 1980, admitted students with the following social background:

Social background	1980	1981	1982	1983	1984	1985 *
Behmina	5	3	2	1	2	–
Rajputs/Kshatriyas	3	–	2	2	–	1
Banias	2	1	2	–	–	–
Patidars	4	9	9	10	10	9
Muslims	2	1	–	–	1	–
Christians	2	2	–	–	2	–
Parsees	–	–	–	–	1	2
Harijans	6	–	3	4	1	2
Scheduled tribes	–	–	–	–	–	–
Barots	2	–	–	2	–	–
Others	3	1	2	–	1	1

* Taken from the register, Karamsad School of Nursing.

The above figures suggest the declining involvement of girls from Christian and Harijan background, who in the past had almost monopolised the profession. Instead, there has been a sizeable increase in girls from the upper castes such as Brahmin, Bania, and Patidar. While there has been an uneven progress in other higher groups, those from the Patidar caste have consistently sought admission to nursing school.

As far as the Harijan and tribal girls were concerned, they were protected by the state policy. There was a provision of 13 per cent of places for the former and 7 per cent for the latter. Such provision for affirmative action recently became a subject of controversy and agitation in the state. For these two backward social groups, a diploma in nursing meant much greater economic advancement, higher status, and an assured vertical mobility through marriage. As opposed to that, to an upper-caste girl, a diploma in nursing gave economic independence, wider choice in marriage, and a possibility of going abroad and settling there.

Such changes in the social background of the students of nursing were not uniform throughout the country. While the social background of the students of nursing has begun to change in recent years, their number was relatively small as compared to those who were already in the profession, often from a lower social background. This fact was borne out by a study in Tamil Nadu in South India where doctors were of higher castes and nurses invariably from the lower social groups (Venkatratnam 1979).

At some of the schools of nursing, especially at Trivandrum in the south, Lady Hardinge College and Rajkumari Amrit Kaur College, New Delhi, in the north, and Karamsad in the west, the instructors were of the opinion that the new entrants at their respective schools came with much greater intellectual preparation and ambition than they had seen earlier. In some cases, they even had science degrees before they came to nursing school. The result was that they have brought a much more trained mind to bear on the profession of nursing. Some of them were highly questioning and a few were even research-orientated. Consequently, in their performance as nurses, they demanded detailed discussion and consultation with the doctors. Often, much to the annoyance of the latter, they even volunteered their own opinions and judgement.

Some of the instructors at the schools of nursing thought that their nursing students were 'technically' far more advanced than those of the last two decades. But then the basic question was whether there was more to nursing than merely technical competence. And it is there that the two generations of nurses parted company. To that we now turn.

THE TWO GENERATIONS

From the point of view of the older generation of nurses, and especially those in their forties and fifties, what the technically more competent younger generation was missing out on was the effectiveness of the 'human care' approach.

In the opinion of the older generation of nurses, antibiotics often replaced human care as far as their younger colleagues were concerned. Thus, there was far too much dependence on the wonder drugs to bring about the recovery process rather than combining the marvels of medical science with good old-fashioned nursing. After all, what wonder drugs can take the place of human beings, especially in areas where genuine human care was needed? Moreover, the excessive use of such drugs had introduced some sort of 'distance' between themselves and their patients.

The old generation, it was obvious, had judged the younger one and its excitement for new knowledge and new approaches against a standard of nursing that it was used to. Over the years that standard itself had become a matter of dispute between the two. For the younger generation, the older one did not want to change and even ruled out any scope for improvement that new advances in medical science continually brought in. The younger generation also believed that, medically speaking, the involvement of nurses in the problems of patients beyond a point did not do much good to the latter. After all, patients came to hospitals for therapy in the first place. What they needed, therefore, was cure rather than a display of human concern.

Such a perspective by the younger generation, although far more professional in its make-up, missed out on what really made nurses in the eyes of the older ones. For the latter, the unconcerned, coldly professional, and seemingly casual approach of the former did not do the profession much good.

The older generation also felt that their colleagues were much more mobile to the point of being unconcerned, uncommitted, and rootless; that sometimes the younger generation went from place to place for the sake of very little extra money. Some of the veterans even saw an element of materialism in the younger generation. Such money-mindedness for them had no place in the profession; one was in it to serve rather than to make money. The veterans also maintained that in the days gone by only the doctors were greedy for money, and now the same shortcoming had spread to the nurses. As a veteran instructor in one of the nursing schools put it in an idealistic vein: 'In the healing profession, what comes first is the care of your patients, the rest is secondary.'

In the old days, when mostly widows and deserted women joined the profession, their commitment to it was very pronounced. The profession gave them a second chance in life, as it were, to be useful and to be with people, a wider family of human beings. What is more, the latter came to the former for help and curative care. Those women never forgot their social ostracism, indignity, and wretchedness in general, prior to joining the profession. When ruthless social exclusion was heaped upon them, the profession of nursing opened up a new door for them and they, for their part, remained grateful and dedicated to the profession for another lease on life. Some among them even felt morally obliged to pay it back, for the rest of their lives, through the people they served. They thus brought into the profession a commitment bordering on dedication and self-sacrifice which did not go unnoticed by those who came in contact with them.

Such an attitude often led to the neglect of the material side of their lives, with the result that most of them were often exploited by their superiors and institutions and had very little to live on in their retirement. While, in their old age, most of them suffered hardship and financial worries, owing to their meagre pension in days of high inflation, they were, nevertheless, full of deeply satisfying memories of how their care and that extra little bit that they brought to bear on their work nursed back to health, and in some cases to life, the patients they happened to serve.

The older generation of nurses also got on very well with the doctors. But then, as they themselves put it, in those days even the doctors were more committed to their work and to the welfare of their patients. They were also highly considerate to the people they worked with, including the nurses. Both groups trusted and appreciated one another and acknowledged their interdependence.

The older generation of nurses viewed sympathetically the demands of the younger generation for higher wages, housing, improvement in working conditions, transport facilities, and educational facilities for their children. The profession, they said, had been neglected far too long. And since women of different background were now entering it, they were not likely to settle for anything less than their fair share. The younger generation was fully aware of the fact that, like the doctors, they too were in great demand abroad. Consequently, most of them did not hide their motives and frankly stated that they wanted to go abroad and make money. But until then they would also demand a decent wage and living and working conditions from the institutions they happened to serve.

In my interviews in various parts of India, nurses from Kerala were described as the most materialistic. They were also seen as very competent and hard-working but yet not willing to settle for anything less and constantly on the look-out for better prospects in different parts of India and abroad. A similar criticism was voiced against girls from the Patidar caste in Gujarat who also did not hide their intention of finding a doctor husband and/or going to America to make more money there.

The older generation of nurses saw the younger as very much a part of mainstream society. For them the latter rarely consisted of women with some matrimonial tragedy or those who chose nursing as a career by sacrificing a possible family life. On the contrary, they were very much like most other educated women, trying to balance married life with their own career and often succeeding in their enterprise. The diverse, and sometimes incompatible, demands of the two often created tension and even occasional neglect of the one or the other, but in the end they all evened out. Part of the credit for this, according to the veterans, must go to the deeper and stronger chords within the Indian family system and the willingness of its members to stand by rather than desert the one who was overstretching his or her capacity.

Members of the younger generation of nurses, despite an outward emphasis on career, going abroad, and claim to remaining in the profession all their lives, were deeply rooted in the family and subscribed to all those values which made it an enduring social institution. They even saw themselves as the centre of their family – as wife, mother, or daughter – rather than one who was totally subsumed in the profession. In that respect they did not subscribe to the view, often held by nurses of the older generation, that as nurses they could not do, or would not be able to do, what married women without careers could do. Despite tensions and occasional lapses, the younger generation did not sacrifice one for the other.

Since the younger nurses had families of their own, they were often seen by the older as very demanding individuals. Their demands included a continual clamour for better wages, cost of living allowance, adequate housing, facilities for schooling of their children, transportation at night, etc. And when they did not get their way, they had no hesitation in resorting to an agitational approach, an approach which did not often find favour with the veterans.

At the other extreme, the younger nurses argued that just because someone was a nurse she did not cease to be a normal human being with needs, that nurses who were treated fairly by society were likely to be more efficient and devoted.

Despite differences in their mutual approaches to the profession, the older generation had a deep admiration for the younger one. As one of the senior instructors pointed out, when New Delhi was burning and innocent people being massacred, soon after Indira Gandhi's assassination in 1983, the younger nurses were all over the town rescuing life and nursing wounds without worrying about their own safety. During those days of terrible carnage, the younger generation showed the other, and much less talked about, side of their commitment to the profession.

Some of the generational shifts that we noticed within the nursing profession can be explained with reference to what has happened within family life itself. The older generation of women depended greatly on their elders for major decisions. Women at that time, as another senior instructor put it, matured much later, leaving major decisions in the household specially to the male elder in the family, as in the western experience of 'father knows best'. But now the younger generation of women, including the nurses, know exactly what they want and go after it in no uncertain terms. Consequently they, the younger nurses, are characterised as self-centred. What in fact has happened is that, with changes within the family, the younger women are no longer as voiceless as they used to be.

RURAL HEALTH WORKERS

Over the years, as a result of the examination of various health policies and health personnel involved in implementing them, it has been increasingly realised that, despite the fact that the bulk of the population lives in rural areas, only a small proportion of public health funds is spent on them and that the new health policies for rural communities should concentrate, along with a provision for greater financial resources, on women and children. And to be able to reach out to them effectively, and in the shortest possible time, women from the rural communities will themselves have to be trained as health workers and then be supervised by nurses and doctors at the sub-district and district level.

Towards such a shift of attention and policy in matters relating to rural health, a number of interesting and in some cases highly effective health schemes have been devised and put into practice. Such a highly successful scheme was put into practice by

47

Tribhuvandas Foundation in Anand for Kaira district, the home of milk co-operative dairying in India. Apart from health, it also brought in a new role for women of rural communities who wanted to participate in it. In the following pages we shall analyse it in some detail.

The Foundation was literally pushed into devising such a programme by means of grass-roots pressure. In the district of Kaira, AMUL Dairy, India's premier milk co-operative, gave to its farmers one of the most efficient programmes for animal health care. The milch animals, in nearly 1,000 villages in the district under its jurisdiction, received high-quality health care (Somjee and Somjee 1976). Over the years, farmers in those villages began complaining that their animals were looked after much better than the human beings. Subsequently, the farmers began pressuring AMUL to start a corresponding health scheme for them. After years of hesitation, it finally came out with a health scheme which is now being implemented by what is known as the Tribhuvandas Foundation or, in short, TK Foundation. In order to implement its own scheme all over the district, the Foundation needed a large number of women health workers, possibly two from each village. The Foundation, therefore, spent a lot of time helping villagers in the careful selection of women who were acceptable to all the social segments of the rural communities they came from. They were then trained as health workers and infant workers. They were trained to diagnose diseases that were common in the community and then administer drugs. If the symptoms were too complicated, then they were asked to take their instruction from a roving team of nurses, nutritionists, child development specialists, and doctors. Such instructions were obtained by means of telephone wherever possible. In more difficult cases, nurses and doctors visited the patients in their villages or took them to the hospital.

For its medical service, each family was required to pay Rs10, which is under one dollar, for the entire year. And as far as the salaries of the two health workers were concerned, they were shared by the village milk co-operative and the Foundation.

From time to time, the Foundation went through its own agonising process of reappraisal and course correction. While the rural communities could not afford doctors, and most government-run health services were remiss in doing their own job properly, there was no alternative for the Foundation but to train the rural communities' own resources and turn them into health workers. What in fact it had established was a health network and linkage of medical personnel, consisting of village-level health workers, nurses, and doctors, whose services were available with reference to the urgency of the situation.

The women health workers, after their initial training, had to face their own problems: social, psychological, and medical. They had to gain access to all the ethnic and religious groups within their own communities. Initially, as could be expected, they were jeered at as 'doctors' (i.e. quacks). Consequently, the fully trained doctors made a point of being seen with them every time they visited the village so as to give to them the shared status of a qualified person.

Then began their work of diagnosing the obvious cases of tuberculosis, malnutrition, stomach upset, cold, malaria, leprosy, etc., and some cases which were beyond them. For such purposes they had their own training and periodic follow-up. But their job as health workers in the field was most difficult in the sense that the people of rural communities often brought their sick to them at an advanced stage of illness. After that, their assistance in getting a nurse or doctor to the village was appreciated by the patients and their families. Like all new health workers, including the fresh doctors, they waited for their chance of success in curing someone and then letting a word go out into the community that they were really good at whatever they were doing. The villagers, the *sarpanch* (village headman), and the members of the *Panchayat*-village councils of several villages that I visited were very appreciative of the excellent doorstep medical service which they provided so promptly.

I interviewed several of these health workers both at the Foundation headquarters and also in their own villages. They all spoke of the extraordinarily tough experience of their first few days as health workers. Nevertheless, not a single worker gave up her work as a result of demoralisation. Those who did give up were involved either in domestic problems or in a second marriage, after widowhood, which their new role had made possible. The rest, and especially the veterans among them, spoke with gratitude of the trust of their communities in their newly acquired skill. Since the scheme's inception in 1979–80, the trained health workers had treated 186,208 patients on the spot and referred 1,341 cases to hospital (Tribhuvandas Foundation *1985–1986 A Review*).

Over a period of seven years, the Foundation had covered 350 villages in the district. In each of them it had given a new role and status to the two women who worked as health workers, and had thereby sent a message to the younger women in the rural communities that, like the health workers, they too could learn new skills and find a new role for themselves. The wider message to those women was one of self-involvement and through it a possible avenue for self-advancement and the development of one's community.

Among the broad category of health workers in rural India are the *dais* or midwives. They have been an integral part of rural India for centuries. Unfortunately, their role and contribution to rural health in general have often been minimised. The colonial health service had a contempt for them and the missionary health institutions and personnel found them far too wanting in basic hygienic standards. Consequently, they rarely received the recognition that was due to them.

One of the few perceptive studies of the role of *dais* is by Kakar (1980). The author points out that while the *dais* are considered to be birth attendants, they in fact play a much wider role in looking after the health problems of rural women. They act as 'lay gynae-cologists, herbalists, nutritionists and psychiatrists', and last but not the least give 'assurance' to their own patients (Kakar 1980).

In recent years the role of the *dais* has been recognised in the most grudging fashion. Various rural health schemes require a large number of health personnel. It is often claimed that close to three-quarters of all deliveries in rural India are supervised by *dais*. Given the scarce material and financial resources, the question then was why not make use of the *dais* by giving them supplementary health education? Finally, the Indian government decided to give one month's training to the 580,000 *dais* spread throughout India.

The trained health workers of the Foundation working in different villages of the district often had to treat pregnant women in the course of their work. They then expressed their desire to be trained also as *dais*. At the other extreme, the Foundation found it very valuable to train the existing *dais* in various villages to act as health workers as well. Such *dais* did not have the problem of acceptance by the bulk of the population of their communities. So, wherever *dais* accepted such responsibilities, they were also trained in more modern and hygienic ways of supervising deliveries.

The *dais* as a rule were either married women or widows but with children of their own. In most cases they had inherited the profession from their mothers, mothers-in-law, or from those to whom they had acted as apprentices. In terms of their social background, there was no uniform caste or religion to which they belonged to but, as a rule, until recently women of higher caste kept themselves away from playing the role of *dai*. This is because, traditionally speaking, birth was considered to be an unclean and even polluting business. The bulk of the *dais* came from lower to untouchable castes. The women of barber caste in particular (barbers come in contact with human body) were often accepted as *dais* by the widest possible spectrum of castes. Then there were cases where even women from untouchable castes had gained the confidence of the highest castes in their communities through their role as *dais*. This can be illustrated as follows.

In a village called Bodal, in Kaira District, with a population of about 5,000, situated about 20km from the town of Anand, Shardaben Maganbhai Makwana, a highly successful Harijan (ex-untouchable) *dai* earned so much respect and affection from the villagers that they sent her for further training as a health worker, constructed a building as a dispensary and a clinic for her, provided her with new equipment and medicine, and patronised her for all their general health problems without hesitation.

Shardaben's work at the dispensary began at 6 a.m. The patients who visited her seemed to have an extraordinary trust in her. In most cases she acted confidently like a doctor and was well received right across all the ethnic and economic groups with different levels of education in the community. Not only did she examine them with a thoroughness that one expects of trained physicians, she engaged her patients in a prolonged process of diagnosis to make sure of her own findings. Once the nature of the disease was recorded and tablets and/or lotions handed over, she went on to discuss how the patient could also help the process of recovery by following her instruction on diet, care in taking medicine, and exercise whenever that was necessary.

The stereotype of *dais*, as illiterate, untrained, and unmindful of hygienic conditions, did not sit well with Shardaben and the way in which she carried her business in the community. To her community, and to the people of all castes and religions in it, she was more than a *dai*. And, despite the social disadvantage of being a Harijan and a *dai* (which till recently was looked down upon as an occupation), she has emerged as a person much above those in her group. And a part of the credit for that must also go to the people of the community whose babies she delivered with utmost care over a period of two decades. After that they went along with her aspiration to become a trained health worker and gave her their support and encouragement. Rural India is indeed full of such surprises.

As the *dais*, spread all over India, get linked up with various health schemes, receive further training, and add to their valuable experience, their image in the eyes of senior health personnel and community as a whole will change. As far as rural communities are concerned, through the ages they have trusted *dais* and depended on them for more than childbirths. Their additional training has not only made them better practitioners of their own occupation, but has also begun to make them look respectable in the eyes of even those who in the past would not have had much to do with them.

CONCLUDING OBSERVATIONS

As we saw in the foregoing pages, while there has been a gradual change in the profession of nursing during the colonial and post-colonial period, the profession has changed substantially only in the last two decades. Such changes were reflected in the social background of those who joined the profession, their motivations, style of working, and, above all, the way in which nursing or the work of health workers and *dais* came to be perceived by society as whole. Thus, over the years the entry of women of higher social background into the profession became socially more and more acceptable.

As we also saw in the foregoing pages, the first break for women to enter the profession was given not by the colonial administration but by the resourceless missionary medical institutions. They trained girls from among those who had embraced Christianity, from lower castes and orphanages. By the time the colonial administration had recognised the usefulness of Indian nurses to the army and civilian hospitals, they were already performing useful and responsible functions within the network of missionary medical institutions.

Before they could join the nursing profession, the women of India had to overcome several obstacles. Among others there was the rigid pollution index, imposed by the traditional social organisation which characterised all the excretions of the human body as pollutants. It therefore ascribed services relating to them to various lower castes in its hierarchically ordered social arrangement. Consequently, the women of upper castes were kept away from the profession for a long time. Moreover, the initial entry into the profession of Christian and Harijan girls also reinforced the view that the profession, even in its modern form, was not for the high castes.

There was, in addition, the problem of having to work with unrelated males, from doctors to patients, and the necessity of moving into the grey and undefined area of comforting and soothing the patients while they were being nursed back to health. In short, nurses were seen as too much exposed and vulnerable to men who would want to take advantage of them.

What helped women overcome such barriers were basically the changes in society itself. To begin with, the economic opportunity which the profession provided – with its assured employment and income and, more recently, highly lucrative job prospects abroad – was one of the greatest single factors in making it acceptable and even apparently respectable to an increasingly large number of women. What is more, unlike in the past, it also began to turn around the matrimonial prospects of women in the profession.

Further, there was the spread of education and the change of attitude towards the family toilet, which in urban apartments had to be looked after by the members of the family. Such changes began dissolving the age-old notions concerning pollution. Besides, in most urban hospitals nurses do all the technical work, often leaving the polluting part of their job to the lower cadres of the service. Finally, as more and more women started joining middle-class professions and coming in contact with men in the course of their work, the objection against working with men has also lost its effectiveness in all walks of life. Nurses are increasingly perceived as being nice to their patients, including male patients, only in the line of their work. This then lends respectability to the profession and also facilitates acceptance of nurses as professionals by the society.

Thus, some of these changes have encouraged girls from higher social background to join the profession and that, in turn, has made the profession look increasingly respectable. Unfortunately, the newcomers began pushing out from the profession the girls of lower castes who, in the past, had monopolised it. These latter needed the access to the profession much more than did the former. Not only that, with their limited education, they stood a limited chance of successfully competing with those who came with a much better educational training and overall confidence.

The newcomers, as we saw in the foregoing pages, brought the profession closer to the mainstream society with all their demands and problems. With them in the profession, it was no longer one where one could find exceptional women or women with no matrimonial or family possibilities. On the contrary, they made the profession one of the many where middle-class women could go without sacrificing their family life as such.

Far more dramatic changes, with limitless possibilities, were noticeable in the life and work of rural health workers, *dais*, and the newly created category of auxiliary nursemaids. They, in fact, opened up for rural women a new world of opportunities.

Social change in the nursing profession, thus, has been basic, widespread, and reflective of the change taking place in society as a whole.

NOTES

1. I am grateful to a number of doctors, academics, nurses, health workers, and administrators connected with health services in different parts of India. I wish to express my deep sense of gratitude to, among others, the following: Dr Uma Vyas, Tribhuvandas Foundation, Anand; Principal Jagtap and Senior Tutor Kausalya Masurkar of Goverdhanbhai Hathibhai School of Nursing, Karamsad; Grace Poonjala, retired matron in Emery Hospital, Anand; Professors A. Bhadhuri and Hashmath Haque of Rajkumari Amrit Kaur College of Nursing, New Delhi; Miss Topo and Miss Dullett of Lady Hardinge Medical College of Nursing, New Delhi; Mr Isaac and the Librarian of the Voluntary Health Association of India, New Delhi; Mrs ChandraKanthy Rajan, Nursing School, Trivandrum; Miss Rema Panikkar, Ass. Librarian, Medical College Library, Trivandrum; and Dr G.K. Goel of NDDB and Mr K.L. Baraya of Rural Health and Development Trust, Jaipur. I also wish to thank a number of

rural health workers and *dais*, in particular Shardaben Makwana
of the village of Bodal in Kaira District and a large number of
students of nursing whom I interviewed in various parts of India
for the preparation of this work. I also wish to thank the
Librarian and staff of the Indian Institute, Bodleian Library,
Oxford University, for tracking down various books, reports, and
journals for my reference.
2. See in this connection, CAHP-TNAI, Nursing Survey in India
Report, 1975, New Delhi, Recommendation of Co-ordinating
Committee for Health Planning, p. ix.

Chapter Four

NURSING IN JAPAN

JOY HENDRY AND LOLA MARTINEZ

Nursing came to Japan in the nineteenth century along with western medicine, and it is still closely associated with western ideas about medicine which exist alongside more traditional notions. A Japanese encyclopaedia entry on nursing refers to Florence Nightingale and the Crimean War as a western one might, and there would not appear to be many corresponding indigenous categories. Developments in western countries are incorporated where appropriate into Japanese nursing and it is not unusual for Japanese nurses to spend a period working or studying abroad during their careers.

However, Japanese hospital patients are often accompanied, where possible for twenty-four hours a day, by a family member who carries out many of the roles usually associated with nursing, and western medicine is also still only one of a number of possible responses to illness in Japan. Before turning to consider nursing in more detail, then, we feel it would be useful to discuss some related aspects of Japanese social organisation and, in particular, some of the attitudes to health and illness. Sections will follow on nursing education and on the current role of nurses and nursing in Japanese society.

ATTITUDES TO HEALTH AND ILLNESS IN JAPAN

There is great concern in Japan with cleanliness and hygiene, but the assumptions behind these concerns are only partly related to western germ theory. There is a clear distinction made, for example, between the clean inside of the home and the dirt and pollution of the outside world. In emphasis of this, members of the family returning home always remove their shoes when entering the house and they frequently wash or bathe and change before they settle down inside. Children are taught from an early age to wash their hands and gargle when they come in, apparently so that the germs of the outside world will not penetrate the inside of the body.[1] These practices are similar to rites of purification on entering a Shinto shrine in Japan, when the hands and mouth are washed, and the anthropologist Ohnuki-Tierney has pointed out (1984) that there is a symbolic equation of the inside of the house with purity and the outside with impurity.

This distinction between inside or *uchi* and outside or *soto* is applied also to people in Japan. Members of one's own family, school, neighbourhood, work group, and so on, are classified as *uchi*, and one of the ways in which close relations are symbolised is in a sharing of sake cups, which could be a literal sharing of germs, as one person drinks from the cup and then passes it immediately to a friend before refilling it. In contrast, one needs purification from even only rather distant contact with unknown people of the outside world, with whom one has perhaps brushed shoulders in shops, buses, or trains. A word for 'crowds' is *hitogomi*, which literally translates as 'people dirt', where the word for 'people' here may also be used to refer to outsiders, as opposed to people of one's own inside group.

Illness is itself polluting, and there is considerable emphasis on prevention in these rites of cleanliness, which also extend to daily bathing and care to avoid draughts, so that a person who falls sick may feel they have failed to keep clean. Mothers keep a close watch on their children for any little signs of change, and they learn to know their weaknesses, and take appropriate precautions. It is the mother, then, who feels guilty if a child falls ill for it is felt that if the body is taken care of properly, it should remain healthy. Nevertheless, there are certain supernatural explanations for illness which are still regarded at least with respect in Japan and many people buy protective amulets in Shinto shrines, or undergo rites of purification at certain appropriate times. It is also possible to have your house purified and many people take their cars for such a rite every New Year.

There is also an idea that individuals are born with a certain constitution, however, which may be vulnerable in certain ways, and, within a family, members come to know each others' weaknesses well. Despite all the concern with preventing illness, most people succumb to colds and other minor complaints quite regularly and the anthropologist Margaret Lock has suggested that illness is perceived in Japan as a time when relatives and friends can express the closeness of their relationships non-verbally. Much has been written about the importance of dependence or *amae* in Japanese relations with each other, and illness is said to be a time when this dependence is evident and members of the surrounding *uchi* group can respond appropriately (Lock 1980: 77–8). Lock also points out, however, that this kind of communication is much more common when the patient is a man rather than a woman.

When more serious illness strikes a Japanese family, there are various responses available and they are by no means exclusive of each other. Western medicine is one of them and, in modern Japan, it is certainly an important one but it is not regarded with unreserved confidence. Hospitals tend to be 'crowded' places and they are, by definition, full of germs. They are also peopled with outsiders and this could be one good reason why a member of the family is often expected to accompany a patient admitted to hospital. In this way, the area surrounding a particular patient's bed may be made a little bit of *uchi* space, kept clean and unpolluted, by a member of one's own *uchi* group. This person also attends to intimate bodily functions, supervises the provision of food, and keeps a constant watch on the patient's progress and development. This last role is related to another common reservation about western medical methods and it is best understood in the context of ideas of alternative, largely East Asian medicine.

One rather basic difference between the two approaches is that western medicine is said to seek to identify symptoms, which treatment aims to remove, whereas many of the East Asian systems look for reasons in the balance of the body as a whole which are causing the symptoms, and aim then to treat the whole person. Generally, this is the ultimate aim of holistic medicine, and thus it is by no means absent from current western thought. In practice, in Japan it means that acute complaints are often successfully treated by the western type of medicine, whereas longer-term, chronic complaints will be taken to other specialists dealing, for example, in Chinese herbalism, acupuncture, or massage. There is an idea, in particular, that too much synthetic medicine, as opposed to that made directly from herbs, is ultimately poisoning the body and it should therefore be regarded with caution.

A further idea of this holistic approach is that the patient's body is affected by interaction with the environment, both physical and social, and thus the focal point of the healing process is not the relationship between the patient and doctor, but that between the family and the community in which the patient lives (cf. Lock 1980: 217–18). This provides reinforcement of the above explanation of the practice of having a family member accompany a patient into hospital, for isolation is thought to have a positively detrimental effect, especially since separation from the *uchi* group is used as a sanction for unacceptable behaviour with both children and adults. It is also customary when a member of a Japanese community falls ill for every neighbour to buy a gift and pay a visit to wish the patient well. Thus, sick beds are often surrounded by well-wishers, and it is another of the roles of the accompanying relative to greet these people and see that the patient is presentable whenever they arrive. A nurse, on the other hand, may find herself in conflict with the well-wishers, especially if she has been charged with maintaining a diet, because they are accustomed to bringing all manner of food to the patient.

Further non-medical help may also be available, possibly even within the *uchi* circle, in the form of a diviner or shaman who can deal with the supposed supernatural causes of illness. Such a person may also have advised a couple about their compatibility for marriage, or have been called in to help with the auspicious design of house reconstruction. A close relative can act on the patient's behalf in seeking this kind of support, but circumstances surrounding and preceding the onset of illness may be relevant here, so a stranger would be no use in this respect. Possible factors may be some recent action which is said to have offended an ancestor or a local deity, and women who have had induced abortions have recently been encouraged to interpret misfortune as the vengeance of the child's soul. In such cases, the specialist may chant over the sick person or recommend some form of action which will appease the wrathful spirit. It is not unusual for amulets and talismans to be taken into hospitals with a patient and various forms of prayer may be practised. Japanese medical staff are quite used to these supplementary aids to the healing process.

One traditional specialist in the realm of health care, whose role is worth considering in that she has now been almost entirely replaced by modern nurses, is the midwife. Until only a couple of decades ago, the local midwife was a woman of some standing in the community who was accorded considerable responsibility for the care of women during pregnancy and childbirth, and who was respected as a specialist in her own right. There is some evidence that women were rather shy about giving birth, the midwife often being the only person present and even she might be excluded from the moment of delivery if all was going well (Smith and Wiswell 1982: 99). She was a well-known member of the community and thus no outsider, so it must have cost them some considerable pain when it became customary for them to have their babies in a relatively impersonal hospital. In fact, many of the old midwives did gain employment in the plethora of private obstetric hospitals which opened up at the time, but they now took on the nurse's more usual role of assistant and those to whom we spoke during research found this adjustment very hard.

NURSING EDUCATION

According to Kodama (1984: 102), 'nursing in Japan emerged only about 20 years after its start in Great Britain and 10 years behind similar changes in the United States'. It was introduced along with foreign hospitals and often by foreign missionaries. Most Japanese doctors of the Meiji and Taisho era (1868–1925) were trained by German doctors.[2] Before the Second World War, the Japanese had adopted nursing to the extent that a Japanese girl could receive her nursing education from Japanese schools which fell under the jurisdiction of the Ministry of Health. A girl would leave school at the age of fifteen, after middle school, and do a two-year course (or three years part-time) which led to the qualification of auxiliary nurse. This was a prefectural qualification and an ambitious girl might work for three further years to gain practical experience and do another two-year course which would give her a national nursing certificate. The emphasis was on learning within the work context. However, nursing was considered a low-status job because the nurse was so closely related to polluting and illness, and the women who became nurses were often from a working-class background.

After the War, with the American Occupation, there were radical changes in the Japanese medical profession. Among nurses, it was the presence of American nurses that occasioned the greatest innovations. American medical training was thought to be better and so was adopted; girls from high-status families took up the profession and many Japanese nurses would train for a year in the USA as well to 'top off' their Japanese education. This does not mean that the modern nursing education system has become more unilinear for, like the American system, the Japanese system has various routes which can lead to a nursing qualification.

The Ministry of Education offers two nursing education courses. A person can attend a junior college and receive an associate nursing degree. This is a two- to three-year course which is mostly taught by nurses. The women who follow this path often become receptionists in private clinics. Alternatively, there is a four-year university course which ends in a Baccalaureate of Nursing.

Most of the public health nurses, however, are trained on the Ministry of Health education courses. There are also two paths a nurse can pursue here. She can study for two years and receive a diploma which makes her an assistant nurse. After this she can enter a two- or three-year (that is, full-time or part-time) course which will help her become qualified at the prefectural level. Yet, for all the changes in programmes which were designed to make the nurse more of a professional, there still remains a tendency for the work to be associated with pollution and many of the women still are recruited from the working or lower classes.[3]

Kodama gives the number of practising nursing personnel at the close of 1980 as:

Table 4.1 Number of nursing personnel in Japan, 1980.

Nurses				261, 613
	Women	258, 504	Men	3, 109
Assistant nurses				257, 219
	Women	248, 381	Men	8, 838
Public health nurses				17, 957
Midwives				27, 388

Taken from Kodoma 1984: 103

Of the nurses and assistant nurses, 73 per cent work in hospitals and 24 per cent in private clinics. Among the public health nurses, 86 per cent work through local health centres or local government, 6 per cent are employed in hospitals or clinics and 5 per cent in industry. Sixty-one per cent of midwives work in hospitals and clinics and 36 per cent in maternity homes where they are independent practitioners or employees. Male nurses are still very few in number and are usually employed in psychiatric care and rehabilitation work.

NURSES IN JAPANESE SOCIETY

Outlined in the first section of this article were various practices relating to Japanese concepts of pollution which would seem to make the nurse's role in hospital care less important than it is in the West. That is, several of the tasks which nurses might perform in the West, such as feeding a patient, supervising the patient's washing, or seeing to the patient's bodily functions, may still, in Japan, be performed by a household member who comes to stay in the hospital with the patient.[4] Even complicated tasks such as cleansing a wound and re-bandaging it will be taught to a family member who will do this for the patient,[5] although it is a nurse, of course, who will teach the family member what needs to be done. Still persistent in modern, urban Japan is the feeling that a patient should be cared for by a member of the household and that a nurse is someone shared among patients (Ohnuki-Tierney 1984: 196). Thus, the notion that a nurse is likely to have other patients' pollution on her is still strongly felt.

This would seem to relegate the nurse in Japan to a rather marginal position: in a hospital, she will dispense medication, supervise visitors, and, perhaps, confiscate gifts of food if she thinks the food will harm a patient's diet. Unlike nurses in Great Britain, neither Japanese nor American nurses are allowed to make decisions about medication nor may they provide treatment which has not been prescribed by a doctor for a patient. A nurse may also be a specialist, such as a radiographer, or simply a clinic secretary who keeps track of appointments and bills for the doctor. To those who know about nursing in the USA, this may sound as if the American system has been fully incorporated into the Japanese medical system.

In fact, there were several similarities in the 1950s and 1960s between American and Japanese images of nurses. According to the Nursing Supervisor at Shima Hospital, Takashi Jinsei, there was a time when it was thought that most girls seeking a nursing degree were actually also looking for a doctor to marry. A number of nurses have married doctors and work with them in the private clinics that dominate Japanese medicine. Many women married and left the profession, which resulted in large gaps in the profession; and those women who did feel that nursing was a vocation often found that they could not combine a career and marriage.

The differences that continue to exist between the images of nurses in Japan and the USA are the result of Japanese cultural expectations of women as well as Japanese notions of hierarchy and pollution. In modern, urban Japan much stress is laid on the value of a woman as housewife and educator and on the old Confucian precept that a woman must obey first her father, then her husband, and finally her son. That these cultural ideals are not always adhered to is to be expected, especially among the working class where women have always had to work.[6] Yet, there persists in modern Japan the idea that woman is but the helpmate of the man: if she is a housewife, then she is to raise the children and look after their education; if she is a nurse, then she is the doctor's helper and, perforce, subordinate to him. There are similarities with the office ladies whose main job seems to be to make tea, supervise the comings and goings of patients and visitors, and act as the intermediary between patient and doctor. It might be inferred that the nurse's job is to deal with and to distance the doctor from the pollution of illness.[7] The idea that she is a professional in her own right is rarely heard.

According to informants, one of the roles which the Japanese nurse has most frequently been called on to fill is that of mediator. The doctor, the *sensei* (literally, teacher), was always a person to be treated with great respect while his assistant, the nurse, was regarded as someone with whom it was easier to communicate and of whom to ask questions. Nurses often use the Japanese terms of address which one applies to children when talking to patients and this further identifies them with the image of someone close and approachable; this contrasts with the doctors who can be very polite or rude in their language.

Another aspect of the nurse's image can be found when analysing the Japanese term for nurse: *kangofu* is a complicated word that does not imply mothering qualities as does the English word but does connote a sort of guardianship. *Kan* can mean to look, gaze, notice; to give attention; to have insight, experience; to give treatment, care, favour; to pity; to have sight or vision. It implies seniority and a rather detached idea of being involved, and seems related to western concepts of what a nurse should do. *Go* is more concerned with the nurse as a sort of guard; it can mean: to defend, protect, keep, observe, obey: to stick by, stick to, be true to. The *fu* means woman or wife while *fu*, meaning husband or man, is also applied to male nurses. The terms may very well relate to western concepts of what a nurse does but for Japanese nurses, this role of protector and observer has begun to seem too passive.[8] Kodama notes that 'until the 1970s Japanese nurses could not identify a unique role for the nurse as a member of the comprehensive health care team' (1984: 104). While American nurses have sought to make the profession more respected, Japanese nurses were looking for a direction and, according to Kodama, they have finally found it in 'what they have been doing every day' (1984: 104). That is, in the day-to-day routine of patient caring and, especially, in treating the patient as a whole individual.

One source of this change in Japanese nursing is the growing concern for the holistic care of the patient, what Lock (1980: 256) sees as a return to Japanese values. This new approach is a mixture of Japanese notions that illness is something that occurs because the individual is somehow physically unbalanced and western notions that an illness consists of symptoms that can be treated. Kodama (1984: 104) also stressed that this change has come about from student nurses' own translations of Florence Nightingale's *Notes on Nursing: What It Is and What It Is Not*' and Hiroko Usui's 'theory of nursing based on Nightingale's principles and views'. Moreover, it is a response to the growing trend in Japan of people demanding to be cared for in their own homes. Hospitals are extending services into the communities, especially for the aged, and nurses are visiting people whose long-term chronic illnesses mean that they have to be treated as whole individuals.

The result of this is that more nurses are needed in Japan and many married nurses are being urged to return to work. There is also a move to phase out the diploma course which produces only assistant nurses and to increase the number of women who are trained as practical nurses in junior colleges and universities. The Japanese Nursing Association wants to raise the status of nurse to practitioner so that they can get on with what they know they have to do for the patient. Kazuko Kodama, whose views have been quoted extensively in this article, sums up the current state of Japanese nursing and what the Japanese nurse feels about her role in the profession:

> For a long time Japanese nurses have looked to nursing in the United States for direction. In the meantime, however, they have begun to formulate something in both practice and education that can be called Japan's own. As a result, Japanese nurses use discretion in choosing what is useful to them from the ideas and experience of their colleagues in other parts of the world. (1984: 106)

The future of nursing in Japan and of the nurses' new image and position, it seems, is firmly in the hands of Japan's nurses. What remains an interesting question is how this shift in the profession may or may not affect continuing Japanese notions of illness as polluting and of nurses as having 'low status in Japanese society due to the nature of their job, which includes handling the bodily dirt of the patients' (Ohnuki-Tierney 1984: 30).

NOTES

1. See Hendry (1984: 215–22) for more detail about how these ideas are taught.
2. In 1869 the government decided to adopt officially the German system of medical education and, until 1946, medical students had to know German. Lock (1980: 235) notes that it was 'usual for diagnosis forms to be written in German'.
3. This is a rather difficult statement to ascertain as most Japanese now call themselves 'middle class', but in this large category (93 per cent of the Japanese population) nurses seem to be found at the lower end of the social spectrum. For example, during fieldwork, it was a surprise to learn that many of the Shima Peninsula Hospital nurses were the daughters of diving women (ama); yet upon talking to their supervisor, it was learned that these women made good nurses, returning to the profession after marriage and childbirth, for that is the work pattern their diving mothers followed.

4. When this chapter was first given as a paper, it was pointed out to the authors that many of these tasks fall in the domain of the nurse's aide; yet it remains important that in Japan these tasks are those of family and that the Japanese Nursing Association is still trying to create the position of nurse's aide.

5. Among foreign students in Japan there is a dread of going into hospital for the very reason that they do not have family members around who will care for them and they are very aware that this means they will not receive what they perceive as proper medical care.

6. See Ueno (1987) 'A new perspective on women's issues in Japan', *Current Anthropology*, for some ways in which modern feminist theories on women in Japan can be re-evaluated in light of Japanese household structure and household division of labour.

7. The idea of the nurse as doctor's *helper* exists in all areas of the profession. Dr von Hardenberg, a German surgeon who worked in Japan, was amazed that in surgery a nurse did not handle the instruments. This was the task of the least senior doctor on the team; the nurse's job was to clean blood and sweat from the surgeon as he worked. According to Dr von Hardenberg, 'Because of the role of the nurse in surgery, Japanese operations are incredibly neat and clean to an almost unbelievable extent yet the nurse was not really counted as part of the surgical team' (personal communication).

8. According to Lia Keneaa, an Ethiopian nurse trained in the USA and currently finishing her Master's Thesis on Nursing Education in Japan, young nurses in Japan have begun to express their unhappiness with this role. One of the queries she put to student nurses in her thesis questionnaire was 'what do you feel is the greatest problem with your training?' One of the most frequent replies was 'lack of confidence'; that is, they were not taught to have confidence in their ability as professionals. When Ms Keneaa pointed this out to a senior nursing supervisor, the reply was 'of course, they are not expected to have confidence; that is not their job. They must do as they are told' (personal communication).

Chapter Five

COLONIAL SISTERS: NURSES IN UGANDA[1]

PAT HOLDEN

This paper is concerned with some of the issues that arise when an essentially western occupation, that of nursing, is transferred to a different cultural setting, in this case Uganda in East Africa.[2] The anthropologist Hilda Kuper, writing about nurses in South Africa, has written of the ambivalence that is experienced by black South African nurses in:

> the contradiction between the traditional systems in which nursing is part of the network of reciprocal rights and obligations that constitute kinship, and the Western system in which illness, not relationship, is a factor which determines institutional care. (1965: 217)

I shall suggest that the 'ambivalence' experienced by Ugandan nurses at present working in Mulago Hospital, Kampala, is related to the fact that their western-style training has left them ill equipped to deal with the situation of crisis that now confronts the hospital. Historical material relating to the colonial period shows that some of the early preoccupations found in the development of nursing in Britain, such as concern with class, with the selection of the 'right type of woman', emphasis on uniform as a symbol of control and order, ideas of separation and the control of sexual morality, were further emphasised and developed during the later colonial period by European nursing sisters working in Uganda. Some of the same preoccupations are still evident in Mulago Hospital today but the crisis situation that has existed in the hospital for some years has led nurses to alter and modify their perceptions of their role and work.

OVERSEAS NURSING: THE EARLY PERIOD

The tradition for women to nurse overseas as part of an organised group had an important precedent in the Crimea, under the direction of Florence Nightingale. Here, women of different social classes and backgrounds are said to have worked together, contributing to the war effort and practising a form of female heroism sanctioned by both the church and the state. Analogies were often drawn between the nurse working overseas and the soldier. Sarah Tooley notes that:

> No place is too remote, no climate too deadly, for the nurse to ply her ministrations. Like the soldier she obeys the call of duty, and if need be gives her life for the cause.
>
> (1906: Preface)

In addition to contributing to the war effort, a number of nurses went out to various parts of the British colonial empire during the second part of the nineteenth century. It was expected in the colonies that every woman would have to be a 'born nurse' but it became increasingly evident that doctors alone could not cope with the illnesses and frequent deaths experienced by the many Europeans who were living and working overseas. In 1892 a nursing association was founded to engage nurses in England to go to nurse Europeans in India, and in 1895 the Colonial Nursing Association (renamed the Overseas Nursing Association in 1919) was founded to send nurses out to government hospitals in the British Crown Colonies and Protectorates and to provide private nurses in centres where the British inhabitants had formed local communities. The first English nurse selected by the ONA went to Mauritius in 1896, followed by two nurses who were sent to Accra in the same year.

In the early colonial period health services were provided primarily for expatriates. However, colonial officers and others often worked closely with native populations and there was an awareness of the need to manage the health of indigenous peoples to avoid threat to the health of expatriates. This was partially achieved by policies of separation, which encouraged the building of expatriate dwellings away from those of natives, or by measures such as advice recommending that native servants should keep separate buckets for their own washing.

However, changing attitudes towards the notion of development during the twentieth century involved an increased sense of responsibility for native health, as well as an acknowledgement of the economic importance of maintaining a healthy working population in a developing country. The early recruitment of nurses for the colonies coincided with the realisation that there was a growing need to train native personnel to assist with health care work. Thus, in 1903, a matron was selected to train native nurses for Sierra Leone, although this was referred to at the time as an 'interesting but not very hopeful experiment' (ONA papers).

Ideas about class played an important part in the recruitment of European women for nursing service overseas. A number of authors have shown that class distinctions were a significant factor in the development of modern nursing in Britain in the nineteenth and twentieth centuries, as is illustrated by the well-known division which was made between 'ladies' and 'probationers' (see e.g. Abel-Smith 1960; Summers 1983). It is arguable that the class divisions and social mores of British life were even more rigidly enforced in the colonial situation than at home because of the need to maintain distance from, and ideas of superiority to, the native races. Thus, the rules relating to the sexual separation of the races were in particular strictly adhered to and, as is usual, the burden for this generally fell upon women. The European nurse was to some extent seen as particularly vulnerable with regard to the various sexual boundaries. Overseas, she might be unmarried or widowed and a working woman in the male-dominated white colonial service where it was the norm for women to be wives. She might be expected to come into contact with the bodies of men. Her work involved close association with native workers to whom she was expected to be an example of morality and discipline.

The need to find the 'right type of women' for this work is reflected in the papers of the ONA. A paper concerning recruitment to the Gold Coast in 1896 notes that it was most desirable that as nice a class of person may be chosen as possible 'for good looks and a cheerful disposition go a long way in the successful management of illness in this colony'. A letter to the ONA from the office of the Under-Secretary of State in the Colonial Office advises that nurses for the colonial hospital in Lagos should not be chosen from the domestic servant class

69

because they would be less able than nurses of higher social standing to resist the temptations to which they would be exposed in a colony. A letter concerning recruitment for Malawi rejects a Mrs Clark on the grounds that her papers show that she is not a lady.

The early recruitment of nurses to the colonies took place during a period when health and morality were still overtly interlinked. As Rosenberg shows, modern nursing developed at a time when illness was still seen as a sign of moral failure in which the body was regarded as 'a constant source of pollution unless vigorously cleansed'. Of Florence Nightingale, he says:

> The hospital seemed to her quite literally a microcosm of
> society, every part inter-related and all reflecting a particular
> moral order. Just as order in the body and an appropriate
> physical and psychological equilibrium constituted health for
> the individual, so order in the hospital implied a low incidence
> of fever and wound infections for its inhabitants. (1979: 124)

This, he adds, accounts for the emphasis on frugality, good housekeeping and the obsessive concern with emptying chamber pots, cleanliness of bedding and endless scrubbing of floors and mackintoshes that were found in hospitals. Hostels for nurses represented a reflection of the world of the hospital. They were places of orderliness and discipline where the practice of good housekeeping could be learnt. Nurses themselves were, in addition, expected to be symbols of order, discipline, and morality with their starched white uniforms and time-pieces reflecting this (Dean and Bolton 1980).

Information for nurses going overseas in the early colonial period, as might be expected, consisted of long lists of uniform requirements. Duty uniform for nurses going to West Africa was to be worn on duty at any hour of the day or night. In 1902 nurses going to Sierra Leone were instructed to wear uniforms indoors when on duty, and also outside the home except by special permission of the superintendent. A letter of 1903 reports on the levity of conduct of some nurses overseas and stresses that nurses should devote themselves to duty and on no account put pleasure first. For this reason, nurses were to wear uniforms at all times to remind them that their first duty was to the sick. Other papers note that nurses should not be invited to card parties at the club or to bachelors' entertainments (ONA papers).

One area in which European nursing sisters were regarded from early times as being particularly influential was that of the education of African mothers. In 1927, a pamphlet published by the Lady Grigg Welfare League drew attention to the importance of mothers as the conveyors of good health practices.[3] Native women were criticised for 'unwise' practices such as carrying their babies strapped to their backs, or placing them on the ground while they worked in the fields, or dancing until the small hours of the morning. The pamphlet concludes:

> The child of today being the father of the man of the future, it is essential that everything possible should be done during the early life of the new generations of Africans to ensure the healthy development and proper care of those untutored mothers of the race who live lives of drudgery under tribal conditions. (1927: 11)

The same theme recurs in a later paper in 1939 which says of the European nurse overseas that:

> through nursing the sick in native hospitals, training local nurses in welfare work among mothers and babies she is brought closely in touch with the life of the people, and her value to the colony increases as she becomes familiar with the language and customs and wins the confidence of the native people, especially woman. (ONA papers)

As I have noted above, the training of local staff was an accepted part of overseas nursing work from the beginning of this century. However, a more systematic approach to the training of local nurses does not appear to have been started until the 1940s. A monograph by Welch (1941) makes the following points and recommendations. Medical training for men in Africa had had a well-defined programme while there had been nothing similar for women. In East Africa nurse training for women had been difficult because of lack of pre-vocational education. There was thus a need for increased educational opportunities for women. Most training of female nurses had been undertaken by missions where there were more European women workers and nurses who had been in close contact with the local community and were therefore able to attract a 'better type of girl' for training than government hospitals.

The paper continues that preventive medicine was in the hands of women who by their position in African society could control the acceptance of new ideas. The key to preventive medicine was to be the newly trained public health nurse who would act both as nurse and educator. The health visitor would supply all these services to families in a given area and act as a family friend. This would mean the broadening of the idea of nursing away from that of a 'recluse' within the four walls of an institution to that of a widely known member of society. Thus, the primary need in Africa was for a non-institutional rural community nursing service, 'an army of public health or community nurses who can reach the hospital-shy population'.

Nutritional deficiency was also recognised at this time as a major medical problem and this was seen as something with which African women as mothers were closely concerned.

Welch's report concludes that 'native' nurses would have to be educated to separate themselves from their previous world of magic and that they would also have to help their patients learn to harmonise the old with the new. Scientific facts could, for example, she adds, be presented in familiar settings. Modern trends would have to be incorporated into nurse training in Africa and these would include the concept of nursing as preventive and involve mental, social, and environmental factors.

The report points to a number of issues that became increasingly significant in the later colonial period with regard to the recruitment and training of African girls: the need for 'better quality' girls and thus for increased educational opportunities for women, the importance of nurses in preventive health work, and the idea that nurses would need to be separated from their home backgrounds in order to become 'good nurses'.

UGANDA IN THE LATER COLONIAL PERIOD

Welch's paper (1941) set out some of the ideals for the future of nursing in Africa. Biographies and reminiscences collected from nurses who worked in Uganda during the 1940s, 1950s, and 1960s describe how the implementation of these plans was constantly beset by problems: insufficient education for girls, resistance in Muslim areas to women working as nurses, lack of accommodation for girls in training, shortage of qualified teachers and girls reluctant to leave their home areas once trained. Colonial medical services were constantly overburdened and under-resourced and frequently forced to concentrate on curative services with their quick results rather than on preventive measures.

The reminiscences provide some indication of why European nurses were attracted to work overseas and what this work entailed once they arrived.

A number already had relatives working abroad. Many were the daughters or sisters of government officials, missionaries, or doctors. Most express some idea of 'calling' to the work and a number mention a religious motive. Relatives and colleagues often opposed the move overseas. Matrons sometimes opposed the idea of recruitment to the colonial service, preferring that their nurses should do mission work or join the forces' nursing services. Some nurses gave up the security of a good job and chances of promotion and were thought 'mad' by their friends and relations.

There were, however, many attractions in overseas nursing. There was the chance for travel to exotic places and the excitement that this promised. Overseas, nurses were given their own or a shared house and this compared favourably with the old-fashioned discipline of nurses' homes in Britain at the time. They were often given responsibility for running small hospitals and health centres when they were still quite young, and there was opportunity for improvisation and initiative in the work they were carrying out. They felt respected in the community by both local people and expatriates. They also earned more money overseas. One complains that she was appointed on the same salary as the governor's chauffeur in 1942, but another notes that in 1945 her salary was £240 which was 'princely' compared with the £65 she was earning in Britain.

A number of nurses felt that the experience gained during the depression and in the war years with evacuees or in bombed areas provided them with important grounding for overseas work. They had learnt in these years to use primus stoves and fish kettles for sterilising. Experience of working in slums was also considered to be useful for those planning to nurse in Africa (Lady Gregg Welfare League 1927).

The selection of the 'right type of woman' for nursing overseas continued to be a preoccupation of the later colonial years. Descriptions of interviews provided by some of the women who were recruited in the 1930s, 1940s, and 1950s give some indication of how this selection took place. The interviewing board is variously described as consisting of 'women who had lived in various colonies but as they were married knew nothing of the work involved', as 'ex-matrons' and 'former colonial people', 'ex-governors' wives', 'a lot of elderly people in hats', 'aristocratic-looking ladies in hats', and 'non-professional people'.

At an interview more interest appears to have been shown in the applicants' hobbies and social background than in their professional skills. They were asked, for example, if they could sew, play tennis, or ride. One was asked if she knew her patients would be black, another if she could get on with other races, and another if she could speak African languages. Others were asked if they knew how to sterilise instruments using a primus stove.

The actual work, once they had arrived in Uganda, consisted largely of general administration and the running of wards, with the actual nursing done by the nurses and orderlies (male nurses) they were training. They checked stores of blankets and linen 'endlessly' and tried to 'keep an eye' on the drugs in their charge. Most of the nursing sisters felt that their trainees did their best but others were more critical, especially of the auxiliaries, who are said to have been unreliable, falling asleep on duty and eating the patients' food. The black-market trade in drugs and the theft of equipment was acknowledged as a perennial problem, and there are many stories told by nurses of practices such as that of the orderly who set up a centre outside the hospital offering injections given with a blunt safety pin.

Serious attempts at systematic training began in the 1940s in Uganda. A recurrent theme of the memoirs of this period is that of the difficulty of finding the 'right type of girl' for training, especially because of the lack of educational opportunities for Ugandan girls at this time. One sister, describing her work at Mulago Hospital (the main native government hospital in the territory), Kampala, in the 1940s, says she felt that she should be trying to raise standards but that girls were of low educational background and knew no English and were barely literate in Luganda. She was assisted in the classroom by a male charge nurse who translated into Luganda as she taught in English. Between them they revised a textbook which had been written by the first matron, into both English and Luganda. Accounts are provided of the efforts made during this period to make do with old buildings as class-rooms and as nurses' homes, to supervise the construction of new buildings, and to rewrite syllabuses to suit local conditions.

From an early period the attempts to feminise the nursing profession in Uganda included the provision of hostels for girls in training. European nurses fought hard to ensure that there was adequate single-sex accommodation for nurses in training. This provided the girls with the rest, food, and recreation seen as necessary for those in training. Implicit in this hostelisation, however, was the idea of 'separation' cited by Welch (1941). The full incorporation of Ugandan girls into a western-style nursing system involved separation from their home background with its associations with superstition and traditional medicines, as well as with indiscipline and loose sexual morals. The ideological importance of the sexual and moral integrity of nurses in the history of the development of modern nursing in Britain is well documented. This took on a slightly different meaning in the colonial situation where African trainees were often seen by the colonial authorities as coming from backgrounds where sexual morals were customarily lax.

Thus, the professionalisation of nursing in Uganda, as in other African countries, involved efforts at control over nurses in training through the 'regulation' of female sexuality. Much effort was expended on this by both mission and government organisations. Such effort often led to frustration and many nurses, in their reminiscences, express their feelings of disillusionment and disappointment which they felt when their 'best girls' became pregnant and had to leave. One nurse says that in 1945 in Mulago many girls became pregnant during training and that this meant instant dismissal. She adds, however, that some had babies already but they had managed to conceal it from the matron who had taken them on. In the process of selection of girls for nurse training, the colonial sisters sometimes felt that the missions, who also provided education for girls, were able to have the 'best pick' of the trainees, with Mulago left to make do with those who were left.

Education for African nurses involved the provision of a new culture, incorporating a 'moral universe' in which the control of leisure also played a significant role. European nursing sisters describe how they bought tennis shoes and netballs for girls, took them on trips to the lake to swim, bought cameras for them, indoor games and wool for knitting. Girls were sometimes invited into their homes for meals, partly to teach them 'European ways' as preparation for going overseas for further training.

The separation and disciplining of girls, many nurses believed, was approved of by local people. A nurse who worked for the Church Missionary Society in the 1940s says that discipline was strict but that parents considered that they held their girls in trust for them. They were helped in recruitment, she adds, by the fact that princesses and senior chiefs' daughters came to them for training.

Uniforms were also considered important and there are many descriptions of tireless efforts made by nurse tutors to produce uniforms out of local cotton, designed in various colours to indicate the nursing hierarchy.

The transference of western-style nursing to Africa thus involved the construction of an organisation which attempted as far as possible to replicate that of the home culture of the colonialists. However, as I have indicated, there was an ever-present awareness among European nursing sisters that this was a task beset by many difficulties. There are many other issues related to this 'transference' which are beyond the scope of this paper, and some of which are summed up aptly by Schuster in her paper on Zambian nurses. She notes, for example, that:

> It does not follow ... that young women recruited to nurse-training programmes in countries of the Third World fit into the western cultural paradigm, either in terms of their own motivation to enter professional training, or in terms of their reception as nurses by their societies. There may instead be serious problems of culture clash. (1981: 79)

However, it should be emphasised that the determined efforts of many European nursing sisters, who were committed to the essential values of the profession in which they were working, did provide the foundation of what has developed into an important career for African women over the last forty years. It is important to note also that, although the response to nursing as a profession for women has been variable in different parts of Africa, it has on the whole become a socially acceptable profession for women which has provided them with status and prestige and has identified them with 'Westernisation and modernisation' (Kuper 1965). As independent career women nurses have also at times

76

been accused of corruption and sexual immorality, and they have shouldered the many criticisms directed at the provision of health services in Africa.

It is the aim of this chapter to consider some of the issues that arise when some of the elements which are associated with western-style nursing become eroded, as has been the case in many African hospitals over the past few years. The brief examination of nurses and current working conditions in Mulago Hospital that follows suggests that the symbolic systems of western nursing are transformed or reinterpreted in response to situations of crisis.

MULAGO HOSPITAL IN THE 1980s

The late 1950s and early 1960s represented a period of considerable expansion of the medical services in Uganda. The prestige of nursing gradually rose and higher educational qualifications were demanded for entry. A new training school opened in 1954 and a well-equipped nurses' hostel was built in 1955. In 1956 a Nurses and Midwives Council was formed. In 1967 there was reciprocity with the General Nursing Council for England and Wales.

The new Mulago Hospital was opened in Kampala in 1962. It is a six-storey building and at its inception was equipped to the highest standards. When it was built it was an important show-piece, desired by both medical personnel and politicians. It symbolised Uganda's intellectual achievements and provided a promise of better treatment for all Ugandans through its outreach programmes. As well as being the major teaching hospital, and the main hospital for Kampala, it is also the main referral system for Uganda.

The hospital today is staffed almost entirely by Ugandan nurses. Some of the older nurses remember the nurses whose memoirs are cited above. These Ugandan nurses have helped to train the subsequent generations who now staff the hospital. But the world of Mulago is very different from that of the late colonial period. Over the years there has been a serious breakdown in the provision of medical services because of the severe economic and political problems that the country has faced. In 1985, at the time of my visit, there was, for example, no proper water supply, soap, disinfectant, or bed linen. Drains and latrines were blocked,

77

windows broken and essential equipment completely out of use.

Since the early 1970s the hospital is said to have declined steadily. Those suffering from the effects of violence have regularly been brought to the hospital but the hospital itself has also been the arena for the playing out of political conflicts. Politicians and military men have been regular users and abusers of the hospital. Many have hidden in it or been dragged away from its sanctuary. In 1979 the hospital suffered severe damage during army looting. Mattresses are said to have been thrown from the windows. Some now-derelict buildings, their damp walls dripping, have bullet marks on the walls and the buildings are used by a few families sheltering inside them.

Remarkably, however, the hospital continues to function and to offer some kind of service. Within this institution it is the nurses who are most visible. Their presence is dignified and enhanced by beautifully laundered uniforms. Visitors to Kampala and others comment on the way in which nurses continue to turn up for work at the hospital looking so well dressed. In the nurses' hostel, now an almost derelict building, the laundry room is kept in good working order.

Doctors are often absent from the hospital, finding that the shortage of staff, equipment, or paper, or the dirty surroundings, makes their job almost impossible. Or, with the current rate of inflation making it impossible to exist on a government salary, they may be away at private clinics or attending to private business concerns. Nurses also do other things to supplement their salaries, activities referred to as *magendo*, strategies for survival that are an accepted part of life in East Africa now. They also work in private clinics when they should be at the hospital. Some take unpaid leave and then fail to return to work, making it impossible for the hospital to replace them. Husbands who once supported women in their nursing careers have been known to hide the uniforms so that they can't go to work. Salaries are so low because of inflation that husbands say that their wives would be better off helping them with their businesses or starting their own. Many nurses have been widowed, or have lost fathers, sons, and brothers in recent years, and they are now struggling to pay school fees, rent, and transport costs.

Security in the hospital is poor. Many people, including patients' relatives and ancillary workers for whom the hospital can no longer afford uniforms, wander freely in the hospital. The building is constructed on an open verandah style with many stairways, making it difficult to police effectively. Nurses on night duty frequently lock themselves in their rooms for fear of violent attack and, not unusually, go to sleep.

So why do nurses continue to come to work at the hospital? In conversation with hospital staff, I was given the following reasons. They can earn money primarily, even though their transport costs may equal their total salary. There are also said to be side benefits (sometimes illegal) such as petty theft and illegal payments demanded from patients. As government employees they are entitled to housing and transport (if these are available). But these are clearly not the only reasons why many nurses continue to turn up at work. Some people said that nurses continued to come to work because they were 'born nurses', others because they were 'religious'. Some came for the social aspects of hospital life; others as an escape from an even more difficult and dangerous home life. In answer to questions as to why they had become nurses in the first place, they gave reasons such as attraction to the uniform, encouragement from parents, or the fact that they were always considered the gentle or caring one in the family.

Almost everyone in the hospital, including nurses themselves, was ready to offer criticisms of the profession. Nurses were said to have 'lost' or 'forgotten their role'. They were said to be no longer interested in the job, but only in the money. The quality of entrant was said to have gone down, with girls entering nursing only if they failed to get into any other form of higher education. One sister said that they no longer knew how to look after patients. They treated them 'as furniture'.

Considerable concern was expressed over discipline. It was said that younger nurses didn't know how to discipline each other. Many middle-range nurses had gone overseas or left the profession because of its difficulties and insecurity, so that nurses were getting promotion too young. Nurses were said to be afraid of each other because of the uncertain political atmosphere. It was still felt by the majority that missions produced better disciplined and in some cases better nurses because, as one nurse said, they are 'more religious'.[4]

Many of the responses thus indicated that there was continuing 'lip service' to ideals such as 'vocation', 'caring', 'devotion to duty' even if these ideals were difficult to maintain. It is arguable that these ideals derived from western-style nurse training have to some extent contributed to a continuing shared collective ideology of what nursing should be, which has in turn both legitimated and reinforced nurses' determination to continue work in the face of extremely difficult circumstances.

CONCLUSION

In conclusion, I would like tentatively to suggest some of the ways in which the colonial legacy of western-style nursing has both provided positive values which can be seen as the basis of the service that is currently being maintained in the hospital under extremely difficult circumstances and at the same time created areas of 'ambivalence' in nurses' attitudes towards their role and work.

Relatives

The development of medicine in the West has involved increased emphasis on the hospital as opposed to the home as a place where patients are both cured and cared for (Abel-Smith 1960). This has of necessity involved the separation of relatives from the hospital routine. Conflicts have clearly been created by this separation in the African setting, where, as Kuper says, 'the obligation to care for the sick was part of a network of kinship obligation' in which the isolated stranger had no place (1965: 216). Missionary hospitals, in particular, have attempted in Africa to involve relatives in the caring process, with the construction of hospitals on one floor and with wide verandahs and waiting areas in the grounds. Nevertheless, this involvement has still been to a large extent controlled by hospital staff.

In Mulago today the control is of a different order. Nurses grudgingly accept the fact that relatives now bring food in, feed the patients, bring in bed linen and clothes, wash the patients, and sit with them day and night, often on the floor surrounded by their pos- sessions. To all appearances, they seem like refugees camped in a modern style hospital with cold marble floors, dirty walls, and rusting beds.

The nurses are uneasy with the situation. Periodically, for example, on the day when doctors were examining medical students, relatives were shooed away. Patients were hastily tidied, their ragged clothes and bed sheets rearranged. The nurses' unease is partly created by the feeling that they are no longer able (or willing) to carry out aspects of nursing which are integral to their western-style training, namely the hands-on care of patients. Hence the accusation that young nurses treat patients 'like furniture'. This unease was also expressed obliquely, through fears that relatives might bring in traditional medicines with the food, by the nurse tutor who said that in a recent examination none of the nurses had been able to answer questions about feeding patients and by the complaints of patients that the nurses don't help them or that they are sometimes cruel. Nurses appear to hover on the edge of wards or sit in the outer office while patients in the wards are clearly in need of attention. They administer injections and carry out certain technical jobs but the overall impression is that they have been peripheralised and have consequently become uncertain of the nature of their role as nurses.[5]

Equipment

This peripheralisation is also related to the question of equipment. Many nurses have never seen much of the hospital equipment in working order. One of the major attractions of western nursing is its association with modernisation, with opportunities for education, travel, and access to new technology. Without these aspects much of the prestige associated with nursing has been lost. For the early European nursing sisters, improvisation meant fish kettles and primus stoves in the tradition of guiding and adventure stories. For nurses in Mulago, improvisation means finding old clothes for patients to wear, rags for them to sleep on, or scraps of paper so that records can be kept and doctors thus persuaded to come and look at a patient. In 1985 nurses were spending many hours a day scrubbing operating floors covered in sewage which had seeped from blocked drains in order to persuade doctors to operate on patients.

Orderliness

The maintenance of 'orderliness' continues to be an important aspect of nursing in Mulago. Many nurses expressed shame that shortage of water and cleaning fluids meant that many wards weren't properly cleaned. One elderly nurse who runs the child malnutrition unit with great success said that during the day she managed to keep relatives' possessions out of the ward but that at night they brought them inside for security's sake creating a 'mess' over which she had no control. In the main hospital, beds continue to be arranged in conventional rows and extra beds were perceived as 'overcrowding' even if this wasn't really the case given the crisis situation currently experienced by the hospital. The notion of 'orderliness', however, might also be seen as providing nurses with some immediately achievable goal in a situation where chaos and disorder threaten constantly to be the prevailing norm.

Uniforms

Uniforms, as I have indicated, continue to be an important aspect of the prestige attached to nursing, and in some cases appear to be the most important reason for nurses' continuing attraction to the profession. I noted above that uniforms played an important part in the symbolic systems associated with colonial nursing, by emphasising order, control, and devotion to duty. In Uganda today, nurses' uniforms have taken on a different symbolic meaning: a reminder of a more ordered past, continuing pride in a profession that has suffered severe difficulties, and perhaps a measure of security for those who wear them. Husbands may hide the uniforms but they cannot detract from what nursing has come to symbolize for those who wear them.

Nurses have been encouraged by their western-style training to regard themselves as an élite, a 'better type of girl'. Changing social circumstances have forced them to re-examine what nursing is without the prestige it once had. Conflicts relating to the transference of colonial medical systems to other cultures continue to create 'ambivalences' for nurses. However, in the context of Mulago Hospital, many of the values derived from western-style training now form the impetus for the service that remarkably continues to be carried out at the hospital.

NOTES

1. Versions of this chapter have been delivered at seminars at the Oxford Women's Anthropology Seminar, at the Institute of Social

Anthropology, University of Oxford, at the Wellcome Institute for the History of Medicine, University of Oxford, at Brunel University, and at the conference 'International Nursing: the Cross-Cultural Context' held in Edmonton, Canada, in May 1986. My visit to Edmonton to give this paper was sponsored by the British Council and the Wellcome Trust. I would like to thank both these organisations for their support.

2. The material on which this chapter is based is drawn from three main sources: (i) papers of the Overseas Nursing Association; (ii) reminiscences and other biographical material collected by Alison Smith for the Oxford Development Records Project for the project Public Health Services in Africa; (iii) interviews and participant observation which I carried out in Mulago Hospital, Uganda in May/June 1985 while undertaking work for the Overseas Development Administration.

3. Advice of this kind is found for example in the 'little green book', *Hints on the Preservation of Health in the Tropics*, 1952, which was given to expatriates going to the tropics in the 1950s and 1960s.

4. Material for the Oxford Development Records Project was collected from approximately 100 nursing sisters who had worked in colonial Africa during this century. Thanks are due to them for the generous way in which they have shared their stories and experiences.

5. In this section I refer to a situation that existed in 1985, and I have accordingly treated it as the ethnographic present.

Chapter Six

A WARD OF MY OWN: SOCIAL ORGANIZATION AND IDENTITY AMONG HOSPITAL DOMESTICS

LIZ HART

INTRODUCTION

This chapter focuses on domestic assistants who work at a large teaching hospital in the West Midlands. The findings presented here are drawn from a comparative study of domestic staff in two different locations – a hospital and a student hostel – although this paper will concentrate mainly on the former. Among other things, the effect of part-time shift work upon social organisation and work identity is discussed, as are the ways the women concerned adapt and respond to working in a hospital situation. In particular, the chapter looks at the informal role played by domestic assistants in patient care and concludes that one possible consequence of privatisation will be to demolish the informal structures which support loyalty and commitment to the ward and the hospital. The material presented here is intentionally descriptive, as one aim of this paper is to understand dimensions of hospital domestic work which lie outside the grasp of quantitative analysis.

METHODOLOGY

For almost twelve months, until December 1985, I worked as a domestic assistant in order to carry out participant research funded by the ESRC.[1] The first period of fieldwork was spent at a student hostel, followed by six months at a large and prestigious teaching hospital. At the hostel I was one of eighteen domestics who cleaned the students' rooms and main buildings, while at the hospital I was one of over 200 other women who worked as domestic assistants on wards, in departments, operating theatres, and the nurses' home.

Research began at a time when domestic services at the hospital were under pressure to make efficiency savings and, shortly before fieldwork started, working hours on some shifts had been shortened. Although both personnel and domestic service managers were interested in the research, they were unable to give the domestic assistants time out to be interviewed. The only way to gain access to the women in their work-place was to work alongside them and make time for them to get to know me. The method adopted is known as 'open participant observation'; it was pioneered in Britain in the late 1950s and early 1960s by researchers at Manchester University and produced two classic workshop ethnographies (Cunnison 1966; Lupton 1963). Although research was carried out openly there were often times when I met people in the hospital who saw me in my green overall as a domestic assistant. This gave me direct experience of the way other groups within the hospital hierarchy responded to domestics in everyday situations. For example, I noticed that caterers – one step up from domestics – generally ignored me, while porters chatted and joked. I was invisible to doctors – particularly when mopping the stairs – while patients' visitors sought me out to ask directions. As my workmates pointed out, there was, however, one important difference between me and them since I did not take sole responsibility for the cleanliness of my work area and always cleaned under a workmate's supervision. In addition, unlike the other domestics, I did not clock on and was not subject to the same work discipline (although on one occasion I was asked by a supervisor to work overtime). Domestic work made structured data collection problematic – methods and the approach had to be flexible – seizing a quiet moment in the kitchen to conduct informal interviews or, as I cleaned the patients' lockers, using the tape-recorder to note everyday conversation. I worked on five different wards, including the cancer ward, the operating theatres, two departments, the doctors' residence, and also interviewed domestic assistants at the nurses' home. Because of the six months' deadline for fieldwork, for several weeks I worked two shifts a day – mornings from 7.30 and evenings from 5 to 9 p.m.

Although relations between domestic managers and staff seemed fairly relaxed and friendly, during the course of fieldwork the domestic assistants grew increasingly uncertain about the future of their jobs if domestic services were contracted out (under the terms of DHSS Circular HC (83) 18) or, even if they stayed in-house, about the likely cut in working hours and staff levels. Insecurity naturally bred suspicion. Some of the women assumed at first that I must be a spy for either management or a private contractor. It seems that these ways of thinking were not confined to this particular hospital. Mailly conducted field research with twelve Health Authorities in England and interviewed managers at both district and unit level, many of whom noted 'a disillusionment and "low-trust" syndrome amongst staff' as an effect of competitive tendering (1985: 14). Without doubt the women to whom I talked felt disillusioned and demoralised by the changes they were witnessing. The longer they had worked at the hospital the more demoralised they seemed to be. Indeed, long-serving domestics perceived privatisation as part of a process of change in work organisation which had begun in the early 1970s and not as an entirely new development. Generally speaking, the domestic assistants were against the contracting-out of domestic services and many of them had joined NUPE in protest. Even so, if and when private contractors took over, they looked forward to the prospect of relatively large redundancy payments. Underlying these attitudes was the knowledge that the shortening of working hours and the introduction of shorter shifts served anyway to erode fringe benefits like sick pay and holiday pay. In addition, the women knew that in the event of redundancy they could easily move in and out of work with a private contractor. Paradoxically, private contractors served both as a threat to their present jobs and as a safety net against unemployment. The women garnered the information on which they based these expectations partly on rumour (NUPE said it would not on principle negotiate redundancy payments) and partly on information from women they knew who worked at other local hospitals or for private contractors. The attraction of lump-sum redundancy payments needs to be seen in the context of low pay and the fact that many of the women were long-serving and expected approximately £1,000.

DOMESTIC ASSISTANTS

Recently growing concern with the worsening pay and working conditions of domestic workers has prompted three separate studies of cleaners, two of them published by the Low Pay Unit

(Beardwell *et al.* 1981; Daley 1985; Coyle 1986). These studies' respective findings suggest that cleaning work is typically married women's work, part-time, low-paid, often involving unsocial hours, poor and sometimes even dangerous working conditions. Two other studies, one by the Manpower Studies Unit (1976), the other by Doyal, Hunt, and Mellor (1981), have looked *inter alia* at ancillary hospital staff and in particular those who came as migrant workers to the NHS. As a recent report by the Labour Research Department (LRD) shows, contract cleaners appear to be by far the worst off: they are largely non-unionised, working part-time hours which are too short to bring them within the range of employment protection, and their working conditions and pay are in some cases described as 'appalling' (1987: 4–7).

In contrast, the domestic assistants with whom this study is concerned are directly employed by the Health Authority.[2] Most of my workmates were members of the National Union of Public Employees, and some of their supervisors members of the Confederation of Health Service Employees. Compared to those of the contract cleaners studied by Daley and by Coyle, working conditions for these hospital workers were relatively good, with access to an occupational health department and adequate health and safety regulations. Relations between the domestic services manager, her assistants, and the domestic staff were informal and fairly relaxed. Although recruitment 'through the grapevine' was not the only way managers recruited new staff, the use women made of their social networks to pass on and obtain job information helped to reinforce a personal style of management.

The Health Authority employs approximately 220 domestic assistants who work on a range of part-time shifts including mornings from 7.30 a.m. to 1.30 p.m.; afternoons from 1 p.m. to 4 p.m.; evenings from 5 p.m. to 8 p.m. (6 p.m. to 9 p.m. for the operating theatre domestics). Three women and one man, the last remaining of the full-time domestics, worked from 7.30 a.m. to 4 p.m. on a once-standard day shift that has now been phased out. Some women worked split shifts and others a two-week repeated pattern in which they always worked one Saturday or Sunday per fortnight. To ensure full cover on the wards the domestic assistants worked a five-day week spread over seven days and were paid a basic hourly rate of 183.95 pence on the wards and 4 pence less an hour when they worked elsewhere in the hospital (i.e. in 1985).

Though not well paid, this compares quite favourably with hourly rates for contract cleaners: Coyle found that, in the West Midlands, contractors have little problem recruiting labour at £1.40 per hour (Coyle 1986: 20). Reinforcing this point, a report by the Labour Research Department found that, where cleaners were unionised, pay was higher on average by 15 per cent (1986).[3]

In the late 1960s incentive bonus schemes and work study were introduced for manual workers in the NHS in an attempt to increase both pay and productivity. At this hospital domestic staff are now assessed at 90 per cent performance, receiving a 20 per cent bonus on their basic hours, with 'time and a half' for Saturday and 'double time' for Sunday working. For example, for a 37-hour week over five days, including weekend working (i.e. two enhanced payment days) earnings would amount to approximately £104 gross, which, with stoppages including tax, national insurance, union dues of 56 pence, and £5 savings, would leave approximately £68 net. In comparison, on the evening shift for a 15-hour week from Monday to Friday net pay would be approximately £31 (with no stoppage for national insurance). This variation in pay indicates quite clearly the wide variation in working hours, fringe benefits, and shift patterns among this particular group of part-time workers – a feature characteristic of part-time work (see for example Perkins 1983; Robinson and Wallace 1981; Lonsdale 1987).

PART-TIME WORK AND SOCIAL DIFFERENTIATION

In common with part-time women workers in industry, the hospital domestics worked a range of different shift patterns. Moreover, many of the domestic assistants regularly worked overtime – covering for women away ill or on holiday – some because they could not find full-time jobs locally. It was my impression, as Coyle also observed in her study, that it 'is not uncommon to find women cleaners who combine two or three part-time cleaning jobs' (1985: 7). As Robinson's survey of part-time employment in the EEC confirms, the growth of the part-time labour force is associated with a gradual contraction of weekly working hours (as among ancillary staff at this hospital). In the service sector for example, 26 per cent of women work fewer than fifteen hours per week (i.e. below the threshold which entitles them to sickness and holiday pay) and 96 per cent fewer than 35 hours (Robinson 1984: 59).

The differing age structure of each shift seemed to support the findings of several recent studies of women's work patterns which show how integral is the connection between age/life cycle stage, domestic responsibilities, hours, and type of work (see for example, Chaney 1981; Elias and Main 1982; Dex 1987; see also Pahl 1984: 81). It was my impression that the age and family structure of the women on each shift varied quite noticeably (as confirmed in an interview with the domestic services manager). Married women in their twenties with young families tended to be concentrated on the evening shift, their husbands looking after the children during this time. In contrast, the day shift tended to be composed of a few single women in their late teens, and a bigger group of married women aged from about thirty years upwards to retiring age with older, less dependent children.

It was my impression that many of the women who worked the shorter evening shift did so because it enabled them and their husbands to take sole responsibility for their children's up-bringing. They saw motherhood as a commitment of time spent with their children and placed great value upon the household's ability to manage itself and be seen publicly to do so. Part-time work supported this culture of independence because it enabled the women's paid work to be structured around child care. Part-time earnings improved the family's standard of living and, in cases where the husband was relatively well paid, provided the children with the material advantages of the respectable working class – holidays abroad with the school, fashionable clothes, computers and so on. Although these women were not highly paid, the money they earned was nevertheless crucial in providing what they termed the 'luxuries' – a label which seemed to cover anything from new shoes to holidays.

Those on the evening shift who were attracted by evening work formed one sub-group within the part-time work-force. In contrast, some women on the day shift wanted full-time jobs but could not find them locally. Others felt that in terms of pay 'it's not worth it' to do full-time hours, preferring instead the longer part-time shifts thereby paying less in national insurance and income tax than if full-time. Many of the first generation Afro-Caribbean women preferred to work the longer day shifts, some expressing the view that the shortening of working hours was tending to make the job less attractive to them and more attractive to younger white women. The women of Afro-Caribbean origin were among the longest serving domestic assistants and among those women who worked the longest shifts. It was recognised by managers I talked to that this group of domestic assistants resented, with some justification, the continued shortening of working hours. Shortly before fieldwork began, I was told that about fifty domestic assistants had taken voluntary redundancy, many of them (though not all) of Afro-Caribbean origin feeling that the hours had been cut beyond a point where 'it wasn't worth it' to do the job. At the present time high unemployment in the area and the shortening of working hours has widened the pool of women from the local labour market available for domestic work. The local residential pattern and the restrictions of low pay also have implications for the labour force. Locally the residential area is predominantly white middle and skilled working class. The Afro-Caribbean women from across town tend to pay higher travelling expenses, weighing these against earnings. All of the women I talked to, black and white, made these fine calculations, carefully weighing the cost of travel against working hours and take-home pay. As working hours get shorter, those with further to travel are reluctant to do so.

The evidence so far available about the work patterns of women who came to Britain from the West Indies suggests that they have high economic activity rates compared with either Asian or white women and that they are more likely to work full-time than women of British origin (see for example Phizacklea 1982; Runnymede Trust/Radical Statistics Group 1981: 103–4). One possible explanation for this is that both slavery and British colonial rule have had effects upon domestic organisation in the West Indies, where it is not uncommon to find the 'mother household' and 'grandmother family' in which the woman is the sole household head and main breadwinner (Phizacklea 1982: 100–2; see also, for a discussion of the West Indian family in Britain, Driver 1982; Barrow 1982). Phizacklea argues that, contrary to popular belief, West Indian women did not migrate to Britain to 'follow their men'; rather they were seeking employment to achieve their own independent socio-economic goals both as workers and as mothers (1982: 100–2). Those with dependent children tended to leave them with their own mothers in the West Indies until they had established a home for them in Britain.

Another factor related to ethnicity which affects attitudes to part-time work is length of service. When the NHS was expanding in the 1950s there was a short supply of indigenous labour coupled with a decline, since the Second World War, of immigrants from Ireland (Doyal *et al*. 1981: 55; Manpower Studies Unit 1976: 91). This was at a time when domestic work was more arduous than now, with longer hours (including full-time shifts), a six-day week, and poorer pay (there were no incentive bonus schemes at this time). As Doyal *et al*. have pointed out, by 1948 the NHS and the then Ministry of Labour were, with the Colonial Office's assistance, recruiting labour in many different countries, including Jamaica. Until the 1962 Commonwealth Immigration Act, the NHS actively recruited ancillary staff from the Caribbean in particular (Doyal *et al*. 1981: 55; see also Mama 1984).

The experience of women who had come originally as migrant workers to the hospital did not necessarily fit the 'married woman returner' pattern now associated with the 'typical' part-timer.[4] For example, one woman had come from Southern Ireland in the 1940s. She had worked for years as a full-time domestic and in that time had seen many different managers come and go and working hours shortened to a point where she felt 'it's not a real job any more'. This attitude was characteristic of domestics in a similar situation – whether from Southern Ireland or the West Indies – who had started work at the hospital when the NHS seemed to offer a 'job for life'. Unlike the younger women who welcomed the shorter shifts, these older domestics felt that the job itself had been impoverished, to the detriment of women, by the continued shortening of working hours. Moreover, at both the hospital and the hostel (with its all white work-force), many of the women over fifty years of age who had come into cleaning when their children were small had originally worked much longer hours than their younger colleagues were now doing, leaving their children with close female kin or neighbours.

Husband's occupation and job status also bore upon a woman's working hours. Those with a husband in a relatively well-paid job could afford to work the shorter hours, thus also protecting their husband's highly valued 'breadwinner' role. It was my impression that the husbands of the domestic assistants from one neighbourhood who were skilled 'time served' men thought it demeaning to have a wife who worked full-time. They seemed to feel that only the most poorly-paid men would welcome a woman's full-time earnings. Among themselves these particular women agreed with these views, being critical of neighbours who left their children with child-minders to go out to work. Individually, however, some women told me that they had wanted a full-time job when their children were small and had even taken up part-time work in defiance of their husbands' wishes. In this particular neighbourhood then collectively sanctioned moral codes took precedence over a woman's individual feelings about her paid work. Even when a full-time job and child-minding facilities were available, these particular women were prevented by the neighbourhood and family culture from taking advantage of them.

These part-time workers are not then a homogeneous group. There are differences in their attitude to the hospital as an employer, in the expectations they bring to their work, and in the way they perceive their mothering role and structure their working lives according to the demands of the family economy. Within the work-place these differences are expressed in various ways. For example, the women say the 'atmosphere' on evenings is quite different to that on days, it is more 'relaxed', the women 'quieter' and less involved in the union. The women on evenings say they feel 'left out' – there is no union representative on evenings and they feel marginalised in other ways, too. 'It's hard to get these evening jobs,' the women say, and they want to hang on to them. Other researchers have come across similar forms of social differentiation between women who work different hours (Yeandle 1984: 109; Wajcman: 1983). In the case of the factory workers studied by Wajcman, the women who worked the longer shifts felt that those on the shorter shift (who had young children) were committed, but in a different kind of way, to the workers' co-operative which lead to a 'polarisation' of the work-force (Wajcman 1983: 85, 119). This was also the case at both of the work-places I studied: the women who worked the longest hours always looked on women who worked the shortest shifts with something akin to suspicion.

Underlying these ways of thinking there is a belief that some cleaners are 'real cleaners' while others are not. Real cleaners are good workers, they work quickly, steadily, and are reliable. They set their own high standards of cleanliness, even defying their managers by bringing in their own wax polish or disinfectant. Understanding the job through long experience, the 'real cleaner' just gets on with it, resenting outside supervision, which is anyway, in her case, unnecessary. Real cleaners – or the 'old ones' as they are also known – make good supervisors, tough yet fair. Women who had been domestic assistants for many years looked on the 'real cleaner' with pride and valued being seen as such by work-mates. But younger women new to the work were more ambivalent in their attitude. For them the 'real cleaner' was associated with the typical 'Mrs Mop' or 'Hilda Ogden' image. But it was not uncommon to find women who remarked that their views of cleaners had changed the longer they had been in the job and who, almost despite themselves, had come to identify with it.

One of the features common to the two different research situations was that at both hostel and hospital the women used the terms the 'young ones' and 'old ones', and made distinctions between the 'real cleaners' and younger women – usually those on the shorter shifts with little experience of the work. These particular assessments drew on factors within the work-place – length of service, experience in the job, and so on. But these were reinfor- ced by social differentiation of another kind based on social age. Distinctions were made between the 'young ones' and the 'old ones' or, among the Afro-Caribbean women, the 'big women'. I realised that to gravitate from the ranks of 'bab' or 'girl' to 'big woman' or 'old one' it was first necessary to have made the social transition from girlhood to motherhood. It was not then simply a matter of chronological age. Although I was nearly forty years old, I was often addressed as 'bab' and on one occasion referred to (not unkindly) as 'the girl'. This can be explained by the fact that I had no children and very little experience of cleaning work. On both counts I ranked as a 'girl'.[5]

Notions of status and authority derived by women from family and neighbourhood are transferred directly to the work-place.[6] As among the women Daley studied in Ireland – three-quarters of whom first heard of their job through a relative, friend, or neighbour – neighbourhood and kinship connections played an extremely important part within the hospital (Daley 1985: 27). Women relied on their social networks for information about available jobs and many of them had 'spoken for' a friend, neighbour, or relative. For example, on one ward, of the four domestic assistants, two had sisters who worked at the hospital – one as a nurse – another had been 'spoken for' by her best friend and neighbour, while the fourth had started work with a group of close neighbours (one of them the sister of the work-mate referred to above). In her quantitative study Chaney found that, although a wide range of women who return to paid employment rely on their social networks for information about jobs, it is mainly those in part-time, local, 'typically female' jobs like catering and cleaning who obtain jobs in this way (1981: 41).

One of the consequences of this is that values and ways of thinking rooted in family and neighbourhood merge with status and authority structures arising from work practices, forming what could almost be described as an informal 'women's promotion ladder'. We have already seen that differentiation along lines of social age served to reinforce collectively sanctioned values and beliefs about, *inter alia*, marriage and motherhood, and to highlight ways of behaving proper to a particular life stage. I found similar ways of thinking about age among men who worked at the local factories, some of whom were married to domestic assistants. In the men's case their age-grade system was inter-woven with a formal system of apprenticeship (apprentices were described as being of a 'lowly age'). Although the women did not have such formal structures to support their social organisation, it was no less complex and intricate than that found among male workers in traditionally skilled occupations. In a similar way to these men the women placed great value upon learning through experience of the job and little value upon 'paper qualifications'.

These views had implications for the way they looked upon their managers and supervisors. From the higher rungs of their status ladder, the older women with grown children looked down at the young women managers – 'I'm not taking it from a girl my daughter's age!' A woman's status position was always relative. On one occasion a domestic in her late fifties, who had been a cleaner most of her working life, even referred to her forty-two-year-old supervisor as 'a slip of a girl'. But this did not totally exclude young women without children from gaining respect. One young super-visor in particular was liked because before her promotion she had been a 'good cleaner' and did not now 'throw her weight around'.

ON THE WARDS

Depending on ward size, there are usually three or four domestic assistants on each of the two day shifts and two on the evening shift, providing domestic cover from 7.30 a.m. until 8 p.m. Although the two-tier domestic grading of 'orderly' and 'domestic' is now obsolete, the domestic assistants continue to make distinctions between 'tops' and 'bottoms' work. Those who do 'tops' work clean the 'clean dirt', i.e. the top surfaces including the patients' lockers and ward sinks, and give out drinks to the patients. 'Bottoms' clean the 'dirty dirt', i.e. the 'bottom' surfaces, like floors and lavatories. In the past, 'bottoms' work was of slightly lower status and the pay a little less than that of the 'tops' or orderly. It was my impression that one or two of the older women who had been orderlies resented having to do bottoms work but younger women, although they used these terms, did not make associations of this kind. For example, one woman in her early twenties explained that she preferred 'bottoms' work because she found the patients less demanding than when doing 'tops'. Although the formal occupational structure has changed since the days of 'orderly' and 'domestic', informally the distinctions have become part of every- day usage, subtly resisting management attempts to introduce greater flexibility into work practices by making tasks interchangeable.

Because they work around patients cleaning lockers and beds, 'tops' tend to have more direct contact with patients than 'bottoms'. Domestic assistants are often asked to find things in the patient's locker, to pour drinks or help someone sit up. Although the latter is strictly a nursing duty, experienced domestics will sometimes lift a patient if a nurse is not readily available. 'Tops' begin the day by preparing the kitchen, the drinks trolley and the patients' dining room and then give out breakfasts and drinks under the direction of the nursing staff. After breakfast the empty trays are collected and stacked on the trolley which goes to the central kitchen. Teacups and beakers are collected, washed, and dried. Then a trolley is made up with cleaning materials which the 'tops' pushes around the ward damp-dusting the patients' lockers and beds, emptying and replacing the rubbish bags attached to each locker. Sinks, taps, surrounds, and mirrors are cleaned and paper towels and other disposables replaced. The patients' drinking water is changed and the ward made generally tidy. The ward kitchen floor is mopped clean twice a day, and there is washing-up to do (teacups and glasses), work surfaces and sinks to clean, and the fridge to be cleaned and occasionally defrosted. There is also the patients' day room to keep clean, ashtrays to empty, and plants to water.

'Bottoms' vacuum all ward areas, adjoining offices, corridors, and landings. Floors are sprayed with a liquid polish and buffed with an electric polisher (sometimes referred to as a 'bumper'). Ward floors are vacuumed, mopped, and polished and throughout the day spillages of blood and urine cleaned up. Lavatories, bathrooms, and sluice are cleaned thoroughly every day. Waste bins are emptied, disposable towels, soap, and toilet rolls replaced and walls and doors cleaned as necessary. The domestic on 'bottoms' work has literally to work around other people on the ward, carefully controlling the powerful polisher as she cleans under and around beds and chairs. Both 'tops' and 'bottoms' recognise that they do more than required in their job description, a fact which prompted a work-mate to remark that 'one day soon with privatisation patients will becomes things to dust around'. Underlying this point a routine health check had found that some domestic assistants who worked on wards where patients were receiving radiotherapy treatment registered radiation levels which, though safe, were nevertheless higher even than those of the nursing staff on the ward. Investigations revealed that these domestics had far more close contact with patients in the course of their work than their job actually required.

Domestics who work on the wards, whether as 'tops' or as 'bottoms', have contact with patients in the course of their daily round. By dealing with patients as 'ordinary people' and not just 'an illness', some of the domestics I talked to quite consciously saw themselves as providing something for patients which they felt the nurses, with their specialised interest, could not. One woman described how a male patient who was very ill with cancer of the pelvis had discussed his illness with her and shown her the open wound. One day she told him truthfully that he looked much better. She felt that this meant more to him than if she had been a doctor or a nurse – 'he really brightened up' – because they had established an ordinary, everyday friendship in which they could chat openly to each other.

In a study of the role of domestic assistants in a psychiatric hospital, Harrisson (who was herself once a nurse) found that domestic staff responded if they saw a patient in need of help and, as they did so, 'patients experienced personal contact and stimulation that, even if brief, they might not have had otherwise' (1986: 7). She concludes that:

> Whereas the content of much of the interaction appeared to be superficial in nature, it resembled the style of association that makes up much of the exchanges of everyday life in public areas by the public at large. (1986: 11)

Harrisson is here referring specifically to a psychiatric hospital where domestic staff were encouraged to be part of the ward team. However, her research shows that domestic assistants can, and do, play a role in patient care the value of which lies in its everyday character.

Although, at the hospital where I worked, domestic assistants were not supposed to spend any time talking to patients, they nevertheless did so as they went about their work. On one ward my two work-mates kept the patients entertained with jokes and friendly jibes as they wiped the lockers and beds. As the following extract from my own notebook shows, domestics can care for patients by simply keeping a friendly eye on them:

> We refer to one of the patients, the gentle, baby-pink old man who's always asleep, as 'Shirley's boyfriend'. 'He's lovely', she says and does his tea especially, keeping him awake while he drinks it, holding the beaker for him as if he were a child.

Older domestics who had worked at the hospital as orderlies or who had many years' experience of ward life were quite confident in their dealings both with patients and nurses: (domestic to elderly man) 'I'll come and smack your bottom if you don't eat that food!'; (domestic quietly to staff nurse with a nudge) 'Quick, move that [used] syringe [left lying about], the nursing officer's coming'. These commonplace exchanges help to create a friendly atmosphere on the ward, a degree of comradeship between domestic and nurse, and, particularly on the male wards, engender the kind of 'leg pulling' that I have often seen take place between male and female work-mates. In addition, the domestic assistant is able to extend the control she exercises over her work environment by encompassing within it 'patient care'. Thus, she is able to exert some control over the patients themselves by involving them in a social way in her work tasks. Only occasionally did I see a domestic assistant becoming short-tempered with the patients, but this does not mean to say that underlying tensions did not exist. For example, some domestics said that they much preferred working on male wards because female patients were less good humoured – a view I have also heard female nurses express. On one occasion, a black domestic drew my attention to the way white patients left blood-stained pyjamas around for her to pick up, commenting that it was these 'little things' that built up over the years and caused trouble between black and white. Another time, when I was working alone, a white male patient in a side ward asked me if my 'ethnic friends were sitting in the kitchen'. The negative attitudes that some patients brought into the hospital thus influenced the way they treated the domestic staff, making the relationship a two-way one.

Domestic assistants who had worked at the hospital for twenty years or more had been expected to carry out tasks which would now be regarded as nursing duties. One woman who started at the hospital in 1949 spoke warmly of the time she had spent working in the intensive care unit (ITU):

> I loved it in the ITU – looked after a patient there – used to feed, wash her – she used to put shit in her hair, shit everywhere. Myself and Joan Woodburn, the orderly, used to look after her and that woman is alive today. I used to 'bag and suck' the patients. Sister used to choose me not a nurse. Wages then were about £13 per week for 40 hours ... at that time we used to do a lot of nursing work. I've laid out dead people, I've shaved fannies! We used to 'milk the tubes' after patients came from heart surgery.

Longer-serving domestic assistants had begun their working lives at the hospital when the domestic or orderly was an integral part of the ward hierarchy, answerable directly to sister and above her to matron. Among other things, changes in work organisation and nursing structure have gradually undermined the domestics' formal role in patient care. But even younger women new to the job and those who have worked at the hospital for only a few years seem also to feel the ambivalence of their situation. Despite the

ever tighter restrictions of their job description, and the increasingly sharp demarcation between specialised nursing and domestic
tasks, they find themselves becoming involved in their ward. Yeandle
also found among the domestic assistants within her larger survey of
working women that they similarly valued being a part of the
'occupational community' of nurses, doctors, and ancillary staff
within the hospital. In addition, they gained job satisfaction because
they could see their labour was directed 'towards genuine human
need', these factors seeming to override even bad working conditions and pay (1984: 113). Some of the domestic assistants I talked
to were motivated by these feelings to move into auxiliary work:

> I'd like to be an auxiliary, since I've worked here and had my
> own ward because of watching them. And also [to work-mate]
> don't you get an awful lot of patients asking you to help them
> and you're not supposed to? It's not your job and you feel
> embarrassed.

Having made the step they find the job more satisfying:

> *Auxiliary:* I love this job!
> *Self:* What do you like about it?
> *Auxiliary:* You've got contact with people and its nice to feel
> that you're doing something really useful. I know how Gladys
> [domestic assistant] feels now mopping that floor and someone
> walks on it. The domestics say it's a step up being an auxiliary
> but I don't feel that. Responsibility I've got mate! If they need
> a bedpan I've got to make sure they're sitting on it properly!

Older women who remembered the days when domestics had
worked as part of what they described as a ward 'team', directly
answerable to the ward sister, viewed the emergence of a separate
domestic management structure in the early 1970s as an erosion
of their status (for an outline of these changes see Levitt and Wall
1984: 234–6). The following comments which illustrate this point
are from a domestic assistant who had come from the West Indies
and had worked at the hospital for over thirty years:

> In morning we would make coffee and toast to take sister and
> the doctors before report, now nobody bothered now,
> everywhere it changed, everything. In the olden days
> anything to be done on the ward the sister come and ask you

99

to do it. Now can't ask you to do anything – ring through to the [domestic] supervisor. It was better. More love on the ward then. In those days the sister would handle you with respect.

Irrespective of length of service the women I talked to, young and old, felt themselves to be in a contradictory situation. A number of related developments have contributed to the changing relationship between domestic and patient, and domestic and nurse. Efficiency-saving measures were restricting their job to cleaning tasks while the everyday demands of their work environment required that they continue to be 'more than cleaners'.

MORE THAN CLEANING

Almost unconsciously the domestic assistants responded to the hospital environment by developing a knowledge of illness and also a personal strategy for dealing with the more distressing aspects of the work. Over time, domestic assistants become sensitised to the presence of death. This heightened sensitivity becomes part of the store of knowledge which the domestic unconsciously acquires with experience. One domestic in her late twenties told me that the third floor of the hospital, where the cancer wards are situated, was always colder than elsewhere, death making it so. Although I was working with her, it did not feel any colder to me – maybe because I had not worked there long enough to become sensitised to the cold. For instance, one work-mate explained that she had trained with an older woman, who had worked at the hospital for years, who asked her one night if she could smell something 'sweet and rotten' and she could not. Then the older woman said 'I can smell death. Someone on this ward is going to die soon', and a few minutes later someone on their ward did die. Some weeks later the younger woman was walking along a corridor when she suddenly became aware of something which smelled 'sweet and rotten'. This time she knew what it was – 'As I turned the corner the porters were bringing the box along [with the dead body in it]'. Encounters with dying patients can also leave lasting impressions on the domestic. As one woman explained:

One evening a male patient caught my arm as I was clearing his locker and said 'I'm thirsty, can I have a drink?' I said 'No, it says not above the bed' [i.e. Nil by Mouth]. He looked at me and said 'Does it matter!' So I went to find and ask a nurse. An hour later that man died. I will never forget it. He held my arm and I can feel it now, and the look on his face because you can see it, see death. You look into the face of death and you can see it. In the eyes – it's though they're not human, not here any more, but very, very distant.

One hot summer's day after helping with 'bottoms' work I sat in the ward kitchen and asked my work-mate, who had worked more than twenty years at the hospital, if she was able to tell when a patient came in whether or not they would get better?

Yes you do. That old man in the first bed on the left in the four-bedder, he won't make it. He's been in lots of times but this time he won't make it. You know when you see them and think to yourself 'you won't go home'.... If they ask what's going to happen and you know it will be painful or they's be ill, you don't tell them. You say 'Oh, you'll be all right', because they're frightened already and it only makes it worse for them. When they're going to die they move them to another ward. You come in one morning and their bed's not there and they [other patients say] 'where has so-and-so gone?' and you say 'he's not well so they've moved him to another ward' ... even when you know they've died. But you don't say. You have to be a hypocrite.

Yet no proper recognition is given to the fact that domestics, like nurses, may be affected in this way by the conditions under which they work. Nurses at this hospital told me that they were encouraged to cry as a necessary safety-valve for their feelings. Yet domestics have to shut themselves up in the lavatory, ward kitchen or, like one woman, the kitchen store cupboard to have a 'good cry'.

Unlike many nurses, once a domestic assistant is allocated to a specific ward, she tends to stay on it for a long time, decades in some cases. In this way the domestic becomes a familiar anchor point for patients in a constantly changing sea of nursing and medical staff. In interviews about their early training midwives and nurses have commented that sister would virtually ignore a first year student nurse – the 'lowest form of life on the ward' – yet she would chat to, and even confide in, an established domestic who had learned from experience 'how sister likes things done'.

Even today familiarity with ward routines and sister's likes and dislikes puts the domestic at an advantage over other nursing and medical staff who are new to the ward. In addition, the domestic gets to know the nurses and is able informally to establish a way of working with them. One of the complaints which nurses level against contracting-out is that they do not know the domestics on their ward and that the shorter shifts that come with privatisation disrupt the sense of continuity in ward routines. On one ward where I worked over a three week period, two of the patients, a man and a woman, were well known to the domestics, who welcomed them like old friends, and seemed to have detailed recall of their medical histories and domestic circumstances. When the male patient left we domestics presented him with a knitted 'willy warmer' because he had complained that the hospital tea had deleterious effects on his libido.

Domestic staff also get to know the patients' visitors. Working evenings with one of the older domestics, I observed that one group of visitors waited anxiously for her to come round with the tea so that they could find out how their relative had been that day. The significance of the domestics' unofficial role in relation to patients' relatives was vividly highlighted by a recent legal case, which the Ealing Health Authority lost, which was reported in the *Guardian* (7 January 1986). A man whose mother was in hospital being treated for cancer learned from a domestic while he was in the hospital canteen that she was in fact dying. The domestic told him that an emergency had happened and he returned to the ward to find his mother dead. Medical staff had not told him of the actual serious state of his mother's illness, so that he was quite unprepared for her death.

After a time, domestics say, they become 'hardened' to illness – their own and other people's. Even their own family notices the change. Experience also brings with it greater confidence in dealing with patients, nurses, and doctors. A feeling of responsibility for 'my ward' develops and with it a sense of identity and belonging. Sometimes patients may indirectly ask for the support of the only person around, and this may be the domestic assistant. For example, as I was leaving the day room of one ward, which was empty except for one elderly male patient, he offered me a drink of whisky. 'I'm celebrating', he said, 'I've just been told I've got three months to live.'

CARRYING THE LABEL: WORK AND IDENTITY

Despite the fact that domestic assistants seemed to gain a feeling of self-worth from their work, all of the women I talked to felt themselves to be stigmatised by their job and by the label of 'cleaner'. Some were more sensitive to this than others. If at all possible they did not use the term 'cleaner', preferring instead 'domestic assistant', although they also found this demeaning. One work-mate said that when she cleaned the public lavatories at the hospital she used to 'dread it' in case she met anyone who knew her or her husband. Meeting her husband's friends socially was an ordeal, as she waited anxiously for the other women to ask her what she did. Usually, when in this situation, the women said they were auxiliaries or nurses. One group of domestics on an evening out claimed to be 'ward sisters' when asking the disc jockey to play a record for them. Sometimes this was done for a laugh. Even so, there was the underlying feeling that there was some shame attached to being publicly labelled 'a cleaner'. But this stigmatised identity could also be used in a more positive and assertive way – when disagreeing with managers or nurses for example or when flirting with men on a night out with the girls – 'We're all scrubbers we are!' This perhaps explains why it was that one nurse who was treating me (as a domestic) for an ankle injury talked in a humouring manner until she realised I was in fact a researcher. Apologising, she explained that domestic staff could be 'a bit militant' if not handled properly. It seemed to me that this assertive behaviour was something of a defence mechanism in a situation in which the women felt themselves to be looked down upon and at the bottom of the hospital hierarchy.

On the other hand, the domestics were critical of women they knew who thought themselves 'too good' to do a cleaning job, expressing views similar to those Gullestad found among women in urban Norway (1984: 188–9). Two work-mates said they were 'disgusted' one night when another domestic told them that her husband thinks a cleaning job is 'the lowest of the low'. They said, 'She's been used to doing office work' and thinks she's 'so high' for this job. This way of thinking focuses on the more positive aspects of cleaning work – 'it's essential work', 'somebody's got to do it 'cause the doctors certainly wouldn't!', 'it's a job like any other', '... there's people here working as domestics who've got high qualifications but it's a job that fits in with the hours they want to do'.

We have already seen that domestic assistants distinguish between 'clean dirt' and 'dirty dirt', taking the patient's middle when in bed as the dividing line. Symbolism and pollution beliefs can also be seen to play a part in other ways in forging work identity, giving rise to what could almost be described, following Searle-Chatterjee, as a 'polluted identity' (1979). Domestic work which, when performed in the home, enhances a woman's status has quite the opposite effect when performed outside it in the public realm. This may perhaps explain why it is that the women seemed to feel the need to establish a personal relationship with those for whom they clean as a kind of shock-absorber against the more polluting aspects of the work. Moreover, by applying her own personal standards of cleanliness to the work-place, the domestic can, as at home, exert control over her work situation and organise her environment in a more satisfactory way, imposing order over the disorder which, as Mary Douglas tells us, is dirt (1975: 2).

The domestic assistants' personal standards of cleanliness, collectively sanctioned by custom and practice, may come into competition with those of the domestic managers. Domestic supervisors attend a day-release course on hygiene science, receiving what one of them described with an ironic chuckle as a 'City and Guilds in Bugs'. Developments in bacteriology have shown that warm water and disinfectant provide a congenial environment for bacteria to flourish. Traditional disinfectants are not now used in hospitals and the domestic assistants are shown how germ cultures grow on damp mops and in dirty water. Despite this fairly new thinking, some women bring in their own disinfectant, surreptitiously adding it to the water in their mop bucket as they were taught to do. In one case this reacted with the official cleaning fluid and the domestic concerned suffered chlorine poisoning.

Because these developments prevent the older domestics from cleaning and polishing to their own personal standards, they seemed to feel that they have gradually lost control of their work situation. While accepting that the hospital 'isn't dirty' they did not accept that it was 'properly clean' – although it might be 'hygienic'. In their eyes it no longer 'looks beautiful', as in the days when it was polished, and they do not now have the time to dust the skirting boards as often as they do at home. Here we see the cleaners' sense of job control, including control over working time and standards of cleanliness, competing with scientific notions of hygiene and cost-based measures of efficiency. Pollution beliefs and related ideas of cleanliness play a central part in the way the domestic assistant relates to and organises her work. As Okely (1983) has shown us through her detailed study of traveller-gypsies, cleanliness is not a fixed category; what for a gypsy is contaminated is clean for a 'Gorgio', i.e. non-gypsy. For gypsies hospitals are part of the outer world of pollution, where Gorgio disease is concentrated, appropriate for handling polluting acts like birth and death or for curing shameful or contaminating illnesses like venereal disease or tuberculosis (Okely 1983: 185). Looked at from this ethnographic perspective, it can be seen that 'cleaning' is a task heavily loaded with symbolism. On all sides the task is bounded by beliefs, commonplace and scientific, which impinge in various ways upon work identity.

It is my view that these ways of thinking also assert the dominance of the collective over the individual and emphasize the importance of shared values and beliefs. In this way the group's social boundary is clearly marked, as are the ways of behaving which reinforce group identity. Those who set themselves apart from the group may incur the ill-will of their work-mates ('you watch her, she's very pally with the supervisor') or you may be called a 'snob' and laughed at for thinking yourself 'middle class'. Along with these notions are commonly held opinions about middle-class people: 'I bet our children are more polite, our homes are cleaner and I bet we've more money – they're probably up to their eyes in debt.' Women play a crucial role in constructing and maintaining these values and beliefs in the home, neighbourhood, and work-place. The domestic assistants identified strongly with a particular estate or local area like the middle-class women studied by Cohen who 'developed and sustained particular cultural forms, which had the effect of clearly marking the boundaries between themselves and outsiders' (1978: 137).

We can see then that work is embedded in a complex of social relationships with female kin, friends, neighbours, and work-mates. A woman's identity derives both from her status within this network and from the way she is viewed by those outside it. Hence the dual, and apparently contradictory, nature of the way domestic work is perceived as a source of both pride and dissatisfaction.

CONCLUSION

There is an integral connection between those tasks defined as 'non-nursing duties' (NNDs) and those which come under the heading of 'nursing duties' proper. The way such tasks as lifting or washing patients, making beds or cleaning up vomit are classified changes over time in response to a range of factors, including staff shortages and changing theories of patient care. Thus, the boundary between nursing and domestic tasks tends to be re-organised to meet changing demands, as too does the working relationship between nurse and domestic assistant. As a recent study by a charge nurse illustrates, a number of factors affect the way NNDs are defined, including the historical framework, custom and practice, and the direct personal demands made by the patient upon the nurse (Macleod, 1985: 5). Consequently, there is a fluid boundary between nursing and domestic tasks. Social historians Bellaby and Oribabor have shown that until the inter-war years, when nurses gradually handed down to domestics the tasks of looking after ward hygiene, this work was considered an essential component of nursing proper (1980: 164). Sister Markham, who trained during the Second World War, writes in her memoirs of the many hours she spent doing domestic work (1975: 64–5) and in his seminal study Abel-Smith reminds us that 'the antecedents of the nursing profession were domestic servants' and not, as popularly supposed, the religious orders who devoted themselves to the sick (1960: 4). Writing in the late nineteenth century Oppert proposed that nurses should be paid wages 'a little higher than of domestic servants, because they run the risk of infection' (1883: 56).

The individual accounts of past work practices I have presented find support in Dale's (1965) study of domestic assistants, carried out over twenty years ago, which undertook a wide-ranging job analysis of work done on hospital wards and found that there was a clear overlap between nursing and domestic tasks. Dale's study was prompted by nurse recruitment problems similar to those we are familiar with today and sought, as now, to make more intensive use of the nurse's skills by making clear the distinction between nursing and domestic tasks (Dale 1965: 164). Dale's study showed not only the extent to which tasks overlapped on the ward but also that domestic staff with part-nursing duties were the most satisfied with their jobs (Dale 1965: 171).

By encouraging more flexible work practices and looking positively on the overlap of nursing and domestic tasks, 'teamwork' appears to offer a satisfactory way of managing the boundary between nursing and non-nursing duties. 'Teamwork' is attractive to managers because it seems to offer a means of improving – cost effectively – the quality of patient care. The research outlined here has already been presented at two conferences for domestic and nurse managers about 'Teamwork' in the NHS (the national one with Sheila Harrisson).[7] This research also relates to current concern about the possible role of the unqualified 'nurse helper' grade envisaged in the United Kingdom's Central Council's 'Project 2000'. In practice, however, cost-effective ways of thinking may make teamwork unworkable – as the following will illustrate: at St Mary Abbots Hospital, Macleod observed that, while nurses on one ward were busy giving out drinks to patients, the domestic assistant, who had finished her allocated tasks, stood waiting for her shift to end. However, this 'waiting time' could not be used, as the charge nurse requested, to assist nursing staff and free them from non-nursing duties like washing up because the job had not been costed and included in the contract for domestic services (Macleod 1985: 21). In Britain, as Coyle (1985) among others has documented, domestic assistants, along with other ancillary staff, have been at the forefront of the government's campaign to privatize an ever-widening range of services in the NHS.[8] This is despite the fact that experience so far suggests that in a number of cases the contracting-out of domestic services may not be the most efficient approach – although it may cut costs.

One perhaps unforeseen consequence of the contracting-out of domestic services may be the demolition of the informal structures of work described in the preceding pages. As we have seen, for example, in the case of social age differentiation, the informal structures of work create their own expectations and internal promotion procedures, giving shape to the otherwise flat horizon of 'unskilled' work. Within the ward hierarchy the experienced domestic is able to construct a place and a social status higher than that formally allocated to her and gain job satisfaction from this. Once domestic assistants have established their own work routines and 'got on top' of the work, a sense of skill and a measure of job control also develop, bringing with them a sense of belonging to a particular ward. It was these related factors which seemed to keep women in the job long after the time when their children had grown up and left home.

Related to this, we have seen that hours of work and job commitment tend to be associated. As hours get shorter job commitment changes with the demands of the family economy taking precedence over paid work. A recent study by Chaney of part-time women workers suggests that special restrictions do apply to women who take jobs like local, part-time cleaning work. This group tends to have relatively little help with domestic tasks and child-care, although in Chaney's view family structure itself does not seem to be a 'significant' factor in this. Rather, it is their belief that women's primary role is domestic which steers certain groups of women towards part-time work (1981: 42). One of the findings of the comparative study from which this paper has drawn is that as hours get shorter and workers are necessarily drawn from a geographically smaller area local loyalties may dominate – and sometimes even override – those to the work-place. The way working hours are structured has social as well as economic implications. Part-time shift workers are, as at this hospital, a heterogeneous group, responding in different ways to those on other shifts, to particular leadership styles and changes in work organisation. Moreover, a number of related factors may combine to intensify the relationship between home and work, neighbourhood and workplace, among them the use of social networks to obtain jobs, the effect of the contraction of working hours on the available labour market, and the differentiation of the work-force along diverse shift work lines. Among other things, this suggests that factors outside the work-place may come to play an even greater part within it than hitherto, further complicating social relations and loyalties within the various sub-groups which form the hospital's domestic work-force.

NOTES

1. This chapter draws on material gathered while doing fieldwork as part of a comparative study of part-time women workers – 'Working Women's Social Worlds: An Anthropological Study in the West Midlands' – funded by the Economic and Social Research Council. The research was directed by Dr Elizabeth Tonkin, to whom I am indebted for her invaluable guidance and friendship. Especial thanks are due to my many work-mates at the hospital who gave

generously of their help and made me very welcome. I would also like to thank their domestic managers and supervisors for their kind assistance, and also NUPE and COHSE for their support. I am also very grateful to the midwives and nurses who have shown an interest in this research and have discussed their working lives with me. My thanks to Angela Coyle for a helpful discussion at an early stage of the research and also to Mary Daley for her help. My thanks to Sheila Harrisson for helpful discussion about our shared area of interest. The librarians at the Nottingham University Medical School have given invaluable assistance, for which I thank them.

2. Since this research was completed the domestic services have been put out to competitive tender. The hospital was successful in its bid and the contract has remained in-house, although in order to cut costs many changes have had to be made.

3. It should be pointed out that there is considerable regional variation in terms of pay and labour markets for domestic assistants. For instance, at least one hospital in the south of England is finding it difficult to compete with the relatively high hourly rates paid by private cleaning firms. 'Efficiency savings' are then being made at the cost of the quality of domestic staff that the hospital can attract with its lower rates of pay. Incentive bonus schemes also introduce pay differentiation between different hospitals and regions, thus further hastening the move towards local pay bargaining in the NHS favoured by the Conservative government. For a discussion of local pay determination, outlining its implications see NAHA (1985) and McCarthy (1985).

4. For accounts of the experiences of black women workers in the NHS see especially Torkingtcn, (1984: 7–12) and Bryan et al., (1985: 43 and 38–50). For a discussion of women who return to the labour market after leaving it for a time to have children see especially Chaney (1981).

5. I found similar distinctions between 'girls' and 'women' among women pottery workers in Stoke-on-Trent. In their case a girl's wedding was made the object of an elaborate factory ritual which I have discussed elsewhere (see Hart 1986: chapter 10). See also Westwood who discusses the girl/woman distinction among women factory workers and describes a similar bride's ritual at the sewing factory she studied (1984).

6 For a discussion of the relationship between home and work and their implications for women's informal authority structures within the work-place see especially Grieco and Whipp (1984).

7. National Conference on Teamwork in the NHS, May 1987, Central London, and Teamwork on the Wards: The Role of Domestic Staff, October 1987, University of Keele. Both conferences were organized by the Dept. of Adult & Continuing Education, University of Keele.

8. For example, at Barking Hospital in 1984 domestics went on strike against the 'slavery' demanded of them by Crothals, a private contractor, and were still on strike a year later; see *Labour Research*, 73, (5) (May 1984) and the *Observer*, 17 March 1985, p. 2. See also Coyle (1985) who highlights the conflicts and pressures faced by union officials who seek to save jobs under these conditions.

Chapter Seven

NURSE OR WOMAN: GENDER AND PROFESSIONALISM IN REFORMED NURSING 1860–1923

EVA GAMARNIKOW

'Nursing is women's work.' It is this explicit gendering of nursing which, according to Lewin (1977), has made its analysis so difficult for feminists. Nursing appears to embody precisely those aspects of femininity which feminism finds problematic – passivity, self-sacrifice, devotion, and subordination. Thus, the content of the job, as well as its occupational social relations, would appear to locate nursing unambiguously within patriarchally constructed femininity.

In this article I shall argue against this view of occupational gendering in nursing. It is certainly true that nursing reform was based on an ideological equation between nursing, femininity, and women's work to which both nurses and doctors subscribed (Gamarnikow 1978). However, the politics of occupational reform suggest that this equation was also a political strategy employed by nursing reformers and doctors to mean different things and to achieve diametrically opposed ends.

FEMININITY AND NURSING REFORM

I have argued elsewhere (Gamarnikow 1984, 1985) that Nightingale and other nursing reformers used ideologies of femininity to legitimate nursing reform. They claimed that women ought to do nursing work because the tasks involved were identical to those which women already performed in the home, and because the caring qualities required in nurses were uniquely feminine.

The crucial issue is that nursing reformers employed ideologies of femininity in an enabling manner. In other words, they did not focus on femininity as a form of restriction, limitation, or disability. Instead, they constructed nursing as 'femininity in

110

action', an occupation of women's work for women. By linking nursing with femininity at the level of tasks and personality, the reformers claimed a right to training, employment, and career.

By contrast, medical men defined femininity in terms of patriarchal female subordination: a restrictive, limiting, and dis- abling view of femininity and nursing. Thus, doctors used the ideologies of femininity to distinguish between dominant and subordinate forms of health care, and to safeguard their own dominance.

Nurses and doctors, therefore, held fundamentally different conceptions of the link between nursing and femininity. This interplay between nursing and medical interpretations of 'nursing is women's work' lies at the heart of the occupational formation of nursing. This makes the gendering of nursing a complex and problematic phenomenon.

NURSING REFORM AS A THREAT TO MEDICINE

1860, the year in which Florence Nightingale opened her training school for nurses at St Thomas' Hospital, is the traditionally accepted starting point for nursing reform. Nursing as a job for women pre-existed this date. For example, St Bartholomew's Hospital had employed nurses since 1549 (Moore 1981) and Guy's Hospital opened in 1725 with a staff of thirty-three nurses (Sheldon 1925). However, the Nightingale reforms created a form of employment which differed fundamentally from the previous one: hospital nursing was removed from the category of domestic service and was redefined as health care. This transformation was institutionalised in a unified hierarchical nursing department and a hospital-based system of nurse training. Both of these changes altered the nature of the nurse–doctor relationship and thus challenged medical predominance in health care.

The nursing department

Under the old system, matrons, sisters, and nurses were recruited separately from the progressively lower strata of the female class population (Abel-Smith 1960). The matron was not a nurse, but a housekeeper, with responsibility for female staff. As hospital employees, ward sisters ran their wards in accordance with the wishes of the medical staff associated with each ward.

111

The Nightingale system, on the other hand, introduced a centralised nursing hierarchy with a matron, a trained nurse, at the top. She remained an administrator, but her duties expanded to include the organisation and supervision of nursing care and nurse training.

Within the voluntary hospital sector, the introduction of the Nightingale nursing department meant that nurses acquired a powerful position within the organisational structure of the hospital. With the centralisation of nursing into a single autonomous department run by the matron, sisters ceased to be directly answerable to doctors in matters relating to patient care, and became instead the matron's subordinates. In addition, ward nursing was restructured in accordance with the requirements of overall hospital nursing policy, organisation, and training.

From the point of view of doctors, the new nursing department altered the organisation of nursing from a *ward system* to a *central system*. Braxton-Hicks, Physician-Accoucheur at Guy's, claimed that the former was preferable because 'the sister and medical staff worked heartily ... together for the common good', whereas the latter made it 'possible for the nursing arrangements to dictate to the medical staff' (1880: 211–12). In other words, doctors experienced nursing re-organisation in the hospital as an encroachment on their control over nursing.

Nurse training

Training was the second pillar of the reform. It consisted of two elements: theoretical instruction and ward work or on-the-job training.

The former took the form of lectures by doctors and, later, sister tutors on medical subjects (like anatomy, physiology, and *materia medica*), which were deemed essential for nurses whose skills and sphere of practice hinged on knowing, as Florence Nightingale put it, 'the reason why' (1882: 1).

Theoretical training had contradictory effects on the medical profession. On the one side it provided doctors with trained 'medical' assistants who could be relied on to carry out orders, knowledgeably rather than mechanically. Doctors desired *skilled* service, on the understanding that they should control the nursing curriculum and hence nursing practice.

Her knowledge of anatomy, physiology, pathology, and the action of drugs, should be thorough, though not necessarily very minute and extensive. She should also understand the value and meaning of symptoms, the means of preventing contagion and infection. She should be able to record the variations of the pulse or thermometer, and know how to act in an emergency in the absence of a doctor.... The hospitals professing to train nurses must give a more thorough and systematic education. Not content with merely teaching them to dress a wound, put on a bandage, or to deliver a woman – acts which require but a small amount of immitative skills to attain unto – they must admit them to the lectures, to teach them the reason for and the value of what they do, so that in their sphere they be no automatic servants of, but rational fellow-workers with, the physician. (*BMJ*, 1873: 14)

Thus, theoretical nurse training cemented the doctor's consultant status, since more and more former medical tasks could be delegated to nurses. But, the more that was delegated, the greater became the involvement of nurses in medical functions.

There was, therefore, a subversive element in nurse training, namely the watered-down medical curriculum. Theoretical training, and the kind of nurse it produced, blurred the division between nursing and medicine: it made the Nightingale nurse into more of a doctor than her untrained predecessor had been.

To give nurses instruction as to the reason why the surgeon or physican considers this or that expedient necessary would be ... to lift them more or less out of their proper sphere ... to demand for them complete education as medical practitioners, and to transform them from nurses into doctors ('Fight', 1876: 71)

Theoretical training thus posed a dilemma for doctors. By integrating nurses into medical education, nurse training blurred the nursing–medical division of labour. However, it also resulted in greater nursing expertise and this, in turn, created skilled assistants who could fulfil their role in the division of labour between nursing and medicine.

Ward work, the other part of nurse training, resulted in the transformation of the ward into a training resource for student nurses. Thus, the organisation and implementation of nursing care at ward level embodied a structure of tasks and responsibilities specifically geared to nurse training. Previously the ward had reflected exclusively the knowledge organisation principle of medicine (Foucault 1976). In the pre-reform ward sisters were individually 'trained' by their doctors, and it was medical men who defined and allotted tasks; in the Nightingale ward pedagogic authority was vested in the sister and she translated medical orders into tasks delegated to her staff.

Medical men regarded this development in ward organisation as a challenge to their right to control ward work in accordance with the needs of medical training.

> Will the medical men and students tamely look on when the nurses dress those who are operated on in the dressing room?.... You students in the hospitals demand the return of your fees, or the exclusion of the trained and training nurses from the wards, which are for your exclusive instruction. University, King's, St Thomas's, Middlesex, Westminster, are with you; arise to your work, and eject them.

Ward work as nurse training therefore also presented doctors with a dilemma. Like theoretical training, ward work produced nurses whose skill and experience made delegation, and consequent consultant status, possible. However, the price was high – loss of control over nursing practice at ward level.

MEDICAL REACTIONS TO NURSING REFORM

Not surprisingly, perhaps, medical attitudes to nursing reform were ambivalent. At one level, doctors regarded nursing as a medically-induced development and welcomed it as an adjunct to their own work.

> Nursing as an art, pure and simple, is an outcome of the reformation that has been gradually taking place in the practice of medicine; for we now know that there are preventive and curative agents other than draughts and pills; that however good the advice given may be, it must be acted upon fully and faithfully; that the ordinary hygiene of the sick-room, and the ordinary as well as special rules of sick diet, must be carried out by persons of intelligence, tact, and

114

unwearying assiduity; and that as physicians and surgeons, we look to the nurse for that helping hand in these things (*Lancet* 1879c: 736)

Doctors recognised that, because of the peculiar division of labour in health care (which necessitated their absence from, rather than presence by, the bedside), medicine depended on nursing for its success. Thus, doctors valued the reforms to the extent that they reflected positively on their own achievements.

However, at the level of inter-professional relations, the nurse was valued solely as a subordinate. What she actually did was far less important than whom she obeyed.

The old system.... had its good points.... Every old nurse was eminently deferential, and in a way thoroughly under the control of the constituted authorities. Though the discipline seemed lax in some particulars, and the work was often more carelessly performed, there was never any doubt as to who was master and who served. (Beale 1873: 630)

Nursing reform shattered this previously unproblematic subordination. The autonomous nursing department and nurse training removed the occupation from direct medical control.

SUBORDINATION AND THE NURSE–DOCTOR RELATIONSHIP

In pre-reform days, the subordination of nursing to medicine was based on the master–servant relationship. The nurse was a 'domestic' servant, employed by the hospital to clean, tend to patients' 'hotel' needs, and personally to serve doctors by obeying their instructions.

Nursing reform redefined nursing as healing. Thus, cleaning became the nurse's contribution to hygiene and patient welfare; the patient's 'hotel' needs became the health needs of sick people enshrined in the 'principles and practice of nursing', systematised and taught by nurse educators; and personal service was transformed into an impersonal, inter-professional relationship.

Nursing reform, therefore, shifted the parameters of the nurse–doctor relationship. Nurses began to theorise their role as one of carrying out orders, while doctors insisted on obedience. As Nightingale put it:

115

It is the duty of the Medical Officer to give what orders, in regard to the sick, he thinks fit to the Nurses. And it is unquestionably the duty of the Nurses to obey or to see his orders carried out. (Nightingale 1874: 5)

The apparently unproblematic 'or' in the second sentence masks an enormous chasm between blind obedience and the nursing deconstruction of medical orders and their reconstitution as hierarchically structured nursing care and ward work or as pedagogically organised ward training. On the whole, nurses tended to define obedience in the latter rather than the former sense.

For doctors, obedience was the single most crucial characteristic of the relationship of nursing to medicine. It signified both the servile status of nursing and the dominant status of medicine within the social organisation of health care. Doctors wanted: a subordinate – 'one to accept his diagnosis and to carry out his instructions' (*Lancet* 1896: 110).

The difference between analysing the relationship in terms of obedience, as doctors did, and of reinterpreting particular instructions by drawing on practical, theoretical, and institutional resources, as nurses did, is not purely a semantic difference between 'obedience' and 'carrying out orders'. The distinction lies in different definitions of nursing and the nurse–doctor relationship. Doctors fell back on power, and hence obedience, whereas nurses interpreted medical orders and redefined them as nursing tasks allotted on the basis of ward organisation, nursing hierarchy, and pedagogic requirements.

Doctors emphasised the fact that they told nurses what to do; nurses stressed their autonomous translation of medical instructions into nursing tasks. This difference in perspectives indicates how far nursing reform altered the nature and extent of nursing subordination.

Another way in which doctors attempted to tackle the problem of nursing subordination was by articulating a division of labour which ensured their dominance and the powerlessness of nursing.

It is important to note that nurses, from Nightingale onwards, also contributed to this elucidation of the nurse–doctor division of labour. And, more crucially still, nursing and medical accounts were practically identical: doctors diagnosed and prescribed, and nurses observed and reported.

Diagnosis and prescription

It was Nightingale who first outlined the division of labour between nursing and medicine. 'Nursing is performed usually by women, under scientific heads – physicians and surgeons.... The physician or surgeon prescribes ... – the nurse carries out' (Nightingale 1882: 6). Writers on nursing in the reform period continued this line of argument. 'It is the nurse's business to observe and report symptoms, but never her business to give a name to the disease or any set of symptoms' (*Nursing Times* 1906b: 457).

Doctors also insisted on this division of responsibilities: they alone diagnosed and prescribed. 'It is the physician's function to discover the cause of his patient's illness and suffering, and to prescribe the proper treatment: it is the nurse's function to carry out that treatment' (Worcester 1905: 404). The nurse was thus to occupy a subordinate position within the structure of health care. It was the doctor's function to diagnose which created this inferior status, since without diagnosis there was no patient and hence no 'need' for nursing intervention. It was diagnosis which initiated health care. Barring nurses from diagnosing subordinated the occupation to medicine.

> Nursing may be roughly defined as the care of patients under medical control.... Such care or treatment is subsidiary simply in the sense that treatment is subsidiary to diagnosis.... This definition of the status and function of nursing is only another way of laying down a proper division of labour (Davies 1912: 251–2).

The strength of feeling among nurses on the issue of medical monopoly of diagnosis can be gauged from a series of letters which appeared in the *Nursing Mirror* in response to a letter in which a nurse, H.W. (1907: 192), criticised doctors for their propensity to operate – 'doctors rush to the knife instead of to medicine or other treatment'.

All the subsequent correspondence attacked H.W.'s attempt to question medical decisions. N.C. (1908: 221) reminded H.W. that diagnosing and prescribing treatment were a doctor's right, and that the nurse's duty was 'to be loyal to her doctor'. F.A.W. (1908: 236) defended doctors on account of 'their good work, with its excellent results'. Welshwoman (1908: 248–9) reminded H.W. that operations were therapeutically useful, and suffering and death were not sufficient reason for condemning them. The letters became more vitriolic after that. Gee-Wiz (1908: 268) expressed 'disgust ... that so few nurses have challenged their statements' because nurses had no right 'to sit in judgement upon our surgeons'. Nurse D.M. (1908: 279) announced that she had 'never before heard of a nurse criticising the work of medical men in black and white'; and IOTA (1908: 279) expressed the hope that no other nurse would venture to express an opinion about whether or not patients needed operations: 'our clever, toiling, self-sacrificing surgeons must decide such vital questions.'

Thus, H.W. was attacked both for expressing doubts about particular diagnoses and prescriptions, and for publicly criticising and questioning medical decisions. She had clearly overstepped the bounds of acceptable behaviour in nursing.

Observation and reporting

Observation and reporting became the complementary functions of nurses.

> In all diseases it is important, but in diseases which do not run a distinct course, it is not only important, it is essential that *the facts the nurse alone can observe*, should be accurately observed and *accurately reported to the doctor*. (Nightingale 1859: 38)

The nurse was expected to observe and report without expressing a (medical) opinion.

Nurses continued to perpetuate this ideology of service to medicine.

> faithful servants we should be, happy in our dependence, which helps us to accomplish great deeds. (Former Matron 1906: 14)

For doctors too, the nurse was: 'a person on whose accurate observation the physician can rely, and in whose intelligent care the patient can rest' (*BMJ* 1873: 14). The nurse monitored the patient's progress and her observations formed the raw data of the doctor's diagnostic knowledge. Without the observations of the nurse the doctor could not perform his role. 'The nurse is always with the patient; the doctor only for a short time.... He is, therefore, dependent on the nurse for an accurate report of what takes place in his absence' (*Nursing Times* 1906a: 177). Yet she was not permitted to doctor. She had to act as if she were the doctor, reconstituting his past and future presences as ongoing presence, but only by means of faithfully carrying out instructions, and never acting independently in anticipation of orders.

Thus, the division of labour between nursing and medicine was not a neutral demarcation of skills, competences, knowledges. It was based on a notion of health care as a stratified and unequal structure of services. The dominance of doctors was established through their control over initiating and directing the healing process. This relegated nursing to a secondary, subordinate position: nursing care could be provided only after a doctor had pronounced a diagnosis, thus transformed a person into a patient, and prescribed an appropriate treatment, thereby constituting the patient as the subject of needs to which nurses could minister and as the object of medical data gathering by nurses.

PROBLEMS IN THE NURSE–DOCTOR DIVISION OF LABOUR

Doctors claimed that: 'the duties of the nurse and the doctor are distinct, and should run parallel without clashing' (*Medical Times and Gazette* 1876: 228). However, observation and reporting could not be rigidly separated from diagnosis and prescription. The nurse's role was to sift through the large number of observations and pick out the ones which were medically relevant. This meant operating the medical diagnostic framework, linking it to her own practical experience of similar cases, and creating a construct – the reporting of symptoms – of medically relevant information.

Thus, the nurse–doctor division of labour in fact made it impossible to separate medical diagnosis totally from nursing observations, since the medical 'gaze' (Foucault 1976) was articulated through and mediated by nursing practice. The nurse was, by virtue of the nurse–doctor relationship, not merely an assistant, but a diagnostician in her own right.

The central reason for this lay in the organisation of health care whereby doctors were primarily absent consultants and nurses ever-present carers for patients. Moreover, medical prestige and status were heavily dependent on this consultant role. Without it there would be no 'need' for a subordinate occupation to implement orders.

Absence, however, forced doctors to rely not so much on direct orders as on conditional ones. And conditional orders locked nurses ever more strongly into the functions of diagnosis and prescription.

> In his presence she has only to do what she is told to do: in his absence she must act for him. And as the science of medicine advances it is becoming more and more impossible for the physician to prescribe just what shall be done by his executive in every possible emergency. He is obliged to rely more and more upon the nurse's commonsense and knowledge of the principles involved. (Worcester 1905: 403)

An absent doctor could not have a monopoly of diagnosis and prescription, and a nurse who was constantly present could not be prevented from diagnosing and prescribing. The separation thus lay not in tasks, but in social relations: doctors had the power to name the diagnosing and prescription performed by nurses as 'following doctors' orders'.

Consultant status and conditional orders significantly blurred the demarcation between nursing and medicine. Medical power was located in the medical monopoly of diagnosis and prescription. However, the social organisation of that power, medical absence and nursing presence, undermined the monopoly considerably. This argument is perhaps best illustrated by a case study.

'PERMISSORY NOTES' AND 'DRUGS': A CASE STUDY OF THE NURSE–DOCTOR RELATIONSHIP

There was a very obvious contradiction between the roles of the nurse as full-time carer and as executrix of doctors' orders. This difficulty was located within the very structure of health care – the doctor was quite simply not available to re-diagnose each change in the patient's condition and prescribe accordingly. The organisation of health care problematised the primacy of medical intervention and this came out very clearly in the debate about drugs.

Nightingale was adamant that nurses never prescribed drugs.

> The nurse, of course, has nothing to do with the prescribing

of stimulants any more than of medicines. But ... the physician expects the nurse to be able intelligently to make the variations he prescribes in giving these things, especially during the night, according to the state of the pulse and other symptoms, which she must know how to observe, in order to follow his conditional directions, upon which hangs the patient's life. (Nightingale 1882: 10)

The conditionality of orders did not, according to Nightingale, turn the nurse into a prescriber of drugs. It merely made her a better nurse.

Doctors were less convinced. Some clearly felt that nurses were given too much latitude with respect to drugs, and that they engaged in prescribing them.

There are sisters and nurses, both in hospitals and private houses, who *will* persistently adopt their line of action in giving the patient stimulants or the reverse, or even in giving or withholding medicines, often in diametric opposition to the direction of the doctor. (*Lancet* 1879a: 570)

Others still recognised the dangers inherent in conditional orders and suggested that nurses should not be allowed access to drugs, other than those explicitly prescribed.

Under no circumstances should an attendant on the sick be placed within reach of drugs other than those she is required to administer. Permissory directions are always fraught with peril.... The only safeguard against this new peril is to give hospital sisters and nurses distinctly to understand that they are personal attendants upon the sick, nothing more, and to lock away beyond their reach every particle of medicine. (*Lancet* 1877: 62)

The contradiction was a glaring one. Without recourse to conditional orders, doctors would lose consultant status and become, like nurses, mere 'attendants upon the sick'. However, it was precisely conditional orders that undermined the medical monopoly on prescribing drugs and turned the nurse *qua* medical assistant into a quasi-doctor. The contradiction lay at the very heart of the division of labour between nursing and medicine.

The following correspondence, entitled 'Hypodermic Medication by Nurses', which took place in the pages of the *British Medical Journal* in 1912, demonstrates the importance of this issue for doctors. The division of labour between nursing and medicine was fraught with tension precisely because it was impossible to state at which point doctoring ended and nursing began. And yet, because this dividing line was not simply a matter of differentiating tasks, but of maintaining inter-occupational power relations, it was a matter of grave concern to the medical profession.

The correspondence was started by 'G.P.' whose patient's life was, ironically, saved by the prompt (diagnostic and prescriptive) actions of the nurse in an emergency.

> May I ask through your columns why the modern nurse should wish to go about with a large assortment of hypodermic tablets in her armamentarium? I had one of these superior beings employed in a case some time ago.... Included were such potent drugs as strychnine, digitalin, atropin, morphine, and last, but not least, hyoscin. Off her own bat, so to speak, she administered one night a hypodermic injection of strychnine.... Such dangerous remedies should not be in the hands of even such a superior person as a modern nurse but should be reserved to the medical attendant ('G.P.' 1912: 644).

'Renlim' agreed with 'G.P.' about the dangers inherent in these developments, but was perceptive enough to locate their origin in the doctor's consultant status.

> The general practitioner has himself to blame in a great measure, for he has gradually allotted to nurses the task of passing catheters and administering enemas, and, occasionally, *to save himself from being called up at night or otherwise disturbed*, the hypodermic injection of morphine.... The time has not arrived when the unqualified woman takes upon herself to 'medicate'. ('Renlim' 1912: 809, my emphasis)

'Woman Practitioner', on the other hand, attempted to support her nursing sisters by distinguishing between the attacks on nurses in the two letters and the 'real' issue, namely, the proper division of labour.

> Without wishing to disagree with 'G.P.'s' point that it is

undesirable for nurses and other unqualified persons to administer hypodermic injections of potent drugs on their own responsibility, I see no reason for his referring in such sarcastic manner to 'such a superior person as the modern nurse'. ('Woman Practitioner' 1912: 809)

At this point the correspondence ceased, probably because it had nowhere to go, having gone full circle through the contradiction of the nurse–doctor division of labour. Diagnosis and prescription as medical monopoly and site of medical power were rendered problematic by medical consultant status. The contradiction in the nurse–doctor relationship persisted; it could not be resolved within the parameters of the division of labour between nursing and medicine.

GENDER AND PROFESSIONAL NURSE–DOCTOR RELATIONS

Nursing reform thus posed a threefold threat to medicine. The new nursing department removed control over ward nursing from doctors and vested it in nurses. Nurse training introduced nurses into the medical curriculum. And the division of labour between nursing and medicine proved difficult to sustain without conceptual acrobatics. Gender alone remained to shore up the increasingly problematic subordination of nursing.

For doctors, gender served as a means of reconstructing threatened power relations within health care. Medical professional power was not sufficiently secure because of the ambiguities created by medical absence and conditional orders. Therefore, by defining medical power as an instance of male power and nursing subordination as a form of female subordination, doctors drew on patriarchal gender relations to reformulate the division of labour. In this they followed a similar line of argument to that which nursing reformers used to legitimate their project.

For instance, doctors also felt that nursing was an occupation particularly suited to women. In his lecture to medical students at King's College Hospital, Lionel Beale claimed that:

Nursing is especially women's work.... It is work which requires care and intelligence, to which the most clever woman might devote herself without feeling that she was

123

fitted for and ought to have been engaged in prosecuting
work of a high kind. Higher or better work there cannot be.
(Beale 1873: 270)

Moreover, in spite of medical opposition to feminism generally
(Delamont and Duffin 1978), nursing, doctors argued, provided a
legitimate outlet for women infected by feminist desires for
employment and economic independence.

Nursing opens a sphere of usefulness to women which those
who profess to be champions of their sex do not sufficiently
appreciate. The social position and the remuneration of
nurses are both improving.... In addition, there is a certain
amount of liberty and independence, as they can walk out
daily at certain times; and their mode of living is regular and
safe.... Here lies a large sphere of work for women, to which
the true friends of the sex and humanity will do well earnestly
and repeatedly to draw their attention'. (*BMJ*,1868: 594).

There were two reasons for these fulsome praises of women's
involvement in nursing. In the first place, nursing was ideal for
women because of their unique capacity for caring.

So far the calling is largely in the hands of women – and,
perhaps, naturally so. They were meant by nature for offices
where gentleness and tenderness of touch count for so much.
(*Lancet* 1894: 280)

The other, more important, reason for arguing that women were
uniquely qualified to nurse was located in patriarchal power
relations. Since nurses were subordinate to doctors, and women to
men, 'natural' female subservience to men could secure professional subservience to medicine. Thus, the nurse's skills and
abilities were collapsed into female obedience to the male doctor.
'Women are particularly fitted for the no less onerous task of
patiently and skillfully caring for the patient in faithful obedience to
the physician's orders' (Worcester 1905: 403). Subordination became
the hallmark of a medically-defined good nurse. 'Speaking ... from
the physician's or surgeon's point of view, the best nurse is she who
can subordinate her own ideas of treatment to those of the medical
attendant' (*Lancet*, 1879a: 570). And subordination was a natural
female condition and, hence, a unique qualification for nursing.

In arguing for the suitability of nursing for women on the grounds of female caring abilities and the natural subordination of women to men, doctors reconstructed the nurse–doctor relationship. It ceased to be a purely professional relationship governed by an allegedly technical division of labour. Medical rights to diagnose and prescribe were no longer justified purely on the grounds of superior knowledge and skills, but on those of a generalised male right to female obedience. Conversely, the duty of nurses to obey and carry out medical orders was transposed from professional secondariness to patriarchal subordination of women to men. Thus, when doctors argued that nursing was women's work, they employed the concept of femininity to impose clear limits on the exercise of female tasks in health care. And those limits were equated with male-medical power.

By contrast, nurses did not define the nurse–doctor relationship as a gendered one, in the sense of locating the power imbalance between the two occupations within a patriarchal gender discourse. In fact, nurses went out of their way to emphasise that the subordination of nursing to medicine was purely professional. If you nurse for him, nurse for his profession (Gould 1910: 189).

Writers on the subject emphasised the fundamental difference between this professional subordination and both social class and gender relations outside health care. Margaret Fox, for instance, told probationers:

This seems very strange ... a complete upheaval of all preconceived notions respecting the relations between modern man and woman. The daughter of a duchess, if she becomes a probationer, has to treat the surgeon, even though he should be the son of a pork butcher, with the same deference, for the reason that in hospital her relations towards him are not social but professional. He is her 'superior officer' and must be recognised as such. (Fox 1913: 142)

This professional subordination was ritualised through deferential behaviour on the wards. If a doctor entered the ward, nurses were expected to rise and open and shut doors for him; not to talk among themselves, move about unnecessarily or make any noise; they were to inform their nursing superiors of the doctor's presence and ensure that patients did not move about or talk.

They were not to speak to the doctor until spoken to and, if and when that occurred, they were expected to address him as 'sir' and answer his questions, but not venture opinions. On arrival, departure and whenever necessary in between, they had to give him water, soap, and towel to wash his hands, and in general 'wait on him quietly and unobtrusively' (Fox 1913: 142).

Margaret Fox argued that this professional etiquette was necessary to preserve order in the health care setting. In other words, subordination was justified, not on the grounds of patriarchal gender relations, but on those of professional hierarchy. In fact, as shown above, by the turn of the century this professional subordination was contrasted directly with 'model' male–female relations where this subordination of women to men did not, allegedly, exist.

However, the nursing representation of the nurse–doctor relationship as purely professional was contradicted by advice given to nurses on how best to handle this relationship. This advice implicitly recognised the patriarchal dimensions of the relationship. It appeared not as a feminist battle-cry demanding the abolition of male-medical power, but took the form of traditional feminine accommodation and manipulation. Nurses were thus advised 'to obey' their professional superiors and to use feminine manipulative tactics to get doctors to do things their way.

Nurses exhorted each other to learn how their doctors wished them to carry out orders and to assure them that they were willing to adapt to medical preferences.

> Sooner or later the nurse will have to give in to her medical man.... Take the trouble to find out his methods of working.... Tell him she is willing and anxious to learn.... Show him she respects his opinion ... realises she is there to see his orders are properly carried out. (*Nursing Mirror* 1909: 71)

Without such apparent servility friction would ensue – 'he proceeds to exert his power'. However, in the next few paragraphs the same writer reminded her co-workers that doctors, 'like most men generally, they can be led where they will not be driven'.

A number of writers drew nurses' attention to the availability of manipulation as a way around difficult doctors or inappropriate, as far as the nurse was concerned, orders or demands. A Matron

(1897: 133) suggested that difficult doctors could be 'managed' by tact and a compromise on methods on the nurse's part. In a quiet happy ward 'the sister studies his wishes and understands his methods of working'; in a badly-managed one, 'she is tactless or injudicious'. Note that the nurse was not castigated for unprofessional behaviour, but for not utilising her feminine resources of 'tact' and 'judiciousness' to manage her man.

Sister Grace went even further and suggested that, behind the facade of professional subordination, the clever, manipulative nurse could twist the male doctor around her proverbial little finger.

> The comfort and well-being of a ward largely depends upon whether the house surgeon and sister work together or swim in different currents. This will rest chiefly with the sister. Never assert your own opinions or wishes, but defer to his and you will find that in the end you generally have your own way. It is always easier to lead than to drive. This is a truly feminine piece of counsel, and I beg you to take it to heart. (Sister Grace 1898: 127)

Thus, at the interpersonal level, nurses gendered professional subordination to encompass the traditional power resource available to women – manipulating the powerful to internalise the outlook and perspective of the powerless.

In spite of the subordination of nurses to doctors which the reformers did not question or challenge, this type of power was available to nurses. It did not address directly institutionalised medical power, but gave space to individual nurses to negotiate as pleasant or non-oppressive a form of subordination as possible. This space was constructed by importing general forms of resistance to patriarchal domination. The following sentiment clearly has a double-edged meaning: 'Honour, commonsense, discretion and tact are generally acknowledged to be peculiar to women. Then nurses should endeavour to acquire a double portion of these qualities' (*Nursing Mirror* 1909: 72). Thus, nurses gendered nursing in two very different ways. In the first place there was the positive 'femininity in action' which stressed tasks and attributes and drew on the sexual division of labour to justify entry into the public sphere. The second type of gendering asserted that, although the power imbalance between doctors and nurses was purely professional, solutions to the problems of professional subordination could be found in the power to manipulate, traditionally ascribed to femininity.

However, what is important about this second form of gendering is that nurses did not locate the whole of the nurse–doctor relationship within this framework: subordination to medicine was justified on professional, not gender, grounds. Gender entered this professional relationship only when nurses conspired to undermine professional subordination by utilising feminine manipulation to get their own way. Thus gendering of nurse–doctor interaction served to empower the nurse at the expense of the doctor. Nurses were thus advised to use gender, not as an adjunct to professional subordination, but to mitigate its effects, or even to overturn it.

CONCLUSION – GENDER: A CONTESTED TERRAIN

Statements such as 'nursing is eminently fitted for women's capabilities' (*Nursing Mirror* 17 April 1920: 40) abounded in the nursing and medical journals of the period. But the similarity of the words employed by both nurses and doctors should not blind us to the different meanings each group attached to them. The difference in meanings had its social origins in the contrasting positions nurses and doctors occupied in relation to the public sphere of occupational and ideological power.

Nurses used the rhetoric of femininity in order to gain access to professional status in the public sphere of employment and occupations. Nursing reformers stressed the task specialisation aspect of the sexual division of labour (Gamarnikow 1984), and, by collapsing the biological female with the social category of woman, nurses inextricably linked women, femininity, and nursing. But this was an active 'femininity' which entailed singling out public sphere tasks and employments which resembled women's work in the home, taking over those occupations or creating new ones, and establishing a sexual division of labour within the public sphere of employment. This strategy of 'active femininity', I have argued, provided the ideological justification for nursing reform.

Doctors, on the other hand, employed the language of femininity to restrict the expansion of nursing and to deal with the threats, real or imagined, posed by nursing reform. They focused on that aspect of the sexual division of labour ignored or avoided by nurses, namely, patriarchal power relations between men and women. Doctors attempted to safeguard their occupational position in relation to nurses by drawing comparisons between patriarchal male domination and female subordination and male-medical power and female-nursing obedience in the nurse–doctor relationship.

Thus, gender became a contested terrain. Nurses used it for empowerment, while doctors employed it for the suppression of empowerment. So, although both occupations operated within the ideology of femininity, each profession drew on different strands and meanings. Thus, even patriarchally constructed femininity proved to be more complex than a simple subordination–domination model would permit: a site of struggle rather than a determined category.

Chapter Eight

HUMAN ABUSE AND NURSING'S RESPONSE

LEE ANN HOFF

History that offers no promise has no meaning.
(Chiaromonte 1985)

INTRODUCTION

Only recently has physical abuse been identified as one of the distinct concerns of nurses. Just ten years ago one found little in nursing literature on violence, let alone an entire issue of a major nursing journal devoted to the topic. Why has the interest of nurses and other health professionals in this age-old problem emerged only during very recent decades? What is the relationship between this development and the fact that most victims are women, most abusers are men, and most nurses – the majority of health professionals – are women, and most members of the politically dominant medical profession are men? What is the meaning and potential of these historical facts for nurses and for numerous victims of violence?

The intent of this chapter is to explore these questions and related issues concerning the history of human abuse. Central to this purpose is examination of the relationship between individual incidents of abuse and broader social-political factors – basically, the translation of 'personal troubles into public issues, and public issues into the terms of their human meaning for a variety of individuals' (Mills 1959: 187). Accordingly, analysis focuses on the social forces, cultural values, and political structures in the United States that have contributed to a history replete with victims' experience of isolation and self-blame for their victimisation. This will include an interpretation of the legacy of blame and neglect

130

of victims by health and social service professionals until very recently – a legacy resulting in further victimisation for many victims. Also analysed is the meaning of nursing's historical and current response to violence as a social issue and its impact on clients. The different historical beginnings of public attention to child abuse, incest, rape, battering, and assault are examined in reference to theoretical currents in academia and social movements in the United States.

HUMAN ABUSE: STATEMENT OF THE PROBLEM

The United States has been called the most violent society in the western world. Between three and four million children are abused by their parents or caretakers each year. Mothers and fathers hit their children with equal frequency, though fathers hit them more severely despite the fact that they spend far less time with children than mothers do. The number of women sexually abused by age 16 ranges between 25 per cent and 50 per cent (Finkelhor 1985). Twenty-five per cent of all couples are violent with each other. Every eighteen seconds, a woman is beaten; between 20 per cent and 25 per cent of adult women have been beaten at least once by a male intimate; while, among pregnant women, 25 per cent are abused during pregnancy (Stark and Flitcraft 1985). Feminists suggest that wife-beating is probably the most unreported crime in the country. American husbands are purportedly hit about as frequently as wives, although women are primarily the victims injured and use violence chiefly in self-defence. In April 1982, Congressional Sub-Committee hearings on problems of the elderly disclosed that up to one million older Americans suffer annually from physical, financial, sexual, and psychological abuse, mostly from their relatives. Among the sub-groups abused, elder abuse is the least researched, with no national survey data available to date (Pillemer 1985).

Illustrating local urban incidence of violence, the Boston Police Department receives forty-five domestic disturbance calls per day and over 17,000 per year. Seventy per cent of assault victims at Boston City Hospital are battered women (Boston Police Department 1980); while 78 per cent of battered women who use psychiatric services did not do so before being abused (Stark 1984). A large percentage of suicidal adolescents and women have histories of incest or battering. More than half of all murders occur in family relationships (Browne 1987). For black men between 15 and 24 years of age, homicide is the leading cause of death (Wolfgang 1986: 11). Among young black men who die between the ages of 20 and 24, one out of three deaths will be by homicide. Figures on domestic violence are regarded by family researchers as underestimated, since violence against family members goes on primarily 'behind closed doors' (Straus, Gelles, and Steinmetz 1980).

The paradoxical and tragic reality is that one's greatest risk of assault or murder comes from intimates and family members, the very persons most relied upon for nurturance, support, and protection. Thus, children, parents, spouses, elders, and friends seem enmeshed in a web of violence that is gaining increasing attention by researchers, practitioners, and, recently, public health officials. During the 1960s, child abuse came to national attention. This was followed by a focus on rape and wife-battering in the 1970s; while elder abuse, child sexual abuse, and black male homicide captured public attention in the 1980s.

These forms of abuse however appear to have been prevalent throughout history. Susan Brownmiller documents the terrorisation of women by rape for many centuries, while anthropological research reveals that even in the most egalitarian of societies, i.e. among hunters and gatherers, women were still subject to rape: 'we tame them with the banana' (Murphy and Murphy 1974: 94–138, Reiter 1975: 15). However, the very absence of historical data on human abuse in health and social science literature speaks to its historical interpretation as a private rather than a public issue.

Thus, for example, even after social and psychological aspects of health care became commonplace in contemporary society, article titles in the *Journal of Marriage and the Family* did not contain the term 'violence' before 1971 (O'Brien 1971). And in 1977 Davidson found in a large library that there was no volume on the history of wife beating in the western world. Yet, while there was and still is no standardised record-keeping on abuse in health and social service agencies (Rosenberg and Mercy 1985), family and psychiatric agency files contain numerous complaints of wife beating (Davidson 1977); while injury from abuse can also be extrapolated from other medical records. The question is: why? Also, when health professionals have dealt with victims of violence, their approaches have often exacerbated rather than relieved the problems and suffering of victims. The meaning of these developments and responses of health professionals, including nurses, becomes clearer by examining the social and political context in which various victims of abuse came to public attention. Theoretical influences on researchers and health practitioners must also be analysed to complete the picture.

THEORETICAL AND POLITICAL INFLUENCES ON SERVICE DEVELOPMENT

In general, the attention of health professionals to violence as a concern within their practice emerged in concert with the Civil Rights and women's movements that began in the 1960s out of concern for the disadvantaged. The focus, theoretical underpinnings, and influence of key characters, however, are inter-twined with historical developments in the social sciences, medicine, and nursing. The following analysis links certain practice problems today with broader social trends and clarifies the relative invisibility of nurses as victim advocates until very recently.

Violence emerged nearly in tandem as a topic of interest to academicians and as a service concern for practitioners. To the detriment of victims and assailants, however, these two groups historically have functioned with little or no explicit cross-fertilisation between them. Academics have often proposed theories with little obvious relevance to practitioners. There is also a general lack of interdisciplinary research on a topic that crosses over several boundaries in theory and practice.

In general, theory about violence falls into three broad categories: intra-individual (including biological), social-psychological, and social-cultural. Intra-individual theories, though popular earlier, are now largely discredited by all serious students of the subject (Gelles and Straus 1979; Breines and Gordon 1983).

Theory development in the violence field parallels theory development in social science as a whole. It can be classified in two broad categories: mainstream and feminist/critical. Mainstream analysts emphasize causal analysis, best represented by Murray Straus and associates at the University of New Hampshire Family Research Laboratory. Mainstream methods most often employ quantitative approaches to data analysis. This group of researchers places great emphasis on the notion of 'objectivity' in the research process and the differences between the 'subjects' of research and the researcher.

Feminist analysts have much in common with critical theorists, reflexive sociologists, and developmental psychologists such as Gergen (1982). This group of analysts focuses on the political-economic and cultural *context* in which violence is thought to flourish with implicit social approval. They assume that the research process itself is value-laden and that the theories and methods chosen to guide research and analyse data are embedded in the values and political context in which the researcher works. They also place heavy emphasis on the ethical norm that research should ideally benefit those being researched. Implicit in such action orientation is alignment by some of these theorists with various social activists and recognition that the knowledge system is often an instrument of oppression. Feminist/critical analysts claim an implicit relationship between the person doing the research, the topic being researched, and the theories and methods used by the researcher (Reinharz 1979; Hoff 1990; Roberts 1981; Oakley 1981; Dutoit 1980; Adams 1981; Cicourel 1964).

In sum, while mainstream analysts ask what *causes* violence, critical analysts begin with explicit acknowledgement of the historical disadvantage of certain groups based on race, sex, age, and economic status; they unravel the *context* in which these persons are victimised, and suggest social change to redress injustices. Paralleling the social conservatism of the 1950s, mainstream analysts have dominated the field. Even after inspiration and support from the Civil Rights movement begun in the 1960s, critical theorists continue as the minority – though increasingly visible – group in social science.

Practitioners, pressed as they are to deliver service, are less overtly interested in theory and indeed have little time to consider its complexities. Also of note is the general reluctance of health practitioners to deal with problems of a psycho-social nature. The implications of this pattern are enormous for any victims of violence who seek treatment for physical injuries that originate from the social act of violence. While most health practitioners disclaim any primary interest in theory, as members of cultural and academic communities, they are nevertheless influenced by historical trends and dominant social theories. Historical highlights in medicine and nursing support this claim.

Hippocrates, a physician of the fourth century BC, laid the foundation for the current emphasis on 'holism' by emphasising the inseparable interaction between a healthy mind and a healthy body. However, Middle Ages and Renaissance medicine was strongly influenced by the Church's contention that study of the mind was the business of the Church. This supported the idea of 'the body as a machine, of disease as a breakdown of the machine, and of the doctor's task as repair of the machine' (Engel 1977: 131). What followed was a general neglect of social-psychological aspects of illness which continued through the seventeenth century. Such practice was profoundly reinforced by the French philosopher René Descartes who emphasized the mind–body dichotomy that influences medicine to the present day. As Dubos states:

> Descartes' philosophy led scientists to neglect questions pertaining to the nature of the mind and the soul and encouraged them to focus their efforts on the much simpler, more concrete, problems of body structure and operation. They could apply knowledge of physics and chemistry ... to the problems of the body without fear of debasing the more lofty manifestations of man's nature, those of his soul. The self-imposed limitations and intellectual freedom that biologists derived from Cartesian dualism gave them a general tendency to study man as a nonthinking, nonfeeling entity. (Dubos 1977: 77)

In spite of the enormous influence of the mind–body dichotomy, public health aspects of medicine linked social and cultural factors to the general health of particular communities during the nineteenth century. Most physicians, however, were less concerned with social reform, public hygiene, and sanitation, than they were with developing medical technology and treatment grounded in exact scientific laboratory procedures. This approach to medicine assumes a specific pathogenic cause for every disease which will respond favourably to laboratory-tested drugs directed to specific pathogens. Today in the violence field it can be seen in the view of parents as the 'pathogen' causing the 'battered child syndrome' (Kempe and Helfer 1980).

Yet a study of the evolution of disease patterns during the last century reveals that physicians affected epidemics no more profoundly than priests did in earlier times. For example, 90 per cent of the decline in mortality from infectious diseases between 1860 and 1965 in industrialised countries occurred before the introduction of antibiotics and widespread immunisation. The recession is instead attributable largely to improved housing, a decrease in the virulence of micro-organisms, and *mostly* higher host-resistance due to better *nutrition* – in general, *ecological* factors rather than scientific medicine.

Thus, analysis of disease trends in the last century shows that *environment* is the primary determinant of the state of general health of any population (Illich 1976: 23–5). In spite of these historical facts, however, when victims of violence or their assailants have come to the attention of health practitioners, the overwhelming trend has been towards 'medicalisation' of such human phenomena – that is, the tendency in the United States to interpret social and other phenomena within a medical paradigm, regardless of the fact that the majority of victims come from groups suffering great disparities in the social structure: women, children, people of colour, the elderly, the poor. Some critics charge that modern medicine can be viewed as a secular religion, with 'medicalisation' replacing the 'theocratisation' or 'criminal-isation' of earlier eras when life's problems were interpreted in a theological or law-and-order framework.

While there are overlapping areas in the modern practice of nursing and medicine, nursing is clearly distinguished from medicine by its different focus. In contrast to the disease emphasis in western medicine, modern nursing focuses on caring and the person's *response* to the disease, while also administering certain treatments (ANA 1979). Since a person's response to disease typically includes emotional and socio-cultural factors, this focus places nursing in a framework closely aligned with Hippocrates, holistic care, and traditional non-scientific healing practices (Ehrenreich and English 1973). While nursing care during early Judaeo-Christian times was administered by women of high social standing, 'nurses' after the Protestant Reformation were various social outcasts working off their debts (Flynn and Heffron 1984: 38–9).

This low point in the history of nursing was followed by reforms associated with the emancipation of women and, finally, the founding of modern nursing by Florence Nightingale during the mid-nineteenth century. Nightingale, highly educated in politics and social science, not only reformed nursing during her pioneering work in the Crimean War, but made major contributions to the advancement of public health. Her model of nursing education was adopted by nurses in the United States and elsewhere, but with one important difference. Because student nurses were supported by the hospitals to which the schools were attached, their formal education took a back seat to the hospitals' immediate labour needs and students were exploited with impunity (Ashley 1976).

Thus, while the nursing profession benefited enormously from the reforms of Florence Nightingale, larger social forces were at work that effectively neutralised much of what was gained to advance the profession. Most central here was the fact that nursing was (and still is) a profession dominated by women. As a consequence, the economic exploitation of nursing students was aided and abetted by Victorian attitudes calling for ladylike, subservient behaviour on the part of women and stressing the danger of too much education to women's essential maternal functions. Together these factors supported the social and ideological forces that shaped the development of modern hospitals and the medical profession. Nursing students were imbued with the notion of loyalty to the institution and tending to the needs of the men (physicians) who controlled the institution. Because of the enormous economic advantage of the nursing apprenticeship system to hospitals and the medical profession, hospital and medical organisations together exerted powerful control over nursing's attempt to reform and take control of nursing education (Ashley 1976; Corea 1985: 59–76; Reverby 1987).

This struggle is highlighted by the fate of the Goldmark Report, the 1923 study of nursing education analogous to the Flexner Report that revolutionised medical education. But unlike the Flexner Report, the results of scientific studies of nursing were not widely publicised and the public remained uninformed about the conditions and needs of the nursing profession. Historians and feminists generally attribute this fact to the low status of women who continue to dominate the profession (Spender 1982). Today, many of the struggles of modern nursing parallel the phases of the women's movement, the primary influence in bringing violence to public consciousness. But, as McBride stated (1983), nursing can

137

also be seen as either the 'antithesis or the epitome' of feminism, a point to be elaborated in a moment in reference to victims.

In summary, the historical attitude of researchers and human service workers towards domestic violence can be described in Dexter's (1958) term as one of 'selective inattention' (Gelles 1974). These omissions imply the high value placed on family privacy and the myth of the family as a haven of love and security (Barrett and McIntosh 1982). They also suggest that researchers and practitioners are less 'neutral' than might be supposed from professional claims of 'objectivity'. Central to this attitude is the role of normative theory as ideology not only in supporting 'selective inattention' to violence. Normative theory has also been a powerful and successful force in the socialisation of boys into dominant, aggressive roles (Broverman *et al.* 1970) and girls (including future nurses) into complementary passive submissiveness (Cloward and Piven 1979; Corea 1985).

While there is as yet no research to explain the current increase in women's use of violence, it is reasonable to speculate that the prevailing dominance and valuation of male traits, in a perverse combination with increased freedom for women resulting from the women's movement, have resulted in some women's emulation of male norms of aggressive approaches to conflict resolution. This notion may also be relevant to understanding the phenomenon of battering among lesbian couples. Sadly, there is little emulation by men of women's traditional traits of nurturance and conflict resolution by mediation and interpersonal concern, as mothers have been doing for centuries in their child-rearing role (Miller 1976; Chodorow 1978; Gilligan 1982; Ruddick 1989). Significantly, to the extent that nurses manifest these traits, they represent the 'epitome of feminism' (McBride 1983). Only history will tell whether aggression and competition will continue to be more valued than nurturance and co-operation.

As ideology, normative theory's systemic model of society provides a convenient 'scientific' justification for consensual support of the traditional structure of society and its major institutions: family, church, economic, health, welfare, and criminal justice systems. The power of normative theory and its implicit approval of wife beating, for example, are revealed in this statement by a Superior Court Judge following the informal settlement of a wife-beating case in 1975: 'This is the best way to handle this without airing a lot of dirty linen' (Davidson 1977: 2). The following 1874 court statement quoted by Davidson suggests that little has changed since Victorian times a century ago:

> If no permanent injury has been inflicted, nor malice nor dangerous violence shown by the husband, it is better to draw the curtain, shut out the public gaze, and leave the parties to forgive and forget.

It is noteworthy that even today, systems theory, a contemporary version of normative theory which is founded on static, mechanical, or biological models of society, is commonly accepted with few questions by many health and mental health professionals, including nurses. Bogard (1984), Hoff (1989, 1990), Taplin (1971), and others have produced critiques of systems theory for its limitations in social analysis. Systems theory is, of course, central to understanding physical phenomena such as heart or kidney disease. But it has little value when applied to one's psychological or social *response* to a particular disease or a life crisis such as victimisation. It is ironic that, while a major nursing focus is on the patient's *response*, nursing's theories draw mostly from general systems theory.

Keeping this historical context in mind, let us now consider the beginnings and development of various programmes for victims of violence. Here we will note the combined influence of mainstream social science and health practice and the political movements of the 1960s and later.

DIFFERENTIAL PROGRAMME BEGINNINGS AND THEIR INFLUENCE ON THE PATTERN OF SERVICES

Children were the first group of abuse victims to receive widespread public attention in the United States. Besides Civil Rights concern for the disadvantaged, this development can be traced to the more easily expressed sympathy for children stemming from their natural helplessness and need of adult support and protection for survival. Public attention to abused children was initiated by the work of paediatrician C. Henry Kempe and colleagues and labelled the 'battered child syndrome' (1962). Basic to Kempe's 'perpetrator–victim model' of aetiology is the 'syndrome' or physical examination findings in the child victim which can be traced to the psychopathology of the parent-perpetrator. This focus flows logically from the history of medicine outlined above.

In contrast, the work of David Gil (1970), a Marxist from the minority group of social scientists, emphasises the social and cultural roots of violence against children, but has had far less influence in the field than the work of pediatricians like Kempe. Newberger (1985), a paediatrician, represents the current attempt to integrate insights from Gil's and related work into paediatric practice with abused children. He notes the unfortunate conse-quences of the perpetrator–victim model that inevitably finds fault with parents. He also suggests the term 'childhood social illness' as more appropriate for considering the complexity of individual cases and de-emphasising the 'criminalisation' of child-abusing families.

However, child sexual abuse received no widespread public attention until two decades later, after the social movements that brought victimisation by rape and battering to public attention. In contrast to child abuse, public attention to victims of rape, battering, and child sexual abuse can be traced chiefly to the women's movement and its corollary, the women's health move-ment. Susan Brownmiller, a journalist, popularised the issue of rape (1975); while Ann Burgess, a psychiatric nurse, and soci-ologist Lynda Holmstrom researched the topic in a clinical setting in 1974, Holmstrom and Burgess (1978). Laywoman Del Martin's book *Battered Wives* (1976), was central to publicising battering in the US and is still one of the most authoritative summaries of the problem. A major reason for the delay in public attention to child sexual abuse and for blaming female victims of abuse can be traced to the enormous influence of Freudian theory on psychiatric practice. In particular, Freud reversed his theory about hysteria originating in childhood sexual trauma. Rather than acknowledge that incest was endemic to the patriarchal family, Freud incriminated the daughters instead of their fathers, and concluded that his patients' reports of sexual abuse were fantasies based on their own incestuous wishes (Herman 1981: 9–10).

In general, service programmes for victims of rape, battering and child sexual abuse have been influenced by the intertwined efforts of grass-roots activities in the women's movement and various professionals, mostly women. For example, one nurse, Ann Burgess, is a recognised authority for her initial work with rape victims and, more recently, with victims of child sexual abuse. Other women professionals combine their professional work on behalf of victims with explicit allegiance to a feminist perspective: e.g. Elaine Hilberman Carmen works as a psychiatrist on the issue of battering. She is one of the first professionals to question publicly the common practice among mental health personnel of attaching psychiatric labels to battered women, thus implying that battering occurs because of the victim's purported psychopathology (Hilberman 1980; Ryan 1970). One of Carmen's collaborators is a sociologist with a feminist perspective, Rieker (1984). Herman (1981), also a psychiatrist, did landmark research and clinical work on father–daughter incest. Russell (1982, 1986), a sociologist, researched extensively the prevalence of marital rape and incest. The exposure of acquaintance rape is even more recent (Warshaw 1988). Sociologist Barry (1979) exposed the international traffic of women sold for sexual purposes. Stanko, a sociologist, and Rafter, a criminologist, documented the discriminatory treatment of women in the criminal justice system (1982), while Jones (1980) and Browne (1987) offer complementary historical and psychological analyses of the criminal justice system's biased disposition of women who kill.

Some professional women in the violence field have been joined by husbands with a feminist/political (vs. psychopathological) perspective on the problem. For example, the sociologist team Rebecca and Russell Dobash (1979) did an exhaustive sociological analysis of wife-battering that emphasises patriarchy as the dominant historical, cultural context of woman abuse. Evan Stark, sociologist, and Anne Flitcraft, a physician, found, through large urban samples of battered women, that health professionals not only most often do not help battered wives, but that their approaches in emergency health settings exacerbate the victims' problems through psychiatric labelling and redefinition of this public issue as a 'private' event (1979, 1984). Schechter, a social worker, has written the most exhaustive history of the battered women's shelter movement, clearly feminist in perspective, but not ignoring traditional professional issues (1982).

Recently, programmes for a special group of victims, Vietnam War Veterans, have been developed. In contrast to most other victims, however, this group consists mostly of men, while their victimisation can be traced to their own participation in socially approved aggression, war – planned and directed by men, conducted in a Third World country, against people of colour. It may be a reflection of male dominance that the 'post-traumatic stress disorder' (PTSD) identified from this population has been proposed as a model for studying stress responses of other victims, thus superceding the earlier 'rape trauma syndrome' identified by Ann Burgess studying female rape victims (NOVA-NIMH 1985).

Services for men who batter are also developing, for example, EMERGE in Boston. The focus of these programmes is on men assuming responsibility for their violent behaviour and stopping it (Hoff 1989: 273–4; Adams 1988). In a Minneapolis police experiment, researchers found that men who were arrested had the lowest rate of repeat battering when compared with traditional police approaches to battering (Sherman and Berk 1984).

This historical overview reveals that, with the exception of Ann Burgess, nurses are conspicuous by their absence from nationally recognised work in the abuse field until very recently. However, in 1984, two nurses, Jacqueline Campbell and Janice Humphreys, wrote the first textbook on nursing care of victims of violence. Hoff (1989) includes a chapter on crises stemming from violence, while traumatic stress is included in the Burgess and Baldwin crisis text (1981). Meanwhile, several nurses have done (or are in process of doing) doctoral or master's theses on victimisation topics: (e.g. Hoff 1990; Trujillo 1985; Campbell, 1986).

However, in spite of nurses' relative invisibility in the historical development of this field, it appears that nursing is on the threshold of a dramatic turn-around in respect to victims. In October 1985, the Surgeon General of the US Public Health Service, C. Everett Koop, MD, convened the first national Workshop on Violence and Public Health in Leesburg, Virginia. Invited participants in this historic event included 150 persons representing the health professions, social sciences, and the criminal justice system. Of this number, twenty-two were nurses, two of whom were included on the thirteen-member planning committee, one functioned as leader of one of eleven work groups and presented testimony at a Senate sub-committee hearing, and another was a recorder. This large representation by nurses is attributed chiefly to the national influence of Ann Burgess and her interdisciplinary research on victimisation. In stark contrast to nurses' previous limited involvement, nurses at this national workshop held a caucus and were the only distinct professional group to issue a public statement supporting the recommendations of the workshop. This activity was followed by a press conference and a news release sent to eleven major nursing journals. During the same week, the University of Massachusetts hosted the first national conference on domestic violence for nurses. And since then, several US nurses have formed a consortium to research violence against women in a feminist perspective.

These contrasting levels of nursing involvement on behalf of victims of violence are clarified in the history of nursing highlighted above and its parallel marginal involvement in the women's movement. It was only in 1972 that the American Nurses Association endorsed the Equal Rights Amendment. And as recently as 1982 the first explicitly feminist group of nurses organised under the title 'Cassandra', commemorating Florence Nightingale's essay likening nurses to the Greek figure Cassandra who cried out but was never heard. While Joanne Ashley's work is a landmark contribution towards the consciousness raising of nurses, it fails to interpret in historical context the apparent collusion of early nursing leaders in their oppression. Thus, while noting the general invisibility of nurses as activists on behalf of victims, it is crucial to consider the number of features that nurses – predominantly women – have in common with victims of violence such as battered women. Nurses and battered women, for example, share a socio-cultural origin of their problem in the devaluation of women; the public's response to their plight is often indifference or blame; and, in turn, both groups' internalisation of society's judgement is often revealed in self-blame (Hoff, forthcoming). Ignoring these commonalities can result in nurses colluding inadvertently in 'blaming the victim' – in this case themselves – much as battered women do when they are isolated and act without benefit of sensitivity to the historical realities of their situation. As Williams states:

> It is precisely a mark of extreme exploitation or degradation that those who suffer it do not see themselves differently from the way they are seen by the exploiters; either they do not see themselves as anything at all, or they acquiesce passively in the role for which they have been cast.
>
> (Williams 1969: 117-18)

143

Historically, and to some extent currently, nurses are prone to blame themselves for the various problems plaguing the profession. Roberts (1983) and Hedin (1986), drawing on Freire's (1970) work, discuss this issue as nurses' oppressed group behaviour. As in the case of battered women, a delicate balance must be struck between accepting personal responsibility for one's plight and recognising the socio-cultural and political forces that usually elude the influence of individuals acting alone without benefit of social support, critical awareness, and joint political action. In this respect the Surgeon General's Workshop on Violence and Public Health represents an occasion when individual effort and group action together 'made a difference' in the public perception and participation of nurses in an historic event.

Only history can tell where this effort will lead and what difference it might make for millions of victims. To paraphrase Chiaromonte (1985: 30), there is no guide other than acting on what we believe about others and the world we live in. Officially, the nursing profession espouses the role of the nurse as patient advocate (ANA 1979) and proposes the concept of 'environment' as central to the nursing paradigm. The most prominent foremother of modern nursing, Florence Nightingale, framed her practice on a very broad definition of environment. Chopoorian (1986) notes that the current very narrow definition of 'environment' has greatly hampered the holistic goals and political potential of nursing. This, along with nursing's definition of 'client/ patient' as primarily the individual – in contrast to the family and community – provides a theoretical basis complementing the poli- tical factors influencing nurses' historical role at the margins of advocacy for victims of violence who in so many ways resemble themselves.

However, there are other historical reasons why nursing and other health professionals have either been marginal to the cause of victims or have actually exacerbated their problems. That is, despite the central influence of the women's movement in drawing attention to victims of rape and battering, there is evidence of a 'pathology' model in most service programmes of traditional health agencies. Even in training programmes for battered women with an explicit feminist perspective, the psychopathological concept of 'battered woman syndrome' (Walker 1979) is widely accepted. Meanwhile, the battered women's shelter movement notes the constant struggle against

144

being co-opted by powerful social service and psychopathology models in services for victims (Ahrens 1980).

In large measure these developments can be traced to the historical influence of the medical model on the various health and mental health professionals concerned with the problem. This development is intertwined with the deeply embedded value of individualism in US society. That is, individual models prevail despite research that provides overwhelming evidence from sociology, anthropology, epidemiology, and social psychology revealing social factors in illness, crisis, and victimisation by violence. A large body of research reinforces the general discrediting of intra-individual theories of violence as noted earlier.[1]

Yet, reams of research notwithstanding, reformers are still trying to overcome the influence of individualism and normative theory in approaches to victimisation and crisis. Complementing this emphasis on individualism and neglect of social factors is the neglect of preventive efforts regarding violence. On the topic of homicide, for example, only seventeen of 364 items in a recent bibliography deal with prevention (Riedel and Zahn 1982).

Besides neglecting prevention, individual models also mask the social reality that women are the predominant victims of abuse by rape, incest, battering, and elder abuse; while men are the predominant assailants. In regard to homicide, men are predominant among both victims and assailants, particularly men in ethnic minority groups. Racism, poverty, and unemployment are highly correlated with victimisation by homicide among minorities. However, common to male dominance in *all* kinds of victimisation by violence is male socialisation to employ violence as a solution to problems and an attitude of entitlement by men that can be traced to their dominance in most aspects of social life.

Emphasis on individualistic/psychopathology vs. social models is all the more striking when considering the Congressional document published in 1960, *Action for Mental Health*. Here, after nearly a decade of research, national recommendations for mental health services included 24-hour emergency mental health and crisis services as essential elements in community mental health programmes. Yet, twenty-five years later, routine crisis services and training of professionals to assist victims of violence and others are the exception rather than the norm in many communities (Hoff and Miller 1987).

Rosenberg and Mercy (1985) suggest, for example, that shelter for battered women may provide an important model for developing comprehensive services to victims of other types of violence. Yet programme developers and practitioners sensitive to the lessons of history might study and compare the shelter movement to an alternative crisis service that preceded it by fifteen years – the suicide prevention movement. Such study should yield successes to emulate and pitfalls to avoid (Hoff 1989a: 14–19; Ahrens 1980: Hoff 1990). Chief among the valuable examples from these alternative models is the need for collaboration between lay and professional groups and the importance of formal training in crisis intervention.

CONCLUSIONS

Widespread action on the lessons of history and current recommendations seem timely, since the battered women's movement and victim advocacy generally appear to be at a crossroads as a result of public consciousness that has emerged from the work of feminists, other social activists, the President's Task Force on Victims of Crime (1982), the Attorney General's Task Force on Family Violence (1984), and, most recently, the Surgeon General's Workshop Recommendations (1986). All who are concerned with victimisation might note that the message of social activists and critical analysts (heretofore the minority voice) is now included in the official documents and testimony of the mainstream: Rosenberg and Mercer of the Center for Disease Control of the USPHS citing shelters as a service model for victims; a police chief, Anthony Bouza of Minneapolis, associating black male homicide with racism and unemployment during the Surgeon General's Workshop; the Surgeon General during Congressional testimony stating that 'the United States is not a safe place for women and children'; the recommendations by authorities in the mainstream and minority to eliminate gender inequality and support more flexible male role models.

The historical moment is both ironic and strategic in that the Federal government has allocated new millions of dollars in services to individual victims, while at the same time curtailing social programmes that aid groups most vulnerable to victimisation in the first place – the poor, women, children, and racial minority groups. While this move corresponds to national trends supporting individualistic solutions vs. prevention and elimination of root causes, still there is an opportunity here to be seized by professional groups such as nurses to use new programme resources in keeping with a holistic social vision as promulgated by Nightingale.

History reveals that 'natural crisis management' has been practised since the beginning of time. Life crises are not merely private events. To avoid catastrophe and even death, community effort is essential. But today in a violent society, the despair and suffering of numerous victims provide poignant evidence that 'formal crisis management' is a critical addition to the strength and coping that individuals bring to bear on resolving a life crisis like victimisation in a positive direction. As front-line health workers, nurses are in a most advantageous position to meet the needs of victims through skilled application of individual and social skills in crisis management. Nurses' recent awakening to their own oppression within the health care system provides them with an important requisite for such sensitive, holistic practice on behalf of victims.

All victims are entitled to the new era of social responsiveness to the disadvantaged and abused in our society that seems on the horizon, not only through immediate assistance but by political efforts to quell the social abuses most influential in producing individual victim states – sexism, racism, ageism, and poverty. As Alice Walker says: Only justice can stop a curse.

NOTE

1. See Hoff (1989: 142, 246–9) for citations of some of this research.

Chapter Nine

GENDER, ROLE, AND SICKNESS: THE RITUAL PSYCHOPATHOLOGIES OF THE NURSE

ROLAND LITTLEWOOD

Witness: I don't know what you mean by kinky. I've had a few
who liked me to dress up in a maid's uniform or a nurse's
uniform....
Mr Justice Caufield: What? Somebody coughed. I thought she
said a matron's uniform.
Mr Michael Hill, QC, counsel for the Star: I think she said a
French maid's uniform.
Mr Justice Caufield: I was a bit surprised at a matron's uniform.
(*The Times*, London, 14 July 1987)

Historical studies of the relationship between patient and healer
in western medicine have always emphasised a special relationship
between patient and doctor. The symbolic attributes of the patient
are taken as characteristically female, those of the doctor as male.
Such an implicit connotation serves to provide a structural model
for the neuroses as socially embedded relationships articulating
this symbolic and political relationship: women in the West are
'medicalised' in everyday life in a way that is not true for men.
Perceived as 'neurotic' they can avail themselves of a small
negotiating space through such neurosis.

The role of the nurse as a characteristically female one, as a
carer, poses certain contradictions within such a rigidly binary
classification. While nursing is a professionalisation of aspects of
women's traditional domestic tasks, an extension of her 'natural'
nurturant and caring activities, her role threatens to approximate
in medical perception to the role of the patient.

Some ambiguities are resolved during the socialisation of the
nurse into her professional role or later in various strategic ways.

Particular problems arise for female doctors in traditionally male specialities such as gynaecology, for male nurses, and for female nurses who themselves have only partial access to the negotiating power afforded to other women by the neuroses. In this paper I consider three patterns of 'abnormal illness behaviour' which the medical profession has perceived among nurses.

IS FEMALE TO MALE AS PATIENT IS TO DOCTOR?

Tullio Maranhão (1986) has reminded us that one characteristic of western therapies is that they take the form of a dialogue between healer and patient. This is taken as a dialogue between doctor and patient. Till recently it has seemed as if this was the only form of serious therapeutic interaction. Doctor and patient. The *doctor–patient relationship*. There is a resonance about it. A salience. It seems the very essence of western healing.[1] Medical textbooks include introductory chapters on it, and since Entralgo's pioneering *Doctor and Patient* (1969) much speculation has centred on its social and historical significance. Maranhão himself relates the therapeutic discourse back to the Socratic method; in psychoanalysis this discourse, purged of any technological interruptions, stands as the very process of healing.

The doctor–patient relationship. By contrast 'the nurse–patient relationship' does not sound so resonant. While nursing textbooks provide chapters on its practice, it always seems contingent on political and symbolic constructs external to the pair. The doctor–patient dyad seems to stand by itself, as if it were a part of the natural order of things. While a preference for binary classifications may or may not be rooted in all human thought (R. Littlewood 1984), here at least we cannot blame the structural anthropologist. A simple triad *patient–doctor–nurse* does not seem right, for the nurse's role is ambiguous, comprising not only nurturance but also passivity. Indeed, as I shall argue, the pair which includes the nurse and which strikes the most powerful resonance in contemporary western medical practice is that of *doctor and nurse*.

In all societies, illness is experienced and manifest through conceptual categories which encode aspects of the social order (Comaroff 1978). While serious illness 'is an event that challenges meaning in this world ... medical beliefs and practices organise the event into an episode which gives form and meaning' (Young

1976). The power of the experience of illness is derived not only from its ability to evoke intense personal affects but also from its evoking deeply felt social responses (Good and Good 1982). Medical intervention in western sickness incorporates the patient into a generally accepted system of biomedical explanation, a common structural pattern which is manifest in the body of every person. Responsibility for the body is, however, shifted. Accountability for the sickness is transferred from the patient to others. While the sick person is usually exempted from fulfilling some of their usual social obligations, and from personal responsibility for the sickness itself, there is a recognition shared between patient and others that the sickness is undesirable and that it involves an obligation first to seek help and then to co-operate with medical treatment (Parsons 1951).

To attempt to question the biomedical schema itself would involve questioning our most fundamental assumptions about human nature and agency. Because it relates the personal experience of distress to the social order through removing personal responsibility and initiating an institutionalised response, together with its justification of ultimate social values through science, medicine offers sickness as a powerful, legitimate, and unquestionable alternative to everyday adult behaviour.

What are the everyday contexts from which the patient's sick role is derived? I suggest that there is a close approximation between the role of the patient *vis-à-vis* the doctor and that of women in relation to men. To be a patient is to be embedded in a web of beliefs, norms, and interests which represent the political and personal relations between the sexes.

> The facts of female physiology are transformed in almost all
> societies into a cultural rationale which assigns women to
> nature and the domestic sphere, and thus ensures their
> general inferiority to men. (La Fontaine 1981: 347)

As Ortner (1974) reminds us, women are 'excluded from participation in or contact with some realm in which the highest powers of the society are felt to reside'. They are excluded from it by a dominant ideology which reflects men's experiences and interests. The fundamental aspects of the female role in western society are reflected in the ideals still held out to women: concentration on marriage, home, and children as the primary focus of concern with reliance on a male provider for sustenance and status. As Beveridge, one of the architects of the British Welfare State, put it: 'Her home is her factory, her husband and children a worthwhile job.' There is an expectation that women emphasise nurturance, that they live through and for others rather than for themselves. By tradition women relinquish their name, occupation, and place of residence when they marry. They are banned from direct assertion or the expression of aggression.

The historical origin of the contemporary role lies in the Industrial Revolution, with a radical division of work by gender and a physical separation between home and work-place which exaggerated the existing social and emotional segregation of women. Turner (1984) and Donzelot (1977) suggest this produced a close relationship between the woman and the family doctor which, in certain areas, replaced that of wife and husband. The move away from the household as a focus for productive work also diminished its responsibilities for religion, education, and recreation, reducing its social significance, contracting women's general responsibilities and isolating them from significant areas of public production.

Woman's lack of power is attributed to her greater emotionality and to her inability to cope with wider social responsibilities. Dependency and passivity are expected of a woman and her normality is that of the neurotic, with a childish incapacity to govern herself and thus a need for male protection and direction (Chesler 1974; Jordanova 1980; Broverman *et al*. 1970). Compared with men, contemporary western women are permitted greater freedom to 'express feelings' (Phillips and Segal 1969), enabling the woman to define her distresses within a medical framework and bring them to the attention of her doctor (Horwitz 1977). The more women take on female role responsibilities, the greater their reporting of medical symptoms (Hillband and Pope 1983). Jordanova (1980) suggests that the action of men on women is characteristic of medicine, in which women are more 'natural', passive, awaiting male ('cultural') organisation. Ingleby (1982) too argues that there is a close historical relationship between the notions of 'woman' and 'patient'. The male patient is inevitably 'feminised'. In a previous paper Maurice Lipsedge and I summarised this relationship as a set of complementary pairs (Littlewood and Lipsedge 1987):

$$\frac{Culture}{Nature} = \frac{Male}{Female} = \frac{Active}{Passive} = \frac{Cognition}{Affect} = \frac{Doctor}{Patient}$$

$$= \frac{Public}{Private} = \frac{Production}{Consumption} = \frac{Desire}{Need}$$

(modified from Jordanova 1980; Turner 1984).

A polythetic classification of this type stresses that it is the relationship between the paired elements which remains constant: there is no equality between either the superordinate or the subordinate elements by themselves taken as a horizontal series. Clearly not all doctors are men. Indeed, medicine has a greater proportion of women than other 'Social Class 1' professions. But the woman doctor's role in relation to her patient replicates the male/female relationship. We may expect a male patient to flirt with his nurse but hardly with his doctor.

The ambiguities of the 'lady doctor' are most manifest in the areas where the doctor/patient relationship closely replicates that of male/female: obstetrics and gynaecology. A British gynaecology textbook reminds its students that 'femininity tends to be passive and receptive, masculinity to be more active, restless, anxious for repeated demonstrations of potency' (James 1963). There are relatively few female gynaecologists compared with women in other medical specialities. Lipsedge and I have argued that the codification of distress to produce many psychiatric 'reactions' – overdoses, agoraphobia, shoplifting, anorexia nervosa – is through a ritual play on the male:female–doctor–patient set.[2] The mediator, the psychiatrist, is thus more 'feminine' than other physicians (Littlewood and Lipsedge 1987). There are many female psychiatrists and paediatricians, but these work in areas of sickness where the male/female bipolarity is muted, where a mother/child opposition becomes appropriate. By contrast gynaecology permits no ambiguities or symbolic play – it is a simple manifestation of the biologically rooted set. Through childbearing, every woman becomes a potential patient. Woman doctors are not allowed to be female through bearing children themselves: a recent questionnaire study reported that they 'were not taken seriously in their career intentions once they had become pregnant' (Stephen 1987). The 'Wendy Savage affair' demonstrates how a female obstetrician who attempts to cut across the symbolic conceptualisations, no longer acting as a classificatory male, creates havoc in the whole system: clearly, natural childbirth and the women's health movements have to adopt an ethic which inverts the traditional relationship.[3]

AND THE NURSE

Nurses in prisons and mental hospitals excepted, the nurse is quintessentially female. She is female both in popular perception and in actual statistics. Jack Goody (1982) has suggested that those occupational roles with which women are now characteristically associated – hairdressing, cleaning, nursing, prostitution, and to an extent infant teaching, catering, and waiting at table – are developments of women's traditional domestic tasks which have become split off and rationalised as separate professions. Nursing is an extension and codification of woman's nurturant role as a mother. To 'nurse' is indeed to be a mother. As Goody notes, these female professions have not developed simply as professions parallel to those of men, for men have now entered them and re-established themselves at the top of the hierarchy. As more men enter, the profession becomes divided into upper (male dominated) and lower (predominantly female) sectors. We have this distinction between *cuisine* and *catering*, between secondary and primary education. The entry of men into general nursing from their traditional area of psychiatric nursing (with its role derived from that of the untrained and custodial mental hospital attendant) has now led to male domination of the Royal College of Nursing and a relative over-representation of men in the newer nursing administrative positions (Gaze 1987). The nursing specialities most closely associated with a traditional female role, midwifery and health visiting, are the last to admit men.

Because of the association of nursing with 'care', with female nurturance and consolation, the male nurse has remained a particularly ambiguous figure: 'Men have always been a touchy topic in nursing' (Gaze 1987). Like the hairdresser, who has also adopted female gender specific tasks, he takes on certain homosexual attributes.[4] The sexual orientation of the male nurse, like that of the female doctor, is a constant matter of interest, while the sexual interests of an engineer or an anthropologist appear irrelevant. A recent supplement on men in nursing carried by a nursing journal was entitled *Man Appeal* and was principally concerned with the popular perception of the male nurse, weighing the images of 'tough' versus 'tender', 'macho' versus 'soft', of custodian versus carer.[5]

In some particulars then, the nurse–doctor relationship presents a standardised system of emotional attitudes in recapitulating professionally that of mother:father, but the immediate popular image of the nurse is of course one who is young, gauche, and sexually attractive, as witness the endless newspaper cartoons and jokes hinting at (never consummated) physical intimacy between male patient and nurse.[6] A concerned *Nursing Times* wonders if 'the average male really does see general nurses as 18-year-old blondes who wear pretty caps' (Gaze 1987: 27).[7] When nurses get older or enter administration the image changes dramatically to that of the well-known 'battleaxe sister' or 'dragon matron', professional but thus defeminised and threatening, wielding bedpan or syringe. Senior nurses do indeed tend to be single, seldom have children, show little interest in life outside the hospital (Hutt 1985). The situation is still that noted by *The Englishwoman* in 1913: nurses who had not left to marry or become matrons were unemployable by the age of forty for doctors preferred young nurses 'who are less likely than older women to interfere' (Simnet 1986).

Patients and nurses then share certain female characteristics: socially ascribed characteristics of gender role, not directly of biological sex, but, as we shall see, the 'natural facts' of biological sex from which they are derived keep breaking in.

Relations with doctors

Nurses perform domestic tasks for doctors – making coffee, running errands, and for surgeons actually helping them wash and dress. If they make suggestions they are careful to do so in a way in which the suggestions can be perceived as actually coming from the doctor (Cassell 1987) – a lateral strategy which if detected in a patient is termed in medical parlance 'manipulation'. Nurses remain defined by the doctor's tasks, mediating between biomedical and lay worlds. In spite of the attempt of nursing academics to establish a professional ethic, a central core idiom which can stand alone, this falters on the question of what it might constitute. Care? Communication?[8]

If, as I have argued, the doctor–nurse–patient triad replicates that of the nuclear family, activity continues to be directed by the doctor who retains the prerogative of deep penetration and control of the body (Armstrong 1983). By contrast, the nurse is an extension of the normal healing processes of the body itself (Henderson 1978). The syringe, bedpan, or enema are, however, threatening in that they too control. The organisation of the hospital replicates that of the domestic economy. The childbirth scene is represented in endless newspaper cartoons of the father, unshaven and smoking, pacing the hospital corridor, excluded and marginal. Inside the delivery suite his role is taken by the doctor. Not surprisingly, the radical midwife endeavours to supplant the doctor, but in this she reintroduces the biological father not as director of the proceedings but as caring assistant.[9]

The self-perception of the doctor, particularly the surgeon, is one of belonging to a confraternity of heroes. Like the gynaecologist, in Britain the surgeon takes the gender-specific title of 'Mr' rather than the gender neutral 'Dr'. Cassell, in a recent paper describes the macho self-assurance of the ideal surgeon: 'The masculine society of surgeons admires cars, sports, speed, competence' (Cassell 1986). She describes the embarrassment caused when one brings his wife to a hospital party where the other surgeons are busily engaged in sexual dalliance with the hospital nurses. Whether at the level of fantasy, flirtation, or actual physical sex, relations between the doctor and 'his' nurse are heavily charged with sexual significance, a favourite theme of television soap opera or Mills and Boon hospital romances.[10] Doctors 'have' their nurses; nurses don't 'have' doctors. Indeed, a doctor who fails to engage in at least the appearance of sexual flirtation with the nurse is a 'wimp', one who is professionally incompetent, slow, unable to act, and thus clinically dangerous through his impotence (Cassell 1987).

By contrast, the notion of a female doctor having sex with a male nurse is incredible and bizarre. If, as I have argued, the patient is quintessentially female, what of sexual relations between her and the male doctor? Again the possibility is abhorrent but not inconceivable, traditionally the worst offence for which a doctor could be summoned before the General Medical Council.[11] Too dangerous a situation to be openly represented, it is the dentist who stands in for the doctor in the numerous soft-core pornographic films which skirt about the issue.[12] By contrast, the female patient is allowed to flirt with the doctor; he responds correctly with anxiety and embarrassment. In the official pre-history of psychoanalysis, it is when Freud's colleague Breuer realises that his patient Anna O. is in love with him and he breaks off the treatment in horror leaving town for a 'second honeymoon' with his wife, that the central idea was generated: patients fall in love with their doctors, the idea that later became developed into the notion of 'transference'.[13]

To summarise:

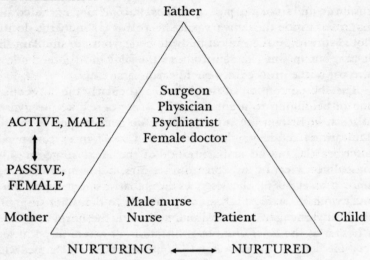

The doctor's perception emphasises the vertical axis, the nurse's emphasises the horizontal.

Socialisation

Student nurses at the London teaching hospitals are usually inducted into their vocation through a period of segregated preliminary training. Throughout their career, the low salary constrains many to spend a considerable period of time in a hall of residence attached to the hospital. There they are treated as younger than their age, in need of protection and surveillance. In contrast with other student hostels, rules are strict and male visitors segregated in a public space during specific visiting hours. Various authors (e.g. Carpenter 1978; Maggs 1983) have noted the tension in the development of nursing between offering the period of training as a type of finishing school for the less affluent young lady, with careful attention to chastity and deportment, and the attempt to train paid and skilled professionals. In the 1970s at St Bartholomew's Hospital the annual Matron's Ball resembled a fashionable 'coming out', the cloistered atmosphere of the Nurses' Home (with its preoccupations with mislaid cap-pins or dieting) enlivened with plans as to whom to invite, what fashionable dress to imitate, how much wine might decently be consumed, the whole recalling more the atmosphere of a girls' public school story than its reality as a rather tawdry piece of glamour punctuating a hot-house atmosphere centred exclusively around the hospital. Sexuality is constrained but highlighted through this constraint. The ideal was marriage to a young doctor and then departure from the hospital. One unfortunate nurse made no secret of her affections for one of the hospital porters and was warned by her ward sister that she would have to choose between her lover and her 'vocation'. Little wonder that so many nurses seemed to marry policemen, affections cultivated in the casualty department or the nurses' canteen in which by tradition policemen in uniform whose work took them to the hospital were allowed to take a cup of tea. There were no male student nurses, whose likely professionalism would doubtless have threatened the notion of 'vocation' (Carpenter 1978).

Relations with patients: the representation of the overdose

Women are closely identified with psychotropic (mind-altering) medications. Seventy per cent of these drugs were found in one study to have been prescribed for women. That we are not concerned with a 'real' gender disparity in psychological distress is suggested by the images of doctor-directed advertising. Women outnumber men by fifteen to one in advertisements for tranquillisers and anti-depressants (Littlewood and Lipsedge 1987). Employed women are rarely portrayed in drug ads, and women are represented as dependent housewives and child-rearers. They inhabit a world which acts on them, they do not act on the world. The treating physician is never depicted as a woman (Prather and Fidell 1975).[14]

Deliberate 'overdoses' with medical drugs are five times more common among women than men, and are especially common between the ages 15–19. The medical explanation of this 'perverse inversion of the medical paradigm' (Littlewood and Lipsedge 1987) is either in terms of symptomatology – expression of underlying feelings or illness, or 'manipulation' – an act unconsciously conceived in terms of its desired consequences, usually increased support or understanding. Faced with an overdose 'doctors feel a sense of irritation which they find difficult to conceal' (*BMJ* 1970). While the rules of play dictate that the patient has access to treatment because she is not responsible for the illness, the 'manipulative' overdosing woman is, to the doctor, clearly responsible. The popular view of the overdose is of something happening to one, an irresistible urge determined by adverse circumstances (Ginsberg 1971). Doctors are prepared to accept the act only as a symptom of an underlying illness or wish to die. Nurses however are more sympathetic to actually expressed instrumental motives (Ramon *et al.* 1975), perhaps because of their anomalous position in the healer–patient relationship.[15] It is not they who have prescribed the drugs. As in other areas they mediate between the lay and biomedical explanatory models and here are able to move beyond a biomedical theory which is shared by the relatives (ensuring the overdose 'works').

PSYCHOPATHOLOGIES OF THE NURSE

Given their position firmly on one side of the patient–doctor paradigm, it is not surprising that doctors are believed (not least by themselves) to make poor patients, failing to accept a novel situation of passivity and obedience. The advantages of the public negotiating strategies of agoraphobia, overdoses, or chronic pain syndrome – psycho-social distress modelled into syndromes – are not available to them. Their psychopathologies are secret – alcoholism, completed suicide, and divorce – for all of which doctors have among the highest rates.[16] To an extent this is true for nurses – while overdoses are relatively common among student nurses, they are rare after they have qualified. In terms of our model they, like the doctors, are too much on the side of the healer in the healer–patient pair to be able to express distress as such. Nor are the more 'transparent' strategies of neurotic patterns (employing a disease idiom for personal distress) available. Nevertheless, hospital doctors have perceived in nurses some characteristic psychopathologies: Loin Pain Haematuria,

Munchausen's Syndrome by Proxy, and Mass Hysteria. Because they lack the 'transparency' of agoraphobia, shoplifting, and other 'neurotic patterns', and use the biomedical idiom more closely, they occasion particular outrage in the doctor.

Loin Pain Haematuria: the case of Edith Owens

The dismay of doctors faced with the patient who takes an over-dose of prescribed drugs reflects a medical preoccupation with 'factitious illness' – apparent diseases induced deliberately by those seeking the advantages of the sick role. Prison doctors in the nine-teenth century discovered 'Ganser psychosis' – the syndrome of approximate answers – a strategy of feigned madness, employing popular ideas of insanity, through which long-term convicts gained the more congenial circumstances of the prison hospital. Junior psychiatrists today are still taught to ask appropriate questions to detect it.[17] While a general acceptance of psychodynamic theories of 'psychosomatic illnesses' and the influences of life events and personality on physical disease are part of the currency of psy-chiatry, these are accepted only grudgingly by many general physicians and surgeons. If the signs and symptoms fail to add up to recognised pathophysiology, or the laboratory tests do not concur, while the patient keeps returning with further episodes and cheerfully accepts hospital admission, then the physicians become suspicious of the possibility of 'factitious illnesses'. They divide them simply into *malingering* (a consciously motivated fabrication of symptoms) or *hysteria* (in which the patient is largely unaware of their production).[18] Malingerers are promptly discharged from hospital, while hysterics are referred to the psychiatrist. Loin pain haematuria was described as a new syndrome in the 1970s – characterised by blood in the urine and pain in the lower abdomen for which no biological cause could be found. The initial studies showed a high proportion of nurses and doctors' wives among the patients and, in the absence of obvious disease of the kidneys, it was suggested to be a factitious illness (Aber and Higgins 1982). Debate has continued as to whether there is a 'real' disease, the patients being nurses only by their proximity to hospital personnel who have a greater readiness to investigate them.

'Edith Owens' is a nursing sister at a small clinic attached to a London teaching hospital, married with two young daughters. Of provincial working-class origin, she was brought up by evangelical parents, left school to enter nursing, and later came to London. She was referred to the hospital renal department at the age of 33 complaining of loin pain and fresh blood when she urinated. Repeated hospital admission for investigations and blood transfusions occurred when her haemoglobin dropped to dangerously low levels. Petite and attractive, looking younger than her age, Edith sat in bed, her face completely white from anaemia, apparently considering her situation with total equanimity and leaving her physicians disconcerted by what they felt was, if not actually flirtation, some type of heavily charged but implicit emotional communication. Concern was also expressed over the large doses of the morphine analogue, pethidine, she required for her pain. She was closely observed and encouraged to see a junior psychiatrist (myself).[19] Formal psychotherapy sessions continued rather fruitlessly for two years, interrupted by Edith's frequent admissions to hospital. Eventually she was detected one night in her hospital bed removing blood from her arm with a syringe (which had been hidden in her handbag) and injecting it into her urethra. She was confronted with the evidence in the presence of her husband by the triumphant physicians while I sat rather uncomfortably at the side. She took up the offer of some time in a psychotherapy ward during which she became considerably more animated and less bland. She recalled the stratagems she used to hide her syringes but said she was never consciously motivated to take her blood: 'It just sort of happened – like in a dream.' Afterwards she had 'just felt – I don't know – well, good'. Her stay was cut short when it was discovered that at home her eldest daughter, aged six, although on the surface comfortably adjusting to her mother's absence, was secretly pulling her hair out in handfuls.

Edith Owen's parental home had been strict but not harsh. Her father was distant and cold while fair, her mother harassed and always worried about money. Disobedience by the seven children was not tolerated by the parents nor apparently ever offered. Edith as the oldest girl adopted enthusiastically the role of a 'little mother' from an early age, looking after the youngest children and at ten was cooking for the family when her mother entered hospital for a few months. There were few family holidays for financial reasons and life centred around the church to which all the children have continued to belong when grown-up. Nursing seemed an obvious vocation for a 'little mother' and she left home to stay in the nurses' hostel. At a hospital dance she was introduced to, and soon married, her only boyfriend, a young businessman of similar background to her own. Life now became transformed as his company prospered – a higher standard of living, two cars, detached house, not to mention sex which Edith suddenly discovered was rather good fun. Although it was not financially necessary, she continued working as a staff nurse in the operating theatre and, while there, in a daze of opening opportunities had an affair with the anaesthetist who happened to be a friend of her husband.

She discovered she was pregnant but whether by her husband or by the doctor she was uncertain. Her father died suddenly and she became depressed; terrified it was not her husband's child, but unwilling to lose it deliberately, she started dieting and using hospital syringes to remove blood from her veins, punishing herself but also hoping through this to lose the baby. Admission to hospital and blood transfusions were followed by 'successful delivery' of the child without any apparent ill effects. The couple moved to London; a second girl was born and Edith continued to work at nights, devoting the day to her husband and children. Her girls were 'perfect', well behaved and loving, and she spent all her spare time with them, a prosperous suburban life enlivened by teaching at the Sunday school, quiet dinner parties, and trips to Glyndebourne. Superficially all was successful but Edith no longer felt 'real', constantly getting thoughts that her children were not hers. In her job she was extremely hard working, a good teacher, and a loyal colleague. She was then offered a year's course to become a nursing tutor and accepted, her husband unenthusiastically agreeing. While waiting for the course to begin, she went to her doctor complaining of passing blood and pain in her lower abdomen. She was forced to take time off from work: her course was postponed. Life continued its sedate public tenor.

Munchausen's Syndrome by Proxy

The most dramatic form of malingering observed by physicians is Munchausen's Syndrome ('hospital addiction syndrome') in which convincing abdominal symptoms in men and women lead to urgent hospital admission and operation. In the extreme form 'Munchausens', as they are called, spend their lives moving from

161

one hospital to another, changing their names, passing an impressive proportion of their lives in hospital beds, sometimes to be operated on yet again, sometimes to be ejected by indignant doctors after consultation of the 'blacklist' in the casualty department (which records their pseudonyms, appearance, and favourite symptoms). While it may be characterised as an extreme form of 'abnormal illness behaviour', psychiatrists usually classify the patients as 'inadequate personalities', citing their incapacity to live any type of conventional life.

A proportion of Munchausen's patients have obtained jobs as hospital porters or orderlies and some studies suggest factitious illness is more common in women who have taken nursing training (Sneddon 1983). A recently studied and related pattern is Munchausen's Syndrome by Proxy [20] in which mothers produce factitious, sometimes real, diseases in their children. Techniques include placing menstrual blood in the child's orifices, contaminating specimens, altering hospital records, or, more seriously, producing rashes on the child with abrasives or caustics, aspirating milk from the child's stomach with a syringe to produce weight loss, or producing fits through asyphyxiation. In one study of forty-seven parents, all were women (Meadows 1984). Seventeen of the group were nurses and another four paramedicals; several claimed falsely to be related to a doctor. The children were admitted to hospital for intensive investigation and operations, including in one case brain surgery.

A common feature of many of the mothers is that they are of a higher 'social and intellectual status' than their husbands, many of whom are absent from the home, working away for considerable periods (Meadows 1984). Reading the case histories it seems significant that a close personal relationship is built up through the child's illness between mother and doctor. In many cases the mother has previously induced or simulated physical illness in herself and Meadows suggests the pattern is related both to personal factitious illness and to child abuse. He emphasises there can be considerable 'gains': 'A medical illness is one of the few available tickets to a source of help. Involve a child and that can be a first-class express ticket.'

Whatever our conclusions as to how 'conscious' a mechanism is involved, how pragmatically it is motivated, in symbolic and political terms we again have a pattern in which doctor–nurse–

father–mother, both united in care of the child. At the same time the principal achieves for herself a role as patient/child/spouse. If we examine an individual instance, the symbolism is more complex and rich, reflecting intense personal affects and contradictions. My model merely sketches out the bare bones of the choreography: out of it the principal develops her own pattern of meanings and expression.[21]

Royal Free Disease

In July 1955 an epidemic occurred among the staff of the Royal Free Hospital in London, the teaching hospital which trained female doctors and which had long been associated with women's medicine. Within two weeks the hospital had to be closed, to open three months later after over 300 people had been affected, the majority women. One hundred and ninety-eight staff needed in-patient treatment, of whom five were men (0.8 per cent of the males) and the rest women (11 per cent). The conclusions at the time were that the illness – headache, malaise, dizziness, nausea, neck stiffness, and limb pain – was caused by a virus; a year later a leading article in the Lancet entitled 'A new clinical entity?' proposed the name of 'benign myalgic encephalomyelitis'. There the matter rested until 1970 when two papers appeared in the *British Medical Journal* suggesting that 'epidemic hysteria' was a more likely diagnosis and noting that 'the occurrence of a mass hysterical reaction shows not that the population is psychologically abnormal but merely that it is socially segregated and consists predominantly of young females' (McEvedy and Beard 1970). The authors detailed fifteen similar epidemics, eight of them involving hospital nurses. An accompanying editorial noted 'the epidemic spread of panic-stricken and hysterical conduct has been more characteristic of women'. A lively storm of abusive correspondence followed.[22] Doctors wrote to say they were 'upset' by the article: 'I regard the conclusions ... as nonsense. Many of these girls were known to me. Illness was alien to their natures.' The editors of the journal were forced to justify having published the papers. One letter pointed out that hysteria had been considered initially at the Royal Free as a likely diagnosis: 'Later, as medical staff of various seniority succumbed, such a suggestion was silenced by unspoken agreement ... even now it is rarely applied except to girls of subnormal intelligence'.[23]

'Epidemic hysteria' is frequently summoned as an explanation in the editorials of medical journals to characterise sudden mass movements of which they disapprove. (Indeed, one doctor wrote in disparaging the critical comments made by others on McEvedy and Beard's papers to characterise such responses as a 'second wave of hysteria'. To doubt hysteria is hysteria.) This is not the place to recapitulate the many sociological studies on hysteria (see Littlewood 1987). Suffice to cite Ellenberger (1970) who describes it as 'a folie à deux ... a culture-bound syndrome emerging from the interaction between the professor and his clientele', or Chodoff and Lyon's famous description of hysterical personality as 'a picture of women in the words of men' (1958).

The notion of 'mass hysteria' has not been examined in the same way. Another nineteenth-century medical category, it emerged in the same sociological climate as Le Bon's study *The Crowd* – where a collectivity of people have a 'mental unity' analogous to a hypnotic trance, in which the individual 'having entirely lost his conscious personality, obeys all suggestions of the operator who has deprived him of it.... His acts are far more under the influence of the spinal cord than of the brain.... Crowds are like savages and women' (Le Bon 1893: 34, 40, 42). The psychological anthropology of Rivers and McDougall also relied on a notion of 'sympathy' or 'psychic contagion' and contemporary psychiatry still regards hysteria as the particular preserve of non-Europeans and women (Littlewood 1987). It continues to be reported in medical journals from closed communities of women and girls – boarding schools, convents, and nursing training schools.[24]

Given its assumption of 'lower mental functioning' and 'psychic contagion', there is no surprise over the furore that McEvedy and Beard's papers generated. Not only had the nurses been affected but female medical students and doctors. And some men. The indignant medical correspondents quite rightly realised that to recognise an episode of mass hysteria in the only 'female medical school' had serious implications for the image of women doctors. Indeed, the Royal Free epidemic still remains part of the folklore of every male student who has never heard of the serious outbreak of poliomyelitis in Britain which preceded it and on which some suggested it had been modelled.

We do not have to follow the medical detectives in choosing between the two explanations – viral or psychological. The experience of illness does not directly reflect a disease process. The disease provides a ground on which personal life, social context, and indigenous theories of sickness erect a pattern of experience, expression, and behaviour. Illness, as I have argued, is embedded in social roles and expectations. Its form may be modelled on pathophysiological changes but be induced by social context, and it may subserve deep-seated personal needs, as psychotherapists maintain.

The perception of the nurse as a woman by male medicine coalesces with a notion of the nurse as a mother. While those not engaged in health care and treatment have relatively easy recourse to 'neurotic' patterns, employing a form of sick role behaviour but with a predominantly psychological idiom, the nurse as a self-sufficient carer has to have recourse to a variety of patterns more closely allied to the presentation of physical disease, patterns more elusive to symbolic analysis, lying congealed in the medical text.[25] Thus, a common measure of nursing 'morale' on a ward is the extent of sick leave.[26]

A common feature of all three patterns is the male doctor as investigator, constantly tracking, suspecting, testing new hypotheses, accusing, while the nurse, elusive behind her sickness, seeks to avoid being caught. Doctors complain bitterly that these patients 'play games' with them, and the rhetoric of theatre or entertainment would indeed be irresistible did not such play involve serious physical risk to the protagonists.

NOTES

1. We have physicians, they have healers. Contrast the titles of two recent influential texts of medical anthropology, Kleinman's pan-cultural *Patients and Healers in the Context of Culture* and Hahn and Gaines's *Physicians of Western Medicine*.
2. We argue that the models derived by anthropologists such as Lewis (1966), in which the idiom of spirit possession in non-Western societies enables women to gain a certain degree of limited control over their circumstances, can be usefully applied to 'neurosis'. Lewis's concept of *mystical sanction* (in which possession both removes personal responsibility and compels others to ameliorative action) is manifest in biomedicine's concept of a *disease*. Women's psychopathologies are an exaggeration of their socially ascribed characteristics, an exaggerated inversion of those held in common with men, and thus at a higher level of classification, those of men.
3. How 'radical' Mrs Savage was at the time of her suspension remains a

matter of debate and some have suggested that her rate of surgical intervention in childbirth was not significantly different from that of male colleagues, and that support for her became increasingly less personal as she evolved into a symbol of opposition to patripotestal gynaecology.

4. This is decreasing with the slow untying of biological sex from social roles (Littlewood 1984), although the heterosexual male nurse has continually to justify his sexual interests without compromising his 'feminine' task.

5. *Nursing Times* 1987a. It is illustrated with a handsome muscle-bound male nurse wielding a threatening syringe, bare-chested beneath his uniform. The male nurse, traditionally at the bottom of the nursing value scale (custodial care) was working class, while the nineteenth-century female nurse was middle class and thus 'charitable' (at least as an ideal). To an extent this compensated for the men at the bottom of the hierarchy. By contrast women doctors are of a higher class status than most nurses, the London teaching hospital nurses perhaps excepted.

6. *Patient:* 'Nurse, kiss me goodnight!'
   Nurse: 'Certainly not!'
   Patient: 'Go on nurse, a goodnight kiss!'
   Nurse: 'I'm sorry, no. I shouldn't even be in bed with you.'

   While Kalisch, Kalisch, and Scobey (1983) suggest this sexualisation of the nurse is a recent phenomenon, a response to the women's movement, the nineteenth-century evidence suggests otherwise (Maggs 1983). To argue, as many apologists do, that a non-consummated sexual flirtation with a nurse may be a way for male patients to reduce their distress in the face of life-threatening illness may be true but this does not explain the social conception of the 'frilly' nurse. In the hospital where I studied it was the orthopaedic ward (where there was no anxiety about serious illness among the men confined to bed) which was characterised by the quantity of sexual bandinage. Flirtation as a response to loss of power yes, but not primarily as a sublimation of terror.

7. See my epigraph. The sexual attributes of the nurse demonstrated in this interchange were the subject of indignant comment in the *Nursing Times* (1987b): 'clearly Mr Justice Caufield sees nothing "kinky" about a prostitute dressing up as a nurse but draws the line at one dressing up as a matron.' On nurses' uniforms, see Littlewood, chapter 10, this volume.

8. Similarly, the wish to ground an alternative to the physician's diagnosis in such categorisations as 'the nursing process'. Recent attempts to provide entry into the profession through a preliminary period of university study are bedevilled by what, apart from biomedical sciences, this might include. Can the professionalisation of the nurse be achieved without loss of the 'nurturant' role? What academic discipline could be central? A promising candidate is social anthropology (as witness this book) which might be felt to offer a rigorous approach to 'healing' and

'care', one grounded in 'holistic' assumptions of 'well-being' with a notion of 'positive health' beyond that of the absence of disease. Chrisman (1982) emphasises that the notion of 'care' is fruitfully open to articulate lay notions of sickness and patterns of health-seeking behaviours.

9. For instance, the interviews in 'The Midwives' Dilemma', *Sunday Times Magazine*, 23 August 1987, in which the radical midwife and the unique male midwife share a similar perspective.

10. And earlier. For a brief review of fictional representations see Maggs (1983: 172–95): 'the nurse as sexual vampire' exploited the patient in the pre-Nightingale period and then turned her attentions to the young doctor to divert him from his work: 'sex and professional incompetence are not too far apart' (p. 178). But see text below.

11. Although the General Medical Council has recently become more lenient in cases of 'love affairs' between general practitioners and their patients. In the past, it was a 'striking-off offence' incompatible with the practice of medicine. As in other areas of Western life there is an increasing loosening of physical sex from gender specific roles. Anne Karpf's *Doctoring the Media* (Routledge 1988) was published after I wrote this paper: she argues that male doctor–female patient sexual relations are suggested in film comedies. I remain unconvinced that this is particularly common.

12. e.g. *Danish Dentist on the Job.*

13. Following the now extensive literature on the history of hysteria in the nineteenth century, I have argued that Freud's theory was a psychological presentation of what was really a sociological relationship of power (Littlewood and Lipsedge 1987). The popular perception of resistance to psychoanalysis as due to its sexualisation of the doctor–patient couple (e.g. John Huston's 1962 film *Freud*) is itself a 'resistance' to the tacit recognition of the power embedded in that relationship.

14. In a recent survey of the imagery of advertisements in the medical press I found only one which portrayed a male nurse (and a female doctor). However, not only was it not concerned with medical treatment but rather with insurance, but the structural 'imbalance' was rectified by the presence of a third figure, an older and, not surprisingly, male hospital consultant. By contrast advertisements featuring male nurses are now commonplace in nursing magazines, but without a doctor.

15. We do not know whether female doctors are more likely to empathise with the overdosing patient than male doctors. From evidence with other medical conditions (Weisman and Teitelbaum 1985) we might predict they would show more 'understanding'.

16. A recent study of junior hospital doctors showed that a fifth had recourse to drinking bouts or drugs (Firth-Cozens 1987).

17. Parodied not entirely unfairly as:
   Q : How many legs has a cow?
   A1: Three (diagnosis – Ganser's syndrome).

A2: I'm a cow (depression).
A3: You're a cow (paranoia).
A4: Four milk bottles (schizophrenia).

18. The British physician appears to lack the rich lexicon available for such patients in America – 'albatross', 'goner', 'turkey', 'crock', and 'troll' (Stein 1986). Helman (1985) introduced the useful notion of *pseudo-disease* to characterise patterns of sickness resembling recognised syndromes but which are not characterised by a discrete and invariate pattern of pathophysiological evidence (clinical signs, laboratory investigations). As he shows, pseudo-disease is a function of personality and current life events and lay explanatory models, with the whole pattern being then developed through biomedical context. 'Factitious illness' is not quite the same, for it includes 'real' pathophysiologies ('diseases') which have been induced by the patient, to an extent shading into 'deliberate self-harm' – mutilations and overdoses. Helman's pseudo-diseases include the iatrogenic development of syndromes through the medical context, a category which most doctors ignore. Scambler (1988) modifies Habermas's (1984) formal pragmatics to apply them to the medical rationalisation of patients' subjective worlds. He suggests we can distinguish strategic communications (those intended to affect the actions of others) which are 'open' from those which are 'closed', dividing the latter into 'conscious deception' (manipulation) and 'unconscious deception' (systematically distorted communication). Doctors as well as patients engage in both.

19. An individual illness is multi-referential, polysemous. I am offering here a simplified account, without details of the psychodynamics of the sessions or of the personal significance of the particular practice she adopted. An external description of this sort does not, of course, do justice to her own feelings and experiences in the face of suffering and death (Davidson and Jackson 1985). 'To determine the extent to which the reactions are "conscious" pragmatic attempts at adjustment is difficult: while to the theorist there is an element of parody in all of them, the irony is only rarely perceived by principal and audience. Participants certainly experience despair and self-hatred' (Littlewood and Lipsedge 1987). Nor should this account be taken as an instance of the superior benefits of psychiatry compared with general medicine: to an extent I was part of the same institutional context, articulating the same set of symbolic values. The justification of an anthropologically informed psychiatry is only that of empowering the individual through constructing with them some more sociologically grounded interpretations of the origins and meanings of their illness and coping strategies. It might be reasonably objected that my use of the term 'ritual' in the title is rather loose, indeed pejorative in the popular sense. Nevertheless, I would maintain that we are dealing here with a situation in which 'inequalities in status are stressed, dramatically displaced

and underwritten by graded mystical powers' (Herdt 1982) if *disease* functions as an ultrahuman 'mystical' sanction (see Note 2). Rituals subsume individuals under specific roles which embody their ideological status, and within which there is room for individual interpretations and personal meanings.

20. Also known as Doctor Shopping or Maternal Hospital Addiction (Meadows 1984). (It is sometimes called Polle Syndrome, after the daughter born to the real Baron Von Munchausen [fictionalised in Raspe's tales] when aged 74 and his 17-year-old wife Bernhardine Von Brunn. Her existence has been doubted.) Meadows, who first described it in 1977, has pointed out that the publicity led to a number of cases of 'factitious MSP' in which he was telephoned by parents who claimed (falsely) to have done it!

21. See note 19.

22. *British Medical Journal* 1970. I have not referenced the quotes separately. The debate has not ended – a recent book (Ramsay 1986) restates the viral hypothesis but agrees there may have been some 'hysterical overlay'.

23. An ironic comment, given that the diagnosis advanced by Ramsay of post-viral fatigue is the one described in the *Sunday Express* (Markham-Smith 1987) in its article 'Career women struck down by yuppie plague'. Irving Salt, the Professor of Medicine interviewed by the paper, pointed out that it affected only professional women in their 'desire to drive to succeed in their professional careers.... This weakens their immune systems.' The social history of 'post-viral fatigue' remains to be written.

24. A more appropriate term for this type of mass hysteria is Kleinman's 'acute somatisation': social stress causes automomic over-arousal leading to physiological symptoms – sweating, trembling, etc. – which are aided by context (including medical interventions) and are systematically focused on and amplified by the individual who minimises and thereby damps down their affective and cognitive concomitants (Kleinman 1986: 61).

25. A situation recalling that of the contemporary Chinese. During and after the Cultural Revolution when depression and mental illness were described as feudal relics (and with a clearer distinction established between political/moral deviation and bodily sickness), they have had recourse to the highly somatic idiom of 'neurasthenia' to express and communicate distress (Kleinman 1986).

26. Now actually codified in new government guidelines for assessing 'quality control' in the economics of hospital service provision. One might speculate that the pattern was pioneered by Florence Nightingale herself: 'If, in her condition of bodily collapse, she were to accomplish what she was determined that she should accomplish, the attentions and the services of others would be absolutely indispensable' (Strachey 1918: 152). As Kleinman puts it, Nightingale's illness 'gave her the sentimental authority of wheelchair and sickbed whilst she negotiated reform' (1986: 150).

Chapter Ten

CARE AND AMBIGUITY: TOWARDS A CONCEPT OF NURSING

JENNY LITTLEWOOD

Virginia Henderson, Professor of Nursing at Yale, has stated that nursing is primarily an intimate and essential service: nurses must learn to develop their caring skills in an age characterised by change and 'ambiguity' (Henderson 1978). In Britain, concerned by the changing roles of the nurse, the Department of Health and Social Security stated that 'no matter what happens at the periphery of her work, *caring* will be the central task of the nurse' (DHSS 1977). In this paper I suggest that the nurse does not so much learn to 'tolerate' ambiguity as to 'manage it', for the central task of caring is the management of ambiguity. In Henderson's paper, ambiguity is equated with uncertainty. Here, the term is explored further through introducing the notion of 'marginals', areas which lie between the formal elements of classificatory systems.

Nursing is work with people who transgress certain social expectations of activity and personal responsibility: that is, individuals who are sick. It is argued that the presence of the nurse maintains the person, encapsulated, in the wider social world during this temporary state of sickness. In so doing, she herself becomes an ambiguous figure. The ambiguity of the nurse centres round two functions: as an advocate on behalf of patients in a predominantly biomedical health system she mediates between lay and professional notions of distress and responsibility and she deals with the disruption of normative time and space caused by sickness. The idea of advocacy has been discussed elsewhere (J. Littlewood 1989), but will be further explored in this chapter in examining information exchange and the notion of hidden texts.

The popular representation of the nurse meeting personal needs is of one associated with bedpans (Salvage 1985). Even in a half-page editorial in the *British Medical Sociology Bulletin*, the editor's own experience of hospitalisation was condensed into one sentence – a quote from the nurse enquiring 'Are your bowels moving?' (Platt 1987). Why is this theme so central to the folk memory of hospitalisation and to the role of the nurse? Nurses are called 'angels' perhaps for dealing with matters no one else would touch, yet they themselves are not perceived as 'dirty'.

In this chapter I will use bodily excretion as a schema for classifying people as in or out of 'control' of themselves, or as being controlled by others. Excreta are ambiguous; they are both part and not part of ourselves – passing from our internal to our external self through the margins of the physical body. The nurse's role is less in pollution control than in interpreting the texts which reinforce our existing notions of control.

CLASSIFYING PEOPLE AS IN OR OUT OF CONTROL

It is a commonplace of social anthropology that the way we experience and categorise the world is a product of social organisation (Durkheim and Mauss 1903). Culture imposes its meanings on the physical world: 'Social concerns are embodied in the raw material of the available experience of the individual: birth, childhood, sex, parenthood and death' (La Fontaine 1978). The body as a symbolic representation can provide a series of formal homologies between the social order and the external world (Turner 1984). As orifices of the body are located at the margins between the self and the external world, they serve as particularly apt symbols for the boundaries of the community (Douglas 1966). Minorities like Jews are faced with the constant threat of assimilation. They may be said to guard the boundaries, entrances, and exits of the body politic through a concern with the boundaries, entrances, and exits of the body physical, through extensive prohibition of certain foods, the practice of circumcision, or rituals and prayers centred around washing and excretion (R. Littlewood 1984).

Social position appears linked with bodily functions, those of highest status generally dealing with the head and heart. Doctors working in gastro-enterology or urino-genital medicine have a low status. Personality too has been 'ordered' through a link with excreta: Freud (1930) links personality with bodily parts: the 'mean' and parsimonious man is the 'anal retentive'.

171

The structure and functioning of the human body provides a physical locus on to which meanings are placed. From birth the child is introduced into human society by constraints upon the body which remain powerful resonances of bodily experience. Psychology (Bruner and Kolowski 1972) has offered the notion of 'scaffolding' in which the mother acts for her child through possessing the cultural blueprints by which the child must organise his life, and linguistics (Vygotsky 1962) has suggested how, as a result of social interaction, these blueprints become internalised. In his examination of intentionality Shotter (1974) goes further:

> to the extent that a mother can interpret her baby's behaviour
> as having a mental content or intentional structure – and the
> extent to which she can do that is up to her – she can attempt
> to complete its content and negotiate 'with him' a satisfaction
> of his needs, i.e. alleviate his state of discomfort or restlessness.
>
> (Shotter 1974: 230)

Her behaviour is a constructive attribution to the baby of intentions. Behaviour is an attempt to realise intentions.

One kind of behaviour may have many meanings. In order to 'disambiguate' meanings (Richards 1974), a culturally distinctive interpretative theory is needed to transform 'natural behaviour' into the behaviour of a social being, and the matter of excretion and excretory behaviour are rigidly controlled. Biological imperatives, however interpreted or emphasised, comprise basic raw materials for thought and action in all human societies. There appear to be particularly strong prohibitions in western societies on the 'free' passage of urine and faeces, prohibitions associated perhaps with the value placed on a post-Cartesian self, contained and indexical (as opposed to the more socially contextual and referential notion of the self in non-literate societies). Culture, comprising the sense of the public standardised values of the community, mediates the physical experience of the individual. It provides in advance the basic categories, a positive framework within which personal violations and imperatives may be tidily ordered, as public matters are cultural categories and not easily subject to revision.

Babies soon find out that approval can be obtained by producing faeces at the right time and in the right place: disapproval if time or place are wrong, or if the faeces are of the

172

wrong colour, consistency, or quality. The baby learns that, through refusing to produce faeces at all, he can inflict pain on those close to him. And on himself. Reciprocity is gradually learned. Achieving continence is regarded as one of the major 'milestones' in childhood (Loudon 1977). In the hospital, requiring permission to 'use the loo' or bed-pan might be interpreted as a partial return of the sick person to the early stage of childhood, to being controlled and liable to humiliation. One function of the nurse as a symbolic mother (Campbell-Heider and Pollock 1987), who uses culturally understood meanings of need (both professional and lay), is to disambiguate the patient's tentative signals.

Excrement commonly represents the potential for fertilisation, a cyclical notion inherent in Egyptian cosmology[1] or in western understandings of the nitrogen cycle. Against this cyclical notion of fertile time we can place the revulsion and depreciatory language associated with faeces that give faeces a limited, disposable, 'linear' time that passes out of life. Prohibitions dealing with faeces are of course extensive. At the extreme, the body as a whole has been equated with dirt and impurities to encourage a view of its transitoriness, [2, 3, 4] its association with madness,[5] danger, or witchcraft.[6] When and where one may excrete in the modern West is rigidly controlled through laws associated with the 'civilised' disposal of our human waste and the increasingly private act of excretion.

Self, shame, and control

With the power to symbolise Man can represent himself to himself as an element of his environment:

> Subjectivity and objectivity are properties of an organised perceptual field in which points of reference are selves (subjects) and objects, and the degree of articulation in this dimension may vary greatly.
>
> (Macleod 1974)

The extent which he does will vary greatly because there is no obvious given point at which an absolute line may be drawn. However, some distinction must be made between the embodied observer and his environment. Any conceptual system embodies some such a distinction (Heelas and Lock 1981). The concepts of self and culture are interdependent. 'Selves are constituted within society, and culture is maintained by the community of selves' (Lock 1980).

Language in the early modern West was believed to have two functions: designation and classification (Givner 1962). This paralleled (and was possibly derived from) the medical language and system of diagnosis. Meaning in medicine is constituted as the relationship between classificatory categories and the diseases they designate. This way of constructing meaning on natural events constrains the way we see the world. In categorising something that 'is', one is automatically rejecting 'what is not'. 'Culture provides external symbols that have emanated from inner experiences – experiences of time and place' (Lock 1980: 21). Nagarjuna (c AD.200) (in Heelas and Lock 1981) in formulating his Sunyavada – a discussion on the relativity of ideas about 'being' or 'knowing' – pointed to the void (Sunya – Doctrine of the void):

'It cannot be called 'void' or 'not void'
or both or neither;
But in order to point it out,
It is called 'the void'

(Madhyarika Shastra: xv, 3)

A statement about something brings with it a gathering of information from many sources and experiences. It focuses down on something having the effect of representing many experiences and aspects of behaviour by one action or statement which automatically implies something else.

Man is a social and cultural animal – with a social and moral order, the moral order being norms of conduct with effective social sanctions, implicit or explicit, to back them up. Self-awareness – the ability to know what is and is not one's 'self' – is culturally constituted.

Excreta and control

If the boundary we have drawn between ourselves and the outside world breaks down, we find it profoundly disturbing:

When this system breaks down it violates something intrinsic to our sense of worth. I was still clearly adult; I no longer felt human. That function of my body had become animal-like.

I dealt with what was happening by denying it. The fact

that it kept happening did not deter me from this denial. It would never happen again, I told myself after each occurrence. I was the only person I spoke to about it, and even I would not listen.

These were the feelings of a person who became unable to control excreta when she developed multiple sclerosis.

If in western culture one can define oneself as 'sick', then acts of excretion 'out of place' are 'forgiven' or are managed in such a way as to ensure the person is not socially ostracised. One such accident occurred at a pensioners' day in a crowded music hall. The urine bag strapped to someone's leg became detached from the tubing. The result? A large pool of urine in the middle of the hall in East London. The reaction? Shouts from immediate neighbours and immediate vacation of their chairs.

As a result, the lady whose bag had burst was left alone in a sea of chairs with people staring at her from a distance. The only thing she felt she could do was faint. She slumped in her chair and the Red Cross took over, lifting her on to a stretcher. The mood of the crowd changed from 'dirty old person, can't she control herself?' to 'leave her alone', 'poor thing, she is ill, let us help' (J. Littlewood 1985). However, if one is not in a position of being able to declare oneself sick – either because one cannot or one does not want to – incontinence can reduce one to a childlike state. As one patient explained:

But incontinence is not merely embarrassing. It is shaming and ignominious. I can still recall with painful clarity the start of my difficulties. Walking along the road I would suddenly feel the urgent desire to empty my bowels. I would stop for a moment to assess how far I was from home. The sweat would break out as I desperately tried to decide what course of action to take. Would it be better to hurry and reach safety as quickly as possible, bearing in mind that hurrying would further excite my gut; or should I slow down, which would be less disturbing to my insides but would prolong the time to get to the loo? Even if I couldn't get to the lavatory, could I at least get through my own front door before noises, stains and smells broadcast my predicament to the outside world? Sometimes I could not, and then my feeling of degradation was complete. I would stand for ages in the shower where the tears streaming down my face didn't show.

Incontinence is clearly extremely upsetting. Many elderly people taking diuretic medication for cardiac failure, for instance, have a fear of not being able to get to the toilet on time. (A frequent comment by professionals is that these elderly people do not take their medication at the prescribed time – they alter the regimen to suit their structuring of time.) Excrement, as we have seen, is 'dirt' and 'disease ridden'. It is to be avoided. If it is found on a chair or in the kitchen for example, it is 'matter out of place' (Douglas 1966) and will offend, confuse, or contradict the ideas of 'usual' in western society:

> excreta are dirt par excellence. Our idea of dirt is compounded into two things: care for hygiene and respect for conventions. The rules of hygiene change of course in our state of knowledge, and friendship. Dirt is a matter out of place; it implies a set of ordered relations and contravention of that order. Dirt, then, is never unique or isolated – where there is dirt there is a 'system'! Dirt is the by-product of a system of ordering and classifying material in so far as ordering involves rejecting inappropriate elements.
>
> (Douglas 1966)

The physical offensiveness of the condition is often associated with the perception of people who are incontinent as being morally weak; guilt feelings and pity may be an onlooker's reaction. Studies looking at the difference between disability and deviance suggest that people do not like to keep themselves apart from those whom they see as responsible for their condition. They disapprove of people they see as responsible such as ex-convicts, people with heart disease, alcoholics, but they do not keep them at a distance. Whereas people who stutter, are paraplegic, are incontinent, or mentally ill are separated off. They are stigmatised. Normal people fear them: they are anxious about actual or anticipated disruption in social interaction, and especially anxious when the disability is particularly visible in specific settings. This may be associated also with some feeling they may be harmed.

How 'disabled' one is, therefore, is context dependent; it depends not first upon the distinct features of one's own condition but on the social and economic environment which has to be negotiated. For example, in London the laundry service for people who are incontinent (actually called the Incontinence

Laundry Service) is financed by the Local Authority's Environmental Health Department – a department associated with pollution, dirt, and disease. It employs a tacit definition of what constitutes 'appropriate faecal matter on the sheets'. 'Excessively' soiled sheets may not be taken to the public launderers but Incontinence Laundry Service staff also decide what constitutes 'enough' faecal matter and will withdraw the service if the sheets are not adequately soiled. Continued use of the Incontinence Laundry Service is defined by laundry workers; if sheets are not soiled enough to warrant the service, the person is removed from the lists. A fastidious old lady however may be disgusted with a few drops of urine and would consider her sheets very soiled. Some people using the Incontinence Laundry Service often wash the sheets *before* they send them to the service as they are too embarrassed by the smell and soiling. Incontinence is therefore the very essence of ambiguity – when is a person incontinent and when are they not?

THE NURSE AS A MEDIATOR OF POLLUTION

The majority of nurses in the UK are women. On becoming a nurse, the woman is separated off and is 'purified' by being 'contained' in a nurses' home and by being 'contained' by her uniform (Mitchell and Oakley 1976; Littlewood 1988). She becomes symbolically pure. Because of her symbolic purity, she herself is 'protected' from being polluted by dirt. Her work is the 'doing for others who are not able to do for themselves'. Sharing dirt depends on knowledge and friendship with a person. The more intimate one is the greater the sharing. To share or care for another's pollution otherwise is a restatement of humility and love (Dunlop 1986). It is the meticulous and ordered attention to personal details – the straightening of drawer sheets, rubbing heels, the taking of temperatures, attending to technical equipment. The nurse's work is enabling patient independence but also the observing and reporting of signs and symptoms – selected criteria for the doctor to make diagnostic judgements. It is encouraging compliance.

Division of labour on the ward is related to division of 'dirt'. Associated with one person's labour is one kind of dirt that is not associated with another. Demarcation disputes have occurred in hospital wards – a bottle filled with urine and accidentally tipped on to the floor was not seen by the ward domestic as being 'her dirt'. The traditional association of women with pollution, low-status work, division of labour within the ward has separated off one form of pollutants – bodily secretions and excretions – from another – dust, spillage from flower vases, and so forth. Nurses are expected to clear up urine, faeces, and vomit. These are 'sick dirt', so highly polluting that they would not be removed by the domestics.

Nurses become intimately involved and identified with the containment of personal pollution. A sick person has undergone several changes – having changed from obeying rules of when to eliminate, eat, or move about according to an accepted social code of being sick and out of control. The sick person has transgressed social rules, has disobeyed accepted ideas on behaviour in space and time. He is separated off, contained, or isolated in order not to contaminate others. His ideas of time and space are disturbed and he needs to go through a cleansing and healing process in order to be made well. For this process to occur, he is traditionally removed to the hospital – removed from his home and his culture – and is subjected to being undressed, given a bath or enema, and placed in a space identical in most respects to that of other sick people on the ward. The nurse helps redefine his space and time: space, by guarding the area around the bed – the sicker the person the greater the space afforded and the closer the guard (nearer Sister's desk). Time is controlled by having ward rules which apply to everyone though they become relaxed as one becomes well. Meals, washes, elimination: a rigorous pattern is imposed on the very sick and becomes more lax as the person gets well and ready for discharge. The nurse's presence shows that something is being done for or with the person. The nurse draws screens around the bed to alter the personal space. The nurse tolerates the person's state of sickness because sickness is a temporary state which nurses are trained to 'contain'. Sickness is a state in which people transgress social codes; a sick person is likely to be rejected or avoided because of this. It is an ambiguous state where the presence of the nurse ensures, even if he is seen as being not responsible, that he is to be forgiven and not isolated. The nurse's presence protects people when they are in an ambiguous state. The nurse mediates not only between the needs of the doctor and the patient, but also between patient and patient, and patient and the 'external' visitor.

Personal space on a hospital ward changes from minute to minute and is affected by population density (bed occupancy), purpose of approaches (injections, casual conversation), fixed locations (beds), character of social occasion (visiting time, ward rounds). The nurse may move the curtains around a bed to expand or contract the patient's personal space. The curtains, bed, and its associated locker define the areas within which one functions. The physical presence of the nurse circumscribes odours and the noise of vomiting or excretion. Humour in wards too may reduce the conventionally offensive behaviour of illness. The nurse guards the person's privacy by her avoidance of eye contact with other patients in the ward during vomiting or defecation of a patient. The patient has a right not to be stared at or defiled. Medical examination of the person by a doctor could leave the person 'defiled' and 'naked'. The presence of the nurse, particularly for someone who is chronically ill, maintains the person's dignity and he becomes *nude* rather than *naked*. The naked 'asocial' state is of use in acute conditions where the urgency of the disorder may be life threatening. In chronic conditions treating the person as asocial or naked is unacceptable. The nude or humanised form must be returned.

The nurse tends the sickest first and the rest of the ward wait their turn. The area around Sister's desk is generally known as a special space. The sicker you are the less responsible you are and the greater your personal space on the ward but the nearer to Sister's desk your bed is placed. In modern wards the most severely ill are placed in cubicles of four-bedded wards within the main ward but nearest to the 'nurses' station'. Voices may be lowered as one passes the very sick person; the nurse consciously limits the number of visitors around the bed, and casual chats by other patients are discouraged.

Nurses guide intrusions and obtrusions in relation to persons who are 'out of control' (the sick). Self-violations (self befoulments) make the individual a particular source of potential contamination. The washing of sick people has been performed as part of ceremonial symbolic inversion by specially venerated figures (such as Jesus and Catherine of Sienna). In doing so they are restating particular subdominant values – those of humility and charity. These ceremonies are conducted ritually to form circumscribed acts that are meaningful to the wider society. Blanket bathing, 'bottle' and 'bedpan rounds' restate a nurse's humility and charity in the wards.

179

The patient has no place in society, that 'outer' social system, as he is not obeying usual codes of time and space. In order to prevent permanent extrusion, precautions against further change must come from others. In a sense, the nurse gives the patient social sanction and conceptual space within which he can pollute. Her presence indicates that what is wrong with him is no longer his responsibility. While the ward contains sick people, the nurse's overlaying of rigorously controlled time and spatial occupation, symbolically representing the outer 'well' society time and spatial arrangements, allows the nurse to encapsulate the spatial and temporal disruptions of the individual sick person on the ward. By doing so she keeps bringing him back into the accepted space–time relations of others on the ward. The ward becomes a whole social body where the individuals form part of that body and their disruption is 'corrected' and fitted back into the social body. She maintains the patient's position (within the ward) and all the ward members are encapsulated from the wider society by being contained in a medicalised compartment. She functions also as the symbolic mother and they the symbolic children in the home.[7]

HIDDEN TEXTS

Let us return to the original stereotype of 'Are your bowels moving?' and examine some of the possible reasons for this being a focus. Suggested earlier was that language has two functions: designation and classification. Meaning, it is held, is constituted as the relationship between classificatory categories and the diseases which they designate. Categories are defined by the distinctive features which they designate, which in turn provide their boundaries. Such a theory of meaning is modelled on the medical activity of diagnosis (Good 1977). This naming activity, he suggests, avoids looking at the manner in which illness and disease are deeply integrated into the structure of a society. Errors in cross-cultural research arise because it looks solely at how societies map classificatory categories on to disease. Rather, it is suggested that a syndrome of experiences needs to be understood which may be condensed to a single term (Lienhardt 1961). Good, for example, examines this through an examination of 'heart distress'. By semantic network analysis Good showed that 'heart distress' related to many aspects of stress in Iranian life that was expressed in these focus words. It is suggested that patients take a stance towards illness (Rhodes 1984). She suggests that explanations of disorder are complex and have contradictory interpretations.

> Treatment, like symptoms, does not consist of an underlying reality overlaid with epiphenomenal cultural 'distortions'.
>
> (Good 1977)

> rather treatment is an interpretive context within which allusive and partially hidden 'texts' unfold.
>
> (Rhodes 1984)

Metaphors provide a dynamic way to approach discrepancies between models of illness and treatment which are available to them, and the actual experience of having to take, or nurses having to give, medication.

Non-compliance in medication has been related to poor communication between doctor and patient, the doctor–patient dyad being perceived as the essential healing relationship – the exclusive relationship in western therapeutic encounters – denying the context of the disorder and the effect or manipulation of the person on his social network. How might the nurse's role be embedded in the exchange of information from the patient for the doctor? The question 'Are your bowels moving?' is associated with many ideas. 'Moving' is associated with change. Nurses are concerned with noting change in relevant signs and symptoms in order to report these to the doctor. The doctor on the other hand is looking for 'fixed' pathology. Movement also suggests activity. The question relates also to control. Are you *in* control or *being* controlled by your bowels? While the overt form is active, the hidden meaning is 'are you in order?', 'have you got a grip on yourself?', or 'do you need help?'

Communication about 'bowels' is more than an exchange of information – it is also an attempt to convey the quality of a particular kind of experience; and it is a means of persuasion. As we have discussed, disruption of bowel function is one of the earliest bodily signs of distress and can produce psychological distress. It is also the focus of an early attempt to control behaviour. It induces anger or anxiety in the mother if the baby produces faeces in the wrong place or at the wrong time, as there is an element of attributed intentionality. The patient likewise must 'behave' in order to be healed.

The citation of nurses in relation to bowels by a social scientist might have been an attempt to humiliate the nurse, to 'get back' at her for demanding a public response to such a private state, the patient-child rebelling, rejecting, and making fun of the nurse-mother, a denigration of the concern, when well, to reduce its power. Within the institution of the hospital, the person becomes the patient, the symbolic child, subject to restrictions and control; outside the hospital the quote of the eliminating nurse/mother shows the symbolic child has now become adult.

Bowel movement is also associated with opening up – allowing entry into the body, the opposite of closing. The associated words, 'empty', ' loosen up', 'unblock', suggest a change in internal space. Empty bowels are a physical reality but are also associated with control of internal space and purity: the person is made clean (empty). The nurse confirms if the patient is 'empty of irrelevant matter' – the content of the bowels. The doctor will then have unimpeded access to the relevant organ which has the pathology.

People are said to locate 'themselves' in their bowels. Removal of the content of the bowel may be parallel to removing the 'self' – becoming void, nothing. The person becomes not just clean, or in control, but someone who is *no* one – a symbolic part of the body of the ward, which in turn is a symbolic piece of the body of the hospital which is 'sliced' into bits for the medical gaze (Foucault 1976).

Bowels are also a defining boundary. The question locates the ordinary/essential, basic, very personal and private functioning of the individual in the public domain. Young (1981) suggests that metaphors emerge at times when understanding is empirical and experiential. Three themes are thought to construct the person's world: time, identity, and communication.

Time he suggests is related to dependence on medical care. In our discussion, responding to 'are your bowels open?' allows a person a public statement of being in control; having an accepted idea of time. There is also a notion of immediacy, of being prepared. They can adhere to their own means of bowel control, for example senna pods, 'I swear by it', 'faithful to it'. Time is imposed if the answer to the question is 'no'. There is also a threat and a punishment (tempered by humour – 'Sister's windy cocktails'). Regularity is imposed. There is also an opportunity for comparison with others as well as observing change in the person himself. There is an imposed new relationship: 'self' as part of its own body or a self as part of the ward.

In relation to identity, it has been suggested that in western society, people have an idealised view of 'self'. If an organ is diseased or not functioning well, it is viewed as 'not self'. 'I'm OK nurse, but my bowels aren't.' The diseased part is taken out of the description of 'self'. The body may be seen as an assembly of autonomous organs. This is how the medical model constructs the body. The nurse links context to questioning as the question itself relates to many levels of meaning. Additionally, people's descriptions of constipation often relate to the use of the term 'self' – 'I'm not myself' meaning 'the person' or soul residing in the bowels. The term bowels is associated with pity and mercy.

Communication takes place at a variety of levels. Bowels or rather bowel action is part of everyday experience. The public statement can unite people in humour – it can provide the patients with a common starting point of camaraderie – 'She's asked us all that, bit of a joke isn't it?' Traditionally, the task of asking about bowels was given to the most junior nurse, the one at the 'bottom' of the hierarchy – the one closest also to the common metaphorical language of lay people. It is often 'binding'; people remember junior nurses and say they are easiest to talk to – their language is still the same as that of the ordinary man. They have not yet absorbed the clinical language and hidden rules of the senior nurse – 'you can get an honest answer out of a junior nurse'. The junior person has 'experience-near' understanding – experience understood effortlessly by others – bowels are the same for everyone.

It has been suggested that bodily excretions are objects of taboo at least partly because they are a potential threat to primary discrimination – benignly ambiguous in so far as they are part of a person's body and at the same time separate from it (both A and not-A) (Ardener 1975). Therefore, contained within the original question are further questions: are the bowels open (a) on purpose or (b) because one is ill? The question is operating between different frames of reference or classificatory systems. 'Are your bowels open?' refers to the person as a person – a public statement of being in control; or it refers to the person as a patient – out of control, dependent, needing help, needing to be controlled. The nurse behaves 'as a concerned mother', ordering, 'disambiguating' the patient/child's world. The nurse is also behaving as controller for doctor. The doctor requires clean, organised patients to be able to focus down and isolate one central problem in order to cure. Bodily impurities will interfere, as might a patient who takes on a 'self' or becomes an active whole person instead of remaining the 'part' that is the focus of the disease. The nurse can therefore use humiliation as a tactic for control. Therefore the question 'are your bowels open?' mediates between different classificatory systems allowing contrasting classificatory systems to co-exist at the same time (see Figure 10.1).

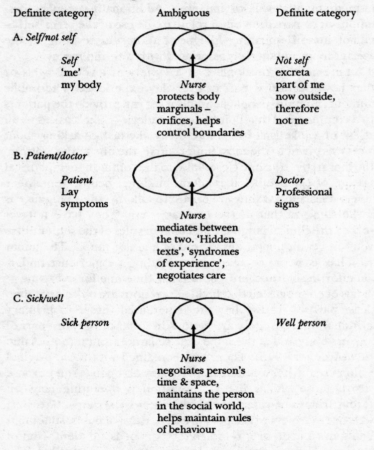

Definite category	Ambiguous	Definite category
A. *Self/not self*		
Self 'me' my body	*Nurse* protects body marginals – orifices, helps control boundaries	Not self excreta part of me now outside, therefore not me
B. *Patient/doctor*		
Patient Lay symptoms	*Nurse* mediates between the two. 'Hidden texts', 'syndromes of experience', negotiates care	Doctor Professional signs
C. *Sick/well*		
Sick person	*Nurse* negotiates person's time & space, maintains the person in the social world, helps maintain rules of behaviour	Well person

Figure 10.1 Care and ambiguity

Caring is manifest in the act of protecting the body marginals, helping to define 'self' and 'not self'; it is the mediation between meaning of illness and meaning of disease, the patient–doctor divide; it is the maintenance of the sick person in the social world. Each culture has its own special risks and problems. In that the nurse articulates these systems by ritually circumscribing the person; the content of her work will vary to an extent in different societies across cultures, but the form remains.

In understanding temporal and spatial order, and elucidating the meaning of illness and negotiating care, she herself becomes an ambiguous figure as she straddles classificatory divides. The classificatory systems will vary in different cultures but classification will exist and will have different points of ambiguity. The concept of nursing as proposed in this paper is that caring, the nurse's central role, is the management of ambiguity.

NOTES

1. Excrement has been incorporated into various cosmologies. Egyptian Khepri, the Scarab God, pushes a ball of dung into the other world in the evening and over the horizon in the morning and is represented by the scarab beetle. For the Egyptians he represented the rising sun, the renewal of life and the idea of eternal existence. Many societies use dung to fertilise crops, suggesting the cyclical nature of events. In some, lavatories have two holes for excretion, one for urine and one for faeces. The faeces drop to the outside of the house and dries. It is then collected and put on to the fields. There has been little exploration of who does the collecting and how they are regarded in their society, though collectors of dung in Auschwitz were seen as having the most abominable task and were ostracised even by those within the camps (*Bulletin*, British Psychological Society 1978).

2. Obscenities and thus kin relationships often refer to excrement. In Firth's *We the Tikopia* (Boston: Beacon Press, 1936) we find the following:

   The obscene in Tikopia is a category defined primarily by relation to situations of constraint in kinship. It is delimited by the recognition of the essential incongruity of a certain type of behaviour – sex reference or exposure – in a situation where a sex bond has been the fundamental factor of association. It can be termed a moral category since its obligations are accepted as binding, not through such influences as political authority or religious fear, but through their own virtue; they are not questioned in their own sphere. A breach of these obligations does sometimes occur but evokes a strong emotional attitude. The reaction to a presentation of the obscene is what may be called behaviour of disorder – symptoms of uneasiness, a tendency to escape, to avoid the situation, maybe in the more extreme cases a strong verbal reaction, as anger. These comprise what the Tikopia subsume under the term *fakama*, which in this connection signifies shame. The citation or admission of obscenity (*tarana pariki*) even in contact between relatives in free relationship means that the category is given autonomy outside its own immediate sphere – it is carried over from situations of constraint to those where the incompatibility exists to a much less degree. Then, too, the curse or indecent expression which associates excrement with a father makes use of a relationship of restraint as an implement of action.

The restraints of *tarana pariki* are wider than the purely sexual sphere: they include also scatalogical references. The close association of the organs of excretion and sex in the human anatomy is said to be responsible. Certain well-recognised forms of cursing by kinship in this way occur and are elicit between persons not under constraint of *tarautau pariki*. The most frequent is what is termed the *kau ki te mana*, the 'command to the father' – to eat ordure. *'Kai te mo te mana'*, 'May your father eat filth' is an expression used with all grades of vehemence, from a merely conventional exclamation of good-humoured repartee to a fling of annoyance or a full-mouthed curse in a blaze of anger. The reaction on the part of the listener or recipient is in corresponding fashion.

3. P. Hershman, (1981) in 'Virgin and mother', In H. Standing, (ed.) *Punjabis Kinship and Marriage*, (Dahli Hindustan Pub. Co., pp.283–5) observes:

Both women and cows are the providers of milk and Punjabis often link the purity of the exudations of the cow with the nature of its diet. Particularly shocking is the idea that a dead mouse might get in the cow's feed and that the cow might swallow it. Similarly, while generally non-Brahmin Punjabi men are meat-eaters, even low caste women are usually strict vegetarians. A woman is particularly careful about the 'purity' of her diet when she is producing milk for her child. Following childbirth, a special gift is made to a woman by her parents which partly consists of a special dish which is composed mainly of clarified butter, almonds, etc. – these types of food are especially eaten in order to strengthen the flow of breast milk.

The cow is not simply identified with the image of mother and child. Whereas the bodily exudations of women (including breast milk) are highly impure and polluting, the products of the cow

186

are empowered in the opposite direction not only being pure in themselves but also being the cleansers of human bodily impurity.

Cow-dung (*goha*) is separated from all other faeces not only linguistically (human, dog and cat faeces are *tatti* or *jhana*; small bird or lizard faeces are *nith*; chicken *cuce*; camel *lid*; and goat *menga*) but also psychologically in that Punjabis feel no repulsion at picking up the dung, warm and fresh, almost as it falls from the animal. The cow-dung is mixed with mud and patted into cakes (*pathia*) and then dried in the sun. Cow-dung cakes are the main source of fuel and are handled freely while cooking. Cow-dung is smeared upon the walls and floor of the house and especially upon the booking place. All sacred rituals are performed on a piece of ground smeared with cow-dung, and a dying man is lowered onto such a surface.

The ashes of cow-dung (*rakh*) are swallowed in order to cleanse the body and especially to expel evil spirits. Cow-urine (*gau pishab*) is drunk by women at the end of the period of ritual pollution following childbirth in order to cleanse themselves 'inside'. Similarly, all the products which come from cow's milk (*dudh*) are used at various times to purify the human body: *kacci lassi* (milk mixed with water) is used in offerings to shrines and to wash the bones following a cremation; clarified butter (*ghi*) is rubbed into the hair and scalp of a woman in the days following childbirth.

It was only when the anthropologist debated with his informants as to whether cow-dung is 'dirty' or not that they produced the argument that the cow only eats grass and therefore its faeces are pure, whereas other animals are omniverous and so their faeces are 'dirty'.

4. Obeyesekere reminds us of the long tradition in Buddhism of meditation on revulsion, on 'foulness' or 'impurity'. The idea is to engender in the meditator a sense of the transitoriness of the body. Lay people conjure up the putrescence of the body in the mind – which leads them to remember the transitoriness of the body and the world. One of his informants said:

The body is full of faeces, it smells badly like a dead rat snake: the body is broken in one hundred and eight places, it is like a lavatory pit used for six months, so cleanse it often and keep it clean. The layman, then, has an especially difficult task. He has no physical object before him in order to conjure up the body's putrescence; he has to evoke this putrescence through various metaphors of revulsion, the most conspicuous being that of faeces. Faeces is the one object par excellence that everyone in the society is familiar with as a revulsive object. It then becomes a metaphor for the revulsiveness of the body in the meditation on revulsion.

Obeyesekere G. (1985) 'Depression, Buddhism and the work of culture in Sri Lanka', in A. Kleinman and B. Good, (eds) *Culture and Depression: Studies in the Anthropology and Cross Cultural Psychiatry of Affect and Disorder*, Berkeley, University of California Press.

5. *Links with madness.* Inappropriate use of excreta has often been linked with madness. Prophylactic protection against madness has been described. Madness has been expressed in terms of eating faeces, essentially an element in some mourning rituals. Preparation of sausages from milled porrage is carried out; they are then sprinkled with powdered medicine and half buried. The mourners are expected to bend down without using their hands and bite off and consume a mouthful of what is quite literally a turd (Loudon 1977). This is to ritually protect the mourner. The corpse and faeces are identified with one another – the corpse is filth, it is excrement, one becomes a madman if one eats turds without the surrounding ritual. Dirt links with symbolism of purity.

6. In the religion of the Dinka, excrement is part of mythology.

> The imagery of the divinities of the Pajieng clan is an illustration of this. It may be said of this clan, by those who are not members of it and when no members are present, that its clan-divinity is Excrement. Pajieng acquired the black cobra as its clan-divinity; this is a deadly snake, and the Dinka regard its swift bite as inevitably fatal. The black cobra is specially associated with night-witches, who are thought to use its blood and venom to injure their victims. The darkness of the cobra and its unexpected and deadly attack connect it with the secret nocturnal operations of the most powerful witches the Dinka can imagine; and as the cobra sheds and leaves its skin (*roc kuac*) and disappears, to appear anew and claim further victims, so witches are thought to renew themselves and return to cause further injury. One of the signs which lead a man to suspect witchcraft is to find human excrement in the homestead: as an anti-social act of particular unpleasantness, this is thought to be a witch's habit. Hence, the total constellation of imagery around the black cobra includes human excrement, and thus the notion that Excrement itself may be the divinity of a clan which respects this creature.

> In this case the set of associations of the black cobra is not accepted by its own clansmen, and they would regard the suggestion that they respected human excrement as disgusting and untrue; but it illustrates the process of associative thought by which divinities and emblems of certain clans may form little groups (Lienhardt, G. (1961) *Divinity and Experience: The Religion of the Dinka*, Oxford: Clarendon Press).

7. Relations in hospital are a 'family', physician-fathers, nurse-

mothers and patient-children (Littlewood, R.) 'Gender, role, and sickness: the ritual psychopathologies of the nurse', see Chapter 9 of this book.

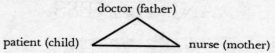

doctor (father)

patient (child)   nurse (mother)

The nurse and the patient spend most time on the ward (the home). The doctor (father) visits at regular but short intervals, spending most of his time 'outside' the ward at the operating theatre, giving lectures, attending meetings. The doctor comes back to check that the patient (child) is all right and that the nurse (mother) knows what to do.

Chapter Eleven

NURSES BETWEEN DISEASE AND ILLNESS

HELLE SAMUELSON

The following dialogue took place during the rounds in a gastro-intestinal surgery ward at a large Copenhagen hospital. The patient had just been operated on for an intestinal cancer and had been given an ileostomy.

Doctor: How are you?
Patient: Under the circumstances, not too bad. I'm dead tired.
Doctor: May I press?
Patient: Yes.
Doctor: Are you nauseated?
Patient: Yes, from time to time.
Doctor: Have you vomited?
Patient: No, I try not to.
Doctor: [to the nurse] Let's take out the catheter.
Nurse: And you also need to get rid of one of the bottles.
Doctor: The skin of the abdomen is a little tense. I think we'll keep you on liquid for a little while – there's no need to provoke it.
Patient: [to the doctor] I'm sorry I didn't catch your name.
Doctor: Petersen.

On another occasion, a nurse working in an out-patient cancer ward said: 'The most interesting thing is the patient, that's the crucial part of the job. For me the treatment itself is not that important, and in any case my knowledge of it is not that great. Those things are only tools around the patient. My job is that of advocate for the patient.'

These two examples demonstrate two different aspects of nursing roles. During rounds, the nurse is merely a technical assistant for the doctor. In interview, she distances herself from

190

biomedical knowledge and treatment and identifies herself with the patient whom she advocates in relation to the doctor.

In this chapter, I shall show that nurses very often find themselves in an ambiguous position. On the one hand, the nurse's job is to implement the orders of the doctor; she is an extension of the doctor and what he stands for. On the other hand, because nursing is associated historically with the female qualities of caring, it involves both understanding of and even solidarity with the patient. Developments in medical technology and in nursing ideology have widened the gap between the two. I suggest that what is really at issue is a new formulation of identity for nurses (Jensen 1943).

The ambiguous position of nurses became apparent while we were working on an anthropological study of cancer patients in Copenhagen. This research focused on patients' conceptions of their sickness and treatment, and on their relationships with the professional medical system, their families, friends, and acquaintances during the course of the sickness. The Danish Cancer Society which funds a considerable amount of biomedical research has recently established a 'psycho-social committee' to support research in this area. We were asked by them to formulate and carry out an explorative, qualitative study of the psycho-social aspects of cancer. We followed nineteen cancer patients over a period of nine months (using loosely structured, informal interviews and participant observation). Although we mainly focused on the experiences of the cancer patients, we also interviewed nurses and doctors in order to obtain an understanding of the professional world. Through these interviews and through daily visits to the hospitals, we learned a great deal about doctors' and nurses' conceptions of sickness, their relations with the patient and to each other.

At the outset of the project, we applied to one of the chief physicians at the National Hospital in Copenhagen for permission to do research in 'his' department. We received a letter from him in reply saying that unfortunately the staff would be unable to co-operate in the project because they were too busy. Eventually, we learnt that the nursing staff had not been informed of our application. At the same time, we applied to the National Cancer Hospital through the head of nursing who showed great interest and support for the project. So we changed our tactics and again applied to the National Hospital through the head of nursing. This time we succeeded. Subsequently, we were permitted to work in a third large modern hospital where again the head of nursing made the arrangements. Throughout the project we observed that the nurses were always very interested in the study, while the doctors – although helpful – were never particularly enthusiastic. In fact, we began to wonder whether the project had an added significance for the nurses – one that we were not sure we could live up to.

NURSES BETWEEN PATIENT AND DOCTORS

A distinction is sometimes made by medical anthropologists between disease and illness as analytical categories. Arthur Kleinman (1980) defines illness as the way sick persons, families, and communities learn to perceive, interpret, communicate, and cope with symptoms. Disease is the way practitioners (professional or folk) learn to reformulate the sick person's illness experience within the theoretical models, taxonomy, and clinical expectations of their therapeutic system (Kleinman 1986a: 146). According to Kleinman, there is a fundamental division between patients and their illness experience, on the one hand, and the healers' interpretation of the illness, on the other hand. Both patient and healer try to give meaning to the sickness episode but their starting points are fundamentally different. The meaning formulated by the patient is neither static nor 'rational'; it will change over time as more knowledge is acquired and as actual experiences are absorbed (Young 1981). He will interpret his symptoms and experiences according to his personal context and feelings.

This research shows that becoming a cancer patient triggers off a process in which individual patients constantly interpret their symptoms and try to understand the disease in their own bodies. They wonder how the treatment affects the disease and the body and speculate on why they have got cancer.

Patients may picture cancer cells as 'wild', 'sick', and 'wild-growing'. One woman said 'Anyhow, you don't know what cancer cells look like. They're like the head of a match, or too small to see at all.' A man who had seen a picture of the lymph gland removed from his groin noticed white spots inside the gland and remarked, 'It's probably some of the cancer stuff'. Another man pictured leukaemia as 'crooked cells' coming out of the spinal cord. Patients also speculate on how the treatment works, what happens during the operation, and how much of the cancer is removed. Chemotherapy is often seen as chemical warfare taking place inside the human body. Most patients treated with chemotherapy know that they receive toxins. In relation to this we heard expressions like, 'I was knocked right down', 'I just hope that they [the cancer cells] really wriggle around in there'.

In attributing meaning to the sickness, patients also consider the question 'Why have I got cancer?'. Some explanations are rejected and some are merely formulated without being definitely accepted or rejected. But all these considerations are part of the process of producing meaning which is more important than the actual conclusions drawn. To our question about what causes cancer, one woman first replied 'I don't know anything about it' and then changed the subject. This response mirrors the 'official' view of the professional sector. But later in the same interview, the woman spontaneously began to talk of possible explanations for her breast tumour; she speculated that it might be the twenty cigarettes that she smoked daily and added – 'But then that would have affected the lungs wouldn't it?' She said that she and her husband had been talking about possible causes of her cancer – was it the position she had been lying in at night, a blow she had received, the bras with wires she had worn in the fifties, something she had done or eaten? Was it hereditary since both her parents had died of it? She thought that the doctors didn't know where it came from and that they put people off with a lot of talk. A couple of weeks later we visited the woman in her home and again spontaneously she began talking about the causes of her cancer, wondering whether it had been caused by pollution or food additives, or even the food colouring in wine gums.

In her attempt to understand her illness the woman had seized upon every explanation she had ever heard of and considered it in relation to her own specific case. Some of the explanations came from the professional sector and some were folk beliefs. She made a retrospective evaluation of her way of living.

Some patients also mention psychological factors as causes of cancer. One woman who had been operated on for breast cancer and was about to have her breast restructured said 'I had heard that it could be caused psychologically, so that was what I thought. I was divorced five years ago, and developed cancer three years after.'

Others made similar observations about the psychological roots of cancer.

Suffering from cancer, however, also involves pain – if not from the disease itself, from the treatment. One man described the side effects experienced after chemotherapy as 'like having wires put to the bones down here [his feet] with the current on ... my bones freeze ... it's just like clay, but if I step on something it's like walking on broken glass'.

In western cultures, the dominant health model is the biomedical one and this provides the theoretical foundation for the healers' interpretation of the patient's illness experience. In talking to doctors and nurses at Danish hospitals about their views of cancer and its treatment, we found that both shared a basic definition of cancer as cellular pathology. A doctor explained: 'Something happens inside the nucleus on DNA level – in the anabolism of amino acid. The cells divide with abnormal speed and destroy the surrounding tissue and can spread to blood vessels and lymph.' When asked what cancer is, nurses give answers like: 'It's a disease, what else? It is changes in cells, it can attack and break through at one point, or run about in the body.... The patient shrinks more and more. Everything is used by those cells.' Although their choice of words is different, nurses are also working within the biomedical paradigm. In interviews we found that they also differed on other issues such as the role they assigned to social and psychological factors in aetiology and prognosis.

The doctors' explanations for cancer start from approved scientific research connecting specific types of cancer with specific genetic or external factors. Thus, it is important to the doctors that the causes of cancer are scientifically shown to be carcinogenic. They talk about smoking, asbestos, ultraviolet rays (skin cancer), all external factors. Although some doctors concur that psycho-social factors may have an influence, these explanations are not seen as 'real' because they are not proven within a traditional medical model. In response to the suggestion that the psychological state could affect a person's vulnerability to cancer, one doctor said 'It is difficult to tell because we can't measure it'; another, a surgeon, added, 'There is no evidence although I always tell a patient to lead as well-adjusted a life as possible' and another said 'It's just a belief on rather shaky ground'. One doctor added, 'Nurses think they can read the prognosis of a patient's disease from his/her attitude, but you could turn this around and say that the disease affects the mood and psyche.'

For the nurses the psychological state appears to be far more important in their explanation of cancer. One nurse said, 'The stronger you are psychologically, the better you can fight the disease. The weaker you are, the more susceptible you are to all kinds of diseases. If you've really been down psychologically all your life, you are more susceptible. That's my experience.' One nurse mentioned radioactivity and viruses as causes of cancer and then confessed that her own theory based on her own experience was that there was a strong relation between external factors and how a person was physically and psychologically. She said they often had people coming into the hospital with newly discovered leukaemia who had recently been involved in stressful situations like divorce or family problems. She felt that these could provoke outbreaks because the resistance against the cells which were always in the body was somehow or other depressed.

Nurses are less dependent on scientific evidence for their explanations of cancer; they are more influenced by their daily experience of working with cancer patients. The notion that mood and attitude affect one's susceptibility to disease is part of Danish folk culture.

Although all healers agree that the treatment of cancer is a great strain for the patients, doctors and nurses make different statements about the actual treatment. Doctors view cancer treatment in terms of statistical outcome. Doctors speak about the probability (in percentages) of curing different forms of cancer. For the doctors, the need to draw conclusions on the basis of a large number of cases is more important than the individual needs of the patients. One doctor said 'As a professional, we have a responsibility to society. We have to give treatment on a systematic basis from which something can be deduced. You can't just give something according to the individual case because then you don't know why it works as it does.' This is used to explain why the treatment of patients with some types of lung cancer is determined by drawing lots. The tendency to perceive the patients more as a collection of diseases than individual sick persons is reinforced by the way hospital doctors' work is organised. At Danish hospitals, doctors do not have continuity in their relationships with individual patients; doctors as a group are responsible for all the patients on a ward and a patient will be seen by a number of different doctors while in hospital. (As one doctor put it, this system is good for doctors because they see a wide variety of cases but not so good for the patients.)

Nurses describe the treatment of cancer from another angle. A nurse said, 'I can't conceive the disease as something you just treat medically because it affects the whole person. The disease and the treatment are interlinked and all-embracing. The patient has to have the bottle [the chemotherapy] for seven days – and you need a strong psyche to stand being chained to that.... A lot of patients say there is poison in the bottle. But at the same time, they know they are getting it to be helped.' Many nurses find the idea of administering a treatment that actually makes the patients even more sick problematic.

Many doctors accept the patient's right to seek alternative therapy. It is not modern to say otherwise. But most were critical of unorthodox treatment for the following reasons: it can unethically exploit sick people and it has not been subjected to scientific verification. Most nurses, on the other hand, were positive about alternative therapy as a supplement. One nurse said, 'As I work here I support the use of the chemotherapy we use here. I more or less have to otherwise it would be unfair to myself and the people I work for. But I definitely don't reject alternative therapy.' The nurses' attitude to alternative therapy is based on their wish to align with the patients' interests. A head nurse said that she felt dissatisfied that they didn't draw the patients' attention to alternative therapies. 'We say: Yes, Mrs So-and-so, now we'll do this and you will get better. We tell people what we feel is best – but people are all different – values are not the same. I have discussed this with the chief physicians but they disagree with me. They think that as therapists they know what's best for the patient. How can you know what's best for someone you don't even know?'

The reasons the nurses give for supporting alternative therapy are not necessarily that it works but that the patient participates actively in the treatment. The doctors' guarded attitude is rooted in their perception of science: the need to prove the validity of treatment through statistical samples.

Thus, although doctors and nurses share the same fundamental definition of cancer as a disease, they differ in important respects. The doctors continually speak as representatives of the biomedical view, while the nurses tend to conceptualise cancer as a disturbance in a more integrated biological, social, and psychological system. From the interviews it appears that the nurses are trying to get close to the patients' experience of the illness and its treatment – and at the same time to distance themselves from the approach of the doctors. When the nurses explain their conception of cancer, they place themselves between doctors and patients. This can be illustrated by the triangle.

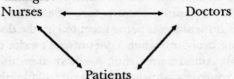

Nurses ←————————→ Doctors

Patients

This position as intermediary between doctors and patients is not in itself ambiguous but nurses are faced with a dilemma when trying to put their views into practice.

NURSES IN THE HIERARCHY

The hospital hierarchy places doctors at the top, nurses and other caring personnel with service functions below, and finally patients at the bottom as receivers of services. This hierarchy is based on different kinds of knowledge. The power of knowledge is the cornerstone in the structure of the hospital.

We have already referred to the idea that technical, impersonal, biomedical knowledge is the dominant form in western healing systems. It is dominant in the sense of being the most valued and authoritative, but it is a model that only doctors can use with ease.

Foucault (1976) describes the historical processes through which the present medical paradigm developed. In an earlier period, symptoms reported by the individual patient were important in the classification of sickness. But the development of hospitals provided doctors with the possibility of comparing clinical cases on the basis of pathological processes. Pathology replaced taxonomy as a major concern of medical practitioners. Foucault described the hospital as a kind of closed system, where the doctors could observe, experiment, and experience on the basis of all cases. The medical gaze was turned upon the signs of sickness. When operating, the doctors were able to see the organs inside the living body and in that way get a visual picture of what earlier could

197

only be sensed or felt. The medical gaze is one of the essential tools for the doctors in their interpretation of sickness as a disease. Hospital doctors are becoming technical experts; their specialised knowledge of specific pathological processes and of technical methods dominates their domain of work. Their specialised and exact knowledge, recognised as scientific, is the basis of authority.

Nurses, like patients, are subjected to the doctors' monopoly of knowledge and the authority structure of the hospital. A nurse expressed the difficulties of being accepted by the doctors: 'Sometimes there are problems when a doctor won't write in the journal things which we consider important. We have to remind them that it is important. Sometimes during rounds you feel foolish trying to tell them things. You can make them listen if you challenge them. When you are new you feel unsure of yourself. As a nurse you also have a mission in the ward. Doctors are not worth more than nurses.'

In the hospital hierarchy, the knowledge of nurses is not accorded the same value as that of the doctors. In this sense their position is similar to that of patients *vis-à-vis* the doctors who have a near monopoly on biomedical knowledge.

Nurses are thus in an ambiguous position, placed somewhere between the disease and illness perspectives. In their conception of cancer and its treatment, they feel closer to the patients than to the doctors; they try to speak about and explain cancer from a holistic point of view, integrating psycho-social aspects. But their daily duties are much more influenced by the perception of sickness as a disease; they rank below the doctors in the hierarchy and are subject to their decisions about treatment. Their position is more like that of assistants to the true representatives of medical science, the doctors, than one characterised by independent tasks in relation to the patients. Of course, in some respects, they do have independent tasks – but these are not seen by the patients as important in treating cancer. And to the patients, the nurses also represent the professional medical establishment; they carry out the doctors' orders and they are the executors of hospital routine. This is the dilemma of the nurses.

NEW PERSPECTIVES

If we look at the objectives which have been formulated for hospital nurses, a distinctive nursing ideology emerges.

Finseninstitutet (The National Cancer Hospital) worked out new guidelines for nursing in 1985: 'Nursing personnel see the person as part of a social context, as an autonomous individual with his/her own life values, obligations, hopes and rights and they [nurses] work to support the patient's potential for deciding and acting independently.' The guidelines for nurses at the National Hospital state: 'Nursing care is carried out as a co-ordination of two equal persons with their own wishes, hopes and rights. Nursing personnel stimulate the patient's desire for self-care, that is, the patient retains the responsibility for himself during admission and treatment.'

Nurses clearly have problems in trying to observe these guidelines in daily practice. For all healers in Danish hospitals the pressure of work is continuously increasing; hospitals in Denmark are subject to budget cuts which also mean staff reductions. The nurses themselves feel this difficulty. This can be illustrated by way of one of the topics nurses sometimes discuss: 'troublesome patients' – that is, patients who are demanding and difficult. One nurse said that she had attended a course in which she learned that troublesome patients did not exist; the problem arose only because healers were not well qualified enough. Nurses had to try to understand and deal with the reasons behind patients' demands, to see them as persons with problems. This might be difficult to achieve under the pressures of a hectic day. As another nurse explained: 'The troublesome patients are those ... who think that the whole world is centred on them. They can be difficult to handle. We have some who call constantly; first they want a bedpan, then they want the bedhead adjusted, then the cup has to be replaced. But now, we have started to ask them to put the requests together ... that is, ask for the bedhead to be adjusted at the same time as asking for the cup.' Then, remembering the need for solidarity with the patient, she added 'By definition, the troublesome patient doesn't exist within nursing. I feel that's right too ... anyhow, they also need good care.'

Nevertheless, the guidelines emphasise a vision of nursing and of nurse–patient relations that corresponds well with what nurses told us about their work with cancer patients. They are concerned with psychological aspects and with the patient's own right to decide. This interest in the individual patient's illness experience will no doubt contribute to better patient care and we do not question the good intentions behind this interest.

However, it is important to recognise the context for this vision of nursing. The new ideology has been articulated at a time when the dominance of doctors is being reinforced by increasingly elaborate technology and by the ever more demanding scientific requirements of the medical 'gaze'. Nurses are challenged by this and one way of reacting is to emphasise those aspects of nursing identity that have to do with humanism and the dignity of the patient as a person. The holistic approach emphasised by the nurses makes sense only in relation to the biomedical one – indeed, it is a creation of it. For nurses it is a way of distinguishing themselves from doctors, or rather forming an identity independent of the doctors and in opposition to the doctors' model of disease. They are forming a counter-model, where the stress is on a holistic perspective and where the knowledge of the patient's illness and experience is central. A nurse says, 'We have struggled a lot with psychological care.' When asked if nurses were properly qualified to deal with that, she replied that they were working a lot in the area and when asked if the doctors were qualified to deal with it, replied 'No they don't go in to the psychological side, they have the knife. We go to psychology courses, but you never see a doctor there.' Another nurse added, 'If you recognise that it is more than a medical defect you're treating, then you have to talk about how people's lives are shaped.'

CONCLUSION

Ardener (1975) drew attention to 'muted groups', those groups who are denied access to the dominant mode of expression and who provide their own alternative models of society. In a hospital, patients are a truly muted group, subject to uncertainty, anxiety, and pain. They are assigned a passive role in a bureaucratic power structure and caught in a routine they cannot influence. Therefore we must welcome the new perspectives the nurses have formulated, emphasising the individual patient's illness experience and the patient's right to decide independently. It is a development very much needed.

However, we have attempted to show that there is a further aspect to nursing ideology; it can be used as part of the conflict between professionals within Danish hospitals. These conflicts have been exacerbated by budget cuts at Danish hospitals, forcing the professional groups to fight for their jobs and assert their importance and indispensability in the cure and care of patients.

Solidarity with patients can be one way in which the professional can express concern about her/his relation (attitude) to the biomedical technocracy. Nurses have been struggling for some time for the acceptance of their work as equally important in the treatment of patients just as the women's movement has been struggling for acknowledgement of the importance of women's work at home. Although some nurses are male, and an increasing number of doctors are female, the nurses' struggle is one between values which in our culture are associated with maleness and femaleness: natural science versus human science, quantitative versus qualitative, impersonal technology versus warm understanding, curing versus caring.

Nurses may eventually improve their position *vis-à-vis* doctors, but the patients with whom the nurses declare allegiance remain muted. The outcome of this could be that the patients remain the passive recipients, sufferers with no possibility of determining or even understanding their treatment, while the nurses use their counter-model claiming solidarity with the patients as a step to improving their own professional position. This can be illustrated in the following way: professional authority over patients.

In that sense the great interest shown by nurses in qualitative methods and the social sciences – and also their positive attitudes and response to this project – may reflect their concern to clothe their new identity with academic respectability – the cloak of science, albeit social science.

In a sense nurses are in a position rather like that of anthropologists. As nurses speak for patients, anthropologists speak for the 'other', expressing solidarity with those who cannot explain themselves in the relevant 'language'. We must all do this with care and continual reflection on the contexts in which we work and on the consequences of our efforts.

NOTES

1. I am indebted to Susan Reynolds Whyte, University of Copenhagen, for her support and inspiration during the research study and in the preparation of this chapter.
2. The research project was carried out by myself and three other students: Sussi Skov Jensen, Helle Nielsen, and Vibeke Steffen whom I also want to thank for their helpful comments on this

BIBLIOGRAPHY

Abel-Smith, B. (1960) *A History of the Nursing Profession*, London: Heinemann.

Aber, S.M. and Higgins, P.M. (1982) 'The natural history and management of the Loin Pain/Haematuria Syndrome', *British Journal of Urology*, 54: 613–61.

Adams, D. (1988) 'Counseling men who batter: a profeminist analysis of five treatment models', in M. Bograd and K. Yllo (eds.) *Feminist Perspectives on Wife Abuse*, Beverly Hills: CA: Sage.

Adams, R.N. (1981) 'Ethical principles in anthropological research: one or many?' *Human Organisation: Journal of the Society for Applied Anthropology* 2: 155–60.

Ahrens, L. (1980) 'Battered women's refuges: feminist co-operatives vs. social service institutions', *Radical America* 14: 41–7, (May-June).

American Nurses Association (1979) *Social Policy Statement*.

Ardener, E. (1975) 'Introduction' in S. Ardener, (ed.) *Perceiving Women*, London: Dent.

Ardener, S. (ed.) (1978) *Defining Females*, London: Croom Helm.

Ardener, S. (ed.) (1981) *Women and Space*, London: Croom Helm.

Armstrong, D. (1983) *Political Anatomy of the Body*, Cambridge: Cambridge University Press.

Ashley, J. (1976) *Hospitals, Paternalism and the Role of the Nurse*, New York: Teachers College Press.

Attorney General's Task Force on Family Violence (1984) *Final Report*, Washington, DC: US Department of Justice.

Austin, R. (1977) *Sex and Gender in the Future of Nursing*, Nursing Times Occasional Papers: 4 August, 1 September.

Barrett, M. and McIntosh, M. (1982) *The Anti-Social Family*, London: Verso Editions/NLB.

Barrow, J. (1982) 'West Indian families: an insider's perspective', in R.N. Rapoport *et al.* (eds) *Families in Britain*, London: Routledge & Kegan Paul.

Barry, K. (1979) *Female Sexual Slavery*, New York: Avon Books.

Beale, L.S. (1873) 'Nursing the sick in hospitals, private families and among the poor', *Medical Times and Gazette* 6 December: 630.

Beardwell, I., Miles, D., and Worman, E. (1981) *The Twilight Army: A*

Study of Civil Service Cleaners, London: Low Pay Unit and Civil Service Union, Pamphlet No.19, November.

Bellaby, P. and Oribabor, P. (1980) 'The history of the present: contradiction and struggle', in C. Davies, (ed.) *Rewriting Nursing History*, London: Croom Helm.

Bogard, M. (1984) 'Family systems approaches to wife battering: a female critique', *American Journal of Orthopsychiatry* 54 (4): 558–68.

Boston Police Department (1980) Boston.

Braxton-Hicks, J. (1880) 'On nursing systems', *British Medical Journal*, 3 January: 11–12.

Breines, W. and Gordon, L. (1983) 'The new scholarship on family violence', *Signs: Journal of Women in Culture and Society* 8: 490–531.

British Medical Journal (1868) 'Nursing in London hospitals', 5 December: 594–5.

British Medical Journal (1873) 'Nursing as a profession', 4 January: 14.

British Medical Journal (1970) Correspondence: 17, 31 January, 7, 21 February.

Broverman, I.K. *et al.* (1970) 'Sex-role stereotypes and clinical judgements of mental health', *Journal of Consulting and Clinical Psychology* 34: 1–7.

Browne, A. (1987) *When Battered Women Kill*, New York: Free Press.

Brownmiller, S. (1975) *Against our Will*, New York: Simon & Schuster.

Bruner, J.S. and Kolowski, B. (1972) 'Visually preadapted constituents of manipulatory action, *Perception* 1: 3–14.

Bryan, B., Dadzie, S., and Scafe, S. (1985) *The Heart of the Face: Black Women's Lives in Britain*, London: Virago.

Bullough, V. (1966) *The Development of Medicine as a Profession: the Contribution of the Medieval University to Modern Medicine*, Basle: S.Karger.

Bullough, V. and Bullough, B. 1979) *The Care of the Sick: The Emergence of Modern Nursing*, London: Croom Helm.

Burgess, A.W. and Holmstrom, L. (1974) *Rape: Victims of Crisis*, Bowie, MD: Robert J. Brady Co.

Burgess, A.W. and Baldwin, B.A. (1981) *Crisis Intervention Theory and Practice*, Englewood Cliffs, NJ: Prentice Hall.

Campbell, J. (1986) *A Nursing Study of Two Explanatory Models of Women's Responses to Battering*, PhD dissertation, Rochester, NY: University of Rochester.

Campbell, J. and Humphreys, J. (1984) *Nursing Care of Victims of Violence*, Reston, VA: Reston Publishing Co.

Campbell-Heider, N. and Pollock, D. (1987) 'Barriers to physician-nurse collegiality: an anthropological perspective', *Social Science and Medicine* 25, 421–5.

Caraka, *Carakasamhita: Carakasamhita, Cakrapanidattaviracitava Ayurveda dipikavyakhyakhyaya samvalita*, Nirnayasagara Press, Bombay, 1941.

Carpenter, M. (1978) 'The new managerialism and professionalism in nursing', in M. Stacey , M. Reid, C. Heath, and R. Dingwall (eds) *Health and the Division of Labour*, London: Croom Helm.

Cassell, J. (1986) 'Dismembering the images of God: surgeons, heroes, wimps and miracles', *Anthropology Today* 2 (2): 13–15.

Cassell, J. (1987) 'Control, certitude and the 'paranoia' of surgeons', *Culture, Medicine and Psychiatry*, 11: 229–49.

Center for Disease Control (CDC) (1983) *Homicide Surveillance, 1970–78*, Atlanta: USPHS Center for Disease Control.

Chaney, J. (1981) *Social Networks and Job Information: The Situation of Women who Return to Work*, Manchester: EOC/SSRC.

Chapman, S. (1979) 'Advertising and psychotropic drugs: the place of myth in ideological reproduction', *Social Science and Medicine* 13: 751–64.

Chesler, P. (1974) *Women and Madness*, London: Allen Lane.

Chiaromonte, N. (1985) *The Paradox of History*, Philadelphia, PA: University of Pennsylvania Press.

Chodoff, P. and Lyons, H. (1958) 'Hysteria, the hysterical personality and "hysterical conversion"', *American Journal of Psychiatry*, 114: 734–40.

Chodorow, N. (1978) *The Reproduction of Mothering: Psychoanalysis and the Sociology of Gender*, Berkeley, CA.: University of California Press.

Chopoorian, T. (1986) 'Reconceptualising the environment', in P. Moccia, (ed.) *New Approaches to Theory Development*, New York: National League for Nursing.

Chrisman, N.J. (1982) 'Anthropology and nursing: an exploration of adaptation', in N. Chrisman, and T.W. Maretzki, (eds) *Clinically Applied Anthropology*, Dordrecht: Reidel.

Cicourel, A.V. (1964) *Method and Measurement in Sociology*, New York: Free Press.

Cloward, R.A. and Piven, F.F. (1979) 'Hidden protest: the channelling of female innovation and resistance', *Signs: Journal of Women in Culture and Society* 4: 651–69.

Cohen, G. (1978) 'Women's solidarity and the preservation of privilege', in *Women United, Women Divided*, London: Tavistock.

Cole, T. (1967) *Democritus and the Sources of Greek Anthropology*, American Philological Society Monograph 25, Cape Western Reserve University Press.

Colliere, M.F. (1986) 'Invisible care and insensible women as health-care providers', *International Journal of Nursing Studies* 23: 95–112.

Comaroff, J. (1978) 'Medicine and culture: some anthropological perspectives', *Social Science and Medicine* 12, 247–254.

Connor Versluysen, M. (1980). 'Old wives' tales? Women in English history', in C. Davies (ed.) *Rewriting Nursing History*, London: Croom Helm.

Corea, G. (1985) *The Hidden Malpractice: How American Medicine Mistreats Women*, New York: Harper Colophon Books.

Coyle, A. (1985) 'Going private: the implications of privatisation for women's work', *Feminist Review* 21.

Coyle, A. (1986) *Dirty Business: Women's Work and Trade Union*

Organisation in Contract Cleaning, West Midlands, Low Pay Unit/Equal Opportunities Commission, October.

Cunnison, S. (1966) *Wages and Work Allocation*, London: Tavistock.

Dale, A.J. (1965) 'Job satisfaction and organisation among hospital domestic workers', *British Journal of Industrial Relations*, 111, (2).

Daley, M. (1985) *The Hidden Workers: The Work Lives Of Part-Time Women Cleaners*, Dublin: Employment Equality Agency.

Davidson, P. and Jackson, C. (1985) 'The nurse as survivor: delayed post traumatic stress reaction and cumulative trauma in nursing', *International Journal of Nursing Studies* 22: 1–13.

Davidson, T. (1977) 'Wifebeating: a recurring phenomenon throughout history', in M. Roy, (ed.) *Battered Woman: A Psychosociological Study of Domestic Violence*, New York: Van Nostrand Reinhold Co.

Davies, C. (1980) *Rewriting Nursing History*, London: Croom Helm.

Davies, D.S. (1912) 'The relation of medical men to nurses', *The Hospital* 8 June: 251–2.

Dean, M. and Bolton, G. (1980) 'The administration of poverty and the development of nursing practice in nineteenth century England', in C. Davies, (ed.) 1980 *Rewriting Nursing History*, London: Croom Helm.

Debabar, B. (1986) *Nursing and the Task of Providing Health for all Through Primary Health Care in India*, New Delhi, Centre of Social Medicine and Community Health, Jawaharlal Nehru University, mimeograph.

Deichgraeber, K. (1970) *Medicus Gratiosus*, Mainz: Akademie der Wissenschaft und der Literatur Wiesbaden Steiner.

Delamont, S. and Duffin, L. (1978) *The Nineteenth Century Woman: Her Cultural and Physical World*, London: Croom Helm.

Deloughery, G. (1977) *History and Trends of Professional Nursing*, 7th edition, St. Louis, Missouri: C.V. Mosby.

Department of Health & Social Security (1977) *The Expanded Role of the Nurse*, HC (77) 22.

Dex, S. (1987) *Women's Occupational Mobility*, London: Macmillan.

Dexter, L.A. (1958) 'A note on selective inattention in social science', *Social Problems* 6: 176–82.

Dobash, R.P. and Dobash, R.E. (1979) *Violence Against Wives: A Case Against the Patriarchy*, New York: Free Press.

Dock, L.L. and Stewart, I.M. (1938) *A Short History of Nursing*, New York: Putnam's.

Dolan, J.A. (1978). *Nursing in Society: An Historical Perspective*, 14th edition of Goodnow, New York: Putnam's.

Dommen T.K. (1978) *Doctors and Nurses: A Study in Occupational Role Structure*, Delhi: The Macmillan Press.

Donzelot, J. (1977) *La Police des Familles*, Paris: Minuit.

Douglas, M. (1966) *Purity and Danger*, Harmondsworth, Middx.: Penguin.

Douglas, M. (1975) *Implicit Meanings*, London: Routledge & Kegan Paul.

Doyal, L. *et al.* (1980) *Migrant Workers in the National Health Service: Report of a Preliminary Survey*, London: Polytechnic of North London/Social Science Research Council.

Doyal, L. *et al.* (1981) 'Your life in their hands: migrant workers in the National Health Service', *Critical Social Policy* 1 (2), Autumn.

Driver, G. (1982) 'West Indian families: an anthropological perspective'. in R.N. Rapoport, *et al.* (eds) *Families in Britain*, London: Routledge & Kegan Paul.

Dubos, R. (1977) 'Determinants of health and disease', in D. Landy, (ed.) *Culture, Disease and Healing: Studies in Medical Anthropology*, New York: Macmillan.

Dunlop, M.J. (1986) 'Is a science of caring possible?' *Journal of Advanced Nursing*, 11: 661–70.

Durkheim, E. and Mauss M. (1903) *Primitive Classification*, London: Routledge (1969).

Dutoit, B.M. (1980) 'Ethics, informed consent and fieldwork', *Journal of Anthropological Research*, 36: 274–86.

Edelstein, L. (1931) 'The Hippocratic physician', in L. Edelstein, (ed.) *Ancient Medicine*, Baltimore, MD: Johns Hopkins University Press, 1967, pp. 87–110.

Ehrenreich, B. and English, D. (1973) *Witches, Midwives and Nurses: A History of Women Healers*, Old Westbury, NY: The Feminist Press.

Eisenberg, L. (1972) 'Disease and illness: distinctions between professional and popular ideas of sickness', *Culture, Medicine and Psychiatry* 1: 9–23.

Elias, P. and Main, B. (1982) *Women's Working Lives: Evidence from the National Training Survey*, University of Warwick, Institute for Employment Research.

Ellenberger, H.F. (1970) *The Discovery of the Unconscious: The History and Evolution of Dynamic Psychiatry*, London: Allen Lane.

Elston, M.A. (1977) 'Women in the medical profession', in M. Stacey, M. Reid, C. Heath, and R. Dingwall, (eds) *Health and the Division of Labour*, London: Croom Helm.

Engel, G.L. (1977) 'The need for a new medical model: a challenge for biomedicine', *Science* 196: 129–36.

Entralgo, P.L. (1969) *Doctor and Patient*, London: Weidenfeld & Nicolson.

Fagin, C. and Diers, D. (1983) 'Nursing as a metaphor', *New England Journal of Medicine* 309 (2).

F.A.W. (1908) 'Nurses and operations', letter, *Nursing Mirror* 11 January: 236.

Ferrari, G.A. and Vegetti, M. (1983) 'Science, technology and medicine in the classical tradition', in P. Corsi and P. Weindling, (eds) *Information Sources in the History of Science and Medicine*, London: Butterworth Scientific.

'Fight' (1876) 'Trained Nurses', letter, *Lancet*, 8 July: 71.

Filliozat, J. (1949) *La Doctrine Classique de la Médecine Indienne, ses origines et ses parallèles grecs*, Paris.

Finkelhor, D. (1985) 'Child sexual abuse', background paper

submitted to Surgeon General's Workshop on Violence and Public Health, Leesburg, VA, October.

Finseninstitutet (1985) 'Idgrundlag og maalsaetning for sygeplejen paa Finseninstitutet', Koebenhavn.

Firth-Cozens, J. (1987) 'Emotional distress in junior hospital doctors', *British Medical Journal* 295: 533–6.

Fitzpatrick, M.L. (1977) 'Review essay: nursing', *Signs* 2: 818–34.

Flynn, J.M. and Heffron, P.B. (1984) *Nursing: From Concept to Practice*, Bowie, MD: Brady Communications Co.

A Former Matron (1906) 'What nurses owe to the medical profession', *The Hospital*, 7 April: 14–15.

Foucault, M. (1976) *The Birth of the Clinic*, London: Tavistock.

Foucault, M. (1984) *Histoire de la Sexualité, 2: L'Usage des plaisirs; 3: Le souci de soi*, Paris: Gallimard.

Fox, M.E. (1913) 'First year nurses: the ethics of nursing', 24 May: 142–3.

Freire, P. (1968) *Pedagogy of the Oppressed*, trans. M.B. Ramon, New York: Continuum Press, 1970.

Freud, S. (1930) *Civilisation and its Discontents*, London: Hogarth Press (1964).

Gamarnikow, E. (1978) 'Sexual division of labour; the case of nursing', in A. Kuhn and A.M. Wolpe, (eds) *Feminism and Materialism: Women and Modes of Production*, London: Routledge & Kegan Paul.

Gamarnikow, E. (1984) 'Nineteenth century nursing reform and the sexual division of labour', *Bulletin of the History Group of the Royal College of Nursing* 4, spring.

Garminikow, E. (1985) *Women's Employment and the Sexual Division of Labour: the Case of Nursing 1860–1923*, Unpublished PhD thesis, LSE.

Gaze, H. (1987) 'Men in nursing', *Nursing Times*, 83 (20): 25–7.

'Gee-Wiz' (1908) 'Nurses and operations', letter, *Nursing Mirror*, 25 January: 268.

Gelles, R.J. (1974) *The Violent Home*, Beverly Hills, CA: Sage Foundation.

Gelles, R.J. and Straus, M.A. (1979) 'Determinants of violence in the family: toward a theoretical integration', in R.Wesley, A. Burr, *et al.* (eds) *Contemporary Theories about the Family*, Vol. 2, New York: Free Press.

Gergen, K.J. (1982) *Toward Transformation in Social Knowledge*, New York: Springer-Verlag.

Gil, D.G. (1970) *Violence Against Children.* Cambridge, Mass.: Harvard University Press.

Gilligan, C. (1982) *In A Different Voice*, Boston: Harvard University Press.

Ginsberg, G.P. (1971) 'Public conceptions and attitudes about suicide', *Journal of Health and Social Behaviour* 12: 200–1.

Givner, D. (1962) 'Scientific Preconceptions in Locke's Philosophy of Language', *Journal of History of Ideas*, 23: 341–54.

Goffman, E. (1969) *The Presentation of Self in Everyday Life*, London: Allen Lane.

Good, B.J. (1977) The heart of what's the matter: the semantics of illness in Iran, *Culture, Medicine and Psychiatry* 1: 25–58.

Good, B.J. and Good, M.J.D. (1982) 'Towards a meaning of symptoms – A cultural hermeneutic model for clinical practice', in L. Eisenberg and A. Kleinman (eds) *The Relevance of Social Science for Medicine*, Dordrecht: Reidel.

Good, B.J., Herrera, H., Good, M.J.D., and Cooper, J. (1985) 'Reflexivity, counter-transference and clinical ethnography', in R.A. Hahn and A.D. Gaines, (eds) (1985) *Physicians and Western Medicine: Anthropological Approaches to Theory and Practice*, Dordrecht: Reidel.

Goodnow, M. (1961) *Nursing History*, Philadelphia, PA: W.B. Saunders.

Goody, J. (1982) *Cooking, Cuisine and Class*, Cambridge: Cambridge University Press.

Gould, Miss (1910) 'The personal factor in nursing: patient, doctor, nurse', *Nursing Times*, 5 March: 186–9.

G.P. (1912) 'Hypodermic medication by nurses', letter, *British Medical Journal*: 644.

Grieco, M. and Whipp, R. (1984) 'Women and the workplace: gender and control in the labour process', Working paper series number 8, Work Organisation Research Centre, University of Aston, May.

Gullestad, M. (1984) *Kitchen-Table Society*, London: Global Books.

Guthrie, D. (1953) 'Nursing through the ages', *Nursing Mirror* 97: 19–25.

Habermas, J. (1984) *The Theory of Communicative Action: Reason and the Rationalisation of Society*, London: Heinemann.

Hahn, R.A. and Gaines, A.D. (1985) *Physicians of Western Medicine: Anthropological Approaches to Theory and Practice*, Dordrecht: Reidel.

Harrisson, S. (1986) 'Teamwork: a valuable part of the team', *Health Services Journal*, 11 December.

Harrisson, S. (1986) 'The contribution of domestic staff to the welfare of mentally ill in-patients', Health Care Research Unit, University of Durham, April, published in edited form.

Hart, E.A. (1986) 'Paintresses and potters: work, skill and social relations in a pottery in Stoke-on-Trent, 1981–1984', Unpublished PhD thesis, University of London, August.

Hedin, B. (1986) 'A case study of oppressed group behaviour in nurses', *Image: Journal of Nursing Scholarship* 18 (2): 53–7.

Heelas, P. and Lock, A. (eds) (1981) *Indigenous Psychologies: an anthropology of the self*, London: Academic Press.

Helman, C. (1985) 'Disease and pseudo-disease: a case history of pseudo-angina', in R.A. Hahn and A.D. Gaines (eds) *Physicians of Western Medicine: Anthropological Approaches to Theory and Practice*, Dordrecht: Reidel.

Henderson, V. (1978) 'The concept of nursing', *Journal of Advanced Nursing* 3, 113–30.

Hendry, J. (1984) 'Shoes: the early learning of an important distinction in Japanese society', in G. Daniels (ed.) *Europe Interprets Japan*, Kent: Tenterden.

Herdt, G.H. (1982) *Rituals of Manhood: Male Initiation in Papua New Guinea*, Berkeley, CA: University of California Press.

Herfst, P. (1922) *Le travail de la femme dans la Grece ancienne*, Amsterdam: Oosthoek, reprinted 1979.

Herman, J. (1981) *Father–Daughter Incest*, Cambridge, Mass.: Harvard University Press.

Hilberman, E. (1980) 'Overview: the "wife beaters's wife" reconsidered', *American Journal of Psychiatry* 137: 1336–47.

Hillband, J.H. and Pope, C.R. (1983) 'Gender roles in illness orientation and use of medical services', *Social Science and Medicine*, 17: 129–37.

Hoekelman, R.A. (1975) 'Nurse–physician relationships', *American Journal of Nursing* 75: 1150–2.

Hoff, L.A. (1989) *People in Crisis: Understanding and Helping*, 3rd edition, Redwood City, CA: Addison-Wesley.

Hoff, L.A. (1990) *Battered Women as Survivors*, London: Routledge.

Hoff, L.A. 'Battered nurses: why don't they leave?' forthcoming.

Hoff, L.A. and Miller, N. (1987) *Programs for People in Crisis*, Boston: Northeastern University Custom Book Program.

Holden, P. (1984a) *Doctors and other Medical Personnel in Nigeria, Uganda and Tanganyika*, Oxford Development Records Project, Report 17, Rhodes House Library, Oxford.

Holden, P. (1984b) *Nursing Sisters in Nigeria, Uganda and Tanganyika*, Oxford Development Records Project, Report 18, Rhodes House Library, Oxford.

Holmstrom, L.L. and Burgess, A.W. (1978) *The Victim of Rape: Institutional Reactions*, New York: Wiley.

Horwitz, A. (1977) 'The pathways into psychiatric treatment: some differences between men and women', *Journal of Health and Social Behaviour* 18: 169–178.

Hudson, L. (1972) *The Cult of the Fact*, New York: Harper & Row.

Hutt, R. (1985) *Chief Nursing Officer Career Profiles: A Study of Backgrounds*, Brighton: Institute of Management Studies.

H.W. (1907) 'Nurses and operations', letter, *Nursing Mirror* 21 December: 192.

Illich, I. (1976) *Limits to Medicine*, Harmondsworth, Middx.: Penguin.

Ingleby, D. (1982) 'The social construction of mental illness', in P. Wright and A. Treacher (eds) *The Problem of Medical Knowledge*, Edinburgh: Edinburgh University Press.

IOTA (1908) 'Nurses and operations', letter, *Nursing Mirror* 1 February: 279.

Jaeger, W. (1957) 'Aristotle's use of medicine as model of method in his Ethics', *Journal of Hellenic Studies* 77: 54–61.

James, C.W.B. (1963) 'Psychology and Gynaecology', in A. Cloge and A. Bourne (eds) *British Obstetrical and Gynaecological Practice*, London: Heinemann.

Jensen, D.M. (1943) *A History of Nursing*, St. Louis, Missouri: C.V.Mosby.

Joly, R. (1983) 'Hippocrates and the school of Cos', in M. Ruse, (ed.) *Nature Animated*, Dordrecht: Reidel, pp. 29–47.

Jones, A. (1980) *Women Who Kill*, New York: Holt, Rinehart & Winston.

Jones, W.H.S. (1923) 'Ancient nursing', in *Hippocrates*, vol.11, Loeb Classical Library, pp.xxx-xxxii.

Jones, W.H.S. (1923) *Hippocrates:* vol. 2 London, Loeb Classical Library. Heinemann.

Jones, W.H.S. (1931) *Hippocrates:* vol. 4 London, Loeb Classical Library. Heinemann.

Jordanova, L.J. (1980) 'Natural facts: a historical perspective on science and sexuality', in C. MacCormack and M. Strathern, (eds) *Nature, Culture, Gender*, Cambridge: Cambridge University Press.

Joshel, S.R. (1986) 'Nurturing the master's child: slavery and the Roman child-nurse', *Signs*, 12: 3–22.

Jouanna, J. (1984) 'Rhétorique et médecine dans la collection hippocratique: contribution a l'histoire de la rhétorique au Ve siècle'. *REG*, 97: 26–44.

Kakar, D.N. (1980) *Dais: The Traditional Birth Attendants in Village India*, Delhi: New Asian Publishers.

Kalisch, B., Kalisch, P., and Scobey M. (1983) *Images of the Nurse on Television*, Berlin: Springer.

Kangle, R.P. (ed.) (1986) *The Kautiliya Arthasastra*, 3 vols., reprint of 2nd edition, New Delhi: Motilal Banarsidass.

Kempe, C.H. *et al.* (1962) 'The battered child syndrome', *Journal of American Medical Association* 181: 17–24.

Kempe, C.H. and Helfer, R.E. (1980) *The Battered Child*, 3rd edition, Chicago: University of Chicago Press.

King, H. (1987) Sacrified Blood: 'the role of the Amnion in ancient gynecology' in M. Skinner (ed.) *Rescuing Creusa: new methodological approaches to women in antiquity*, Helios, n.s. 13: 117–26.

King, H. (1989) 'The daughter of Leonides: reading the Hippocratic corpus', in A. Cameron, (ed.) *History as Text*, London: Duckworth.

Kleinman, A. (1980) *Patients and Healers in the Context of Culture*, Berkeley, CA: University of California Press.

Kleinman, A. (1986a) 'Anthropology and psychiatry: the role of culture in cross cultural research on illness and care', in M.L. Rosenberg, G. Raben, *et al.* (eds) *Psychiatry and its Related Disciplines, the Next 25 Years*, Copenhagen.

Kleinman, A. (1986b) *Social Origins of Distress and Disease: Depression, Neurasthenia and Pain in Modern China*, New Haven, Conn.: Yale University Press.

Kodama, K. (1984) 'Nursing in Japan', *Nursing Outlook* 32 (2): 102–6.

Kuper, H. (1965) 'Nurses' in L. Kuper, (ed.) *An African Bourgeoisie: Race, Class and Politics in South Africa*, New Haven and London: Yale University Press.

La Fontaine, J.S. (1978) *Sex and Age as Principles of Social Differentiation*, London: Academic Press.

La Fontaine, J.S. (1981) 'The domestication of the savage male', *Man (n.s.)* 16: 333–49.

Labour Research Department (1984) 73, (5), May.

Labour Research Department (1987) Bargaining Report 59, February.

Labour Research Department (1986) Bargaining Report 53, July.

Lady Grigg Welfare League (1927) 'Child welfare in Kenya: how the British public can help', Nairobi.

Lancet (1877) 'Skilled nursing', 13 January: 62.

Lancet (1879a) 'Nursing', 19 April: 569–70.

Lancet (1879b) 'Nurses for all classes', 26 April: 604.

Lancet (1879c) Untitled, 23 May: 736.

Lancet (1894) Untitled, 3 February: 280.

Lancet (1896) Untitled, 11 January: 109–10.

Le Bon, G. (1893) *The Crowd*, London: Unwin.

Lewin, E. (1977) 'Feminist ideology and the meaning of work: the case of nursing', *Catalyst*, 10: 11–18

Lewis, I.M. (1966) 'Spirit possession and deprivation cults', *Man (n.s.)* 1: 307–29.

Levitt, R. and Wall, A. (1984) *The Reorganised NHS*, London: Croom Helm.

Lienhardt, G. (1961) *Divinity and Experience: The Religion of the Dinka*, Oxford: Clarendon Press.

Littlewood, J. (1985) 'No flag day for incontinence', *Self Health* September 32–4.

Littlewood, J. (1988) 'Nurses and alcohol or why the image of the nurse as angel persists', paper presented at Gender and Addiction, Centre for Cross-Cultural Research on Women, Oxford. (Publication forthcoming in McDonald, M., *Gender and Addiction*, Berg.)

Littlewood, J. (1989) 'A model of nursing using anthropological literature', *International Journal of Nursing Studies* 23: 221–29.

Littlewood, R. (1984) 'The individual articulation of shared symbols', *Journal of Operational Psychiatry* 15: 17–24.

Littlewood, R. (1987) *Pathology and Identity: The Genesis of a Millennial Community in North-East Trinidad*, DPhil thesis, Oxford University.

Littlewood, R. and Lipsedge, M. (1987) 'The butterfly and the serpent: culture, psychopathology and biomedicine', *Culture, Medicine and Psychiatry*, 11: 289–335.

Littré, E. *Oeuvres complètes d'Hippocrate*, 10 vols (Paris, 1839–61); reprinted Hakkert, Amsterdam, 1962.

Lloyd, G.E.R. (1979) *Magic, Reason and Experience*, Cambridge: Cambridge University Press.

Lloyd, G.E.R. (1983). *Science, Folklore and Ideology*, Cambridge: Cambridge University Press.

Lock, M. (1980) *East Asian Medicine in Urban Japan*, Comparative Studies of Health Systems of Medical Care, Number 4. Berkeley, CA: University of California Press.

Lonie, I.M. (1981) 'Literacy and the development of Hippocratic medicine', in F. Lasserre and P. Mudry (eds.), *Actes du Colloque hippocratique de Lausanne*, Geneva: Droz, pp. 145–61.

Lonsdale, S. (1987) 'Patterns of paid work', in C. Glendenning and J. Millar (eds) *Women and Poverty in Britain*, Sussex: Wheatsheaf Books.

Loudon, J. (1977) 'On bodily products', in J. Blacking (ed.) *The Anthropology of the Body*, New York: Academic Press.

Lupton, T. (1963) *On the Shop Floor*, London: Pergamon.

McBride, A. (1983) 'The nursing profession: the antithesis or epitome of feminism', paper presented at Boston Area Colloquium on Feminist Theory, October.

McCarthy, Lady M. (1985) 'A new approach to NHS pay', *Health and Social Service Journal* 3 October.

McEvedy, C.P. and Beard, A.W. (1970) 'Royal Free epidemic of 1955: a reconsideration', 'Concept of benign myalic encephalomyelitis', *British Medical Journal* 17–11, 11–15.

McKinlay, J.B. (1973) 'Social networks, lay consultation and help-seeking behaviour', *Social Forces* 51: 275–92.

McKinlay, J.B. (1981) 'Social network influences on morbid episodes and the career of help-seeking', in L. Eisenberg and A. Kleinman, (eds), *The Relevance of Social Science for Medicine*, The Hague, Netherlands: Reidel.

Macleod, R.B. (1974) 'The phenomenological approach to social psychology', *Psychological Review* 54: 193–210.

Macleod, M.F. (1985) 'Charge nurse "non-nursing duties": a research project, St Mary Abbots Hospital, July 1985', *Nursing Times*, 18, (48).

Maggs, C. (1983) *The Origin of General Nursing*, London: Croom Helm.

Mailly, R. (1985) 'Contracting out of ancillary services in the National Health Service: its impact upon management/staff relations', unpublished paper, Nuffield Centre for Health Service Studies, University of Leeds, July.

Mama, A. (1984) 'Black women, the economic crisis and the British state', *Feminist Review*, 17, autumn.

Manpower Studies Unit (1976) *The Role of Immigrants in the Labour Market*, London: Department of Employment.

Mansfield, J. (1983) 'The historical Hippocrates and the origins of scientific medicine', in M. Ruse, (ed.) *Nature Animated*, Dordrecht: Reidel, pp. 49–76.

Maranhão, T. (1986) *Therapeutic Discourse and Socratic Dialogue*, Madison, WI: Wisconsin University Press.

Markham, J. (1975) *The Lamp was Dimmed: The Story of a Nurse's Training*, London: Robert Hale.

Markham-Smith, I. (1987) 'Career women struck down by yuppie plague', *Sunday Express*, London, 22 March.

Martin, D. (1976) *Battered Wives*, San Francisco: Glide Publications.

A Matron (1897) 'The power of management', *The Hospital* 10 July: 133.

Meadows, R. (1984) 'Factitious illness: the hinterland of child abuse', in R. Meadows, (ed.) *Recent Advances in Paediatrics*, Edinburgh: Churchill Livingstone.

Medical Times and Gazette (1876) 'The doctor's aide-de-camp', 26 February: 228.

Miller, J.B. (1976) *Toward A New Psychology of Women*, Boston: Beacon Press.

Mills, C.W. (1959) *The Sociological Imagination*, London and New York: Oxford University Press.

Mitchell, J. and Oakley, A. (1976) *The Rights and Wrongs of Women*. Harmondsworth: Penguin.

Moore, N. (1981) *The History of St Bartholomew's Hospital*, Vol.2, London: Pearson.

Murphy, Y. and Murphy, R.F. (1974) *Women of the Forest*, New York: Columbia University Press.

NAHA/King's Fund (1985) *NHS Pay: A Time for Change*, London.

N.C. (1908) 'Nurses and operations', letter, *Nursing Mirror* 4 January: 221.

Newberger, E.H. (1985) 'Child abuse', background paper submitted to Surgeon General's Workshop on Violence and Public Health, Leesburg, VA, October.

Nightingale, F. (1859) *Notes on Nursing: What it is and What it is not*, London: Harrison.

Nightingale, F. (1874) *Suggestions for Improving the Nursing Service of Hospitals and on the Method of Training Nurses for the Sick Poor*, London: Imprint, BLPES Nightingale Collection.

Nightingale, F. (1882) 'Training of nurses and nursing the sick', reprinted from Dr Quain (ed.) *Dictionary of Medicine*, London: Spottiswoode.

NOVA-NIMH (1985) 'The aftermath of crime: a mental health crisis', Service Research and Evaluation Colloquium sponsored by National Organisation for Victim Assistance and National Institute of Mental Health, Washington, DC, 28 February–3 March.

Nurse, D.M. (1908) 'Nurses and operations', letter, *Nursing Mirror* 1 February: 279.

Nursing Mirror (1909) 'The relationship between nurse and medical officer', 30 October: 71–2.

Nursing Times (1906a) 'The home preparation of a probationer', 3 March: 176–8.

Nursing Times (1906b) 'The nurse's limitations', 2 June: 457.

Nursing Times (1987a) 'Man appeal', 83 (20): 24–30 (supplement).

Nursing Times (1987b) 'First among equals?' 83 (32): 27.

Nutton, V. (1979) *Galen on Prognosis* (edition, translation and commentary), Corpus medicorum graecorum 8: 1, Berlin: Akademie Verlag.

Oakley, A. (1981) 'Interviewing women: a contradiction in terms, in H. Roberts, (ed.) *Doing Feminist Research*, London: Routledge & Kegan Paul.

O'Brien, J.E. (1971) 'Violence in divorce prone families', *Journal of Marriage and the Family* 33: 692–8.

Odlum, D.M. (1954) *Psychology – The Nurse and the Patient*, New York: Philosophical Library.

Ohnuki-Tierney, E. (1984) *Illness and Culture in Contemporary Japan, an Anthropological View*, Cambridge: Cambridge University Press.

Okely, J. (1983) *The Traveller-Gypsies*, Cambridge: Cambridge University Press.

Oppert, F. (1883) *Hospitals, Infirmaries and Dispensaries*, London: Churchill.

Ortner, S.B. (1974) 'Is female to male as nature is to culture?', in M.A. Rosaldo, and L. Lamphere (eds) *Women, Culture and Society*, Stanford, CA: Stanford University Press.

Pahl, R.E. (1984) *Divisions of Labour*, Oxford: Blackwell.

Parsons, T. (1951) 'Illness and the role of the physician', *American Journal of Orthopsychiatry* 21: 452–60.

Pavey, A.E. (1938) *The Story of the Growth of Nursing as an Art, a Vocation and a Profession*, London: Faber & Faber.

Pavey, A.E. (1959) *The Story of the Growth of Nursing: As an Art, a Vocation and a Profession*, 5th edition, London: Faber & Faber, p. 36.

Perkins, T. (1983) 'A new form of employment: a case study of women's part-time work in Coventry', in M. Evans and C. Ungerson, (eds) *Sexual Divisions: Patterns and Processes*, London: Tavistock.

Phillips, D.L. and Segal, B. (1969) 'Sexual status and psychiatric symptoms', *American Sociological Review* 29: 678–87.

Phizacklea, A. (1982) 'Migrant women and wage labour: the case of West Indian women in Britain, in J. West, (ed.) *Work, Women and the Labour Market*, London: Routledge & Kegan Paul.

Pillemer, K. (1985) 'Domestic violence against the elderly', background paper submitted to Surgeon General's Workshop on Violence and Public Health. Leesburg, VA, October.

Platt, S. (1987) 'Editorial', *Medical Sociology Bulletin* 12 August: 3.

Prather, J. and Fidell, L. (1975) 'Sex differences in the content and style of medical advertisements', *Social Science and Medicine* 9: 23–6.

President's Task Force on Victims of Crime. 1984 *Final Report*, Washington, DC: US Government Printing Office.

Pyle, F. (1981) 'From project to program', Cambridge, Mass.: MIT, unpublished thesis.

Radhalaxmi, K.K. and Rao, M.N. (1956) 'Nursing under ancient Indian systems (as described in ayurveda classics)', *Indian Journal of the History of Medicine* 1: 36–40.

Ramon, S., Bancroft, J.H.J., and Skrimshire, A.M. (1975) 'Attitudes to self-poisoning among physicians and nurses in general hospital', *British Journal of Psychiatry* 127: 257–64.

Ramsay, A.M. (1986) *Post-viral Fatigue Syndrome: The Saga of the Royal Free Disease*, London: Glover.

Rây, P.C. (1909) *History of Hindu Chemistry*, 2 vols, 2nd edition, London.

Ray, P.C. and Gupta, H. N. (1965) *Caraka Samhita (a scientific synopsis)*, New Delhi: The National Institute of Sciences of India.

Ray, P., Gupta, H., and Roy, M. (1980) *Susruta Samhita (a scientific synopsis)*, New Delhi: The Indian National Science Academy.

Reinach, S. (1904) 'Medicus', in C.V. Daremberg and E. Saglio, (eds) *Dictionnaire des Antiquités*, Paris: Hachette, pp. 1887ff.

Reinharz, S. (1979) *On Becoming A Social Scientist*, San Francisco: Jossey-Bass.

Reiter, R.R. (ed.) (1975) *Toward an Anthropology of Women*, New York: Monthly Review Press.

Renlim (1912) 'Hypodermic medication by nurses', letter, *British Medical Journal* 6 April: 809.

Report on the papers of the Overseas Nursing Association (1973) MSS Brit. Emp. s 400 Rhodes House Library, Oxford.

Reverby, S.M. (1987) *Ordered to Care: The Dilemma of American Nursing: 1850–1945*, Cambridge: Cambridge University Press.

Rhodes, L.A. (1984) ' "This will clear your mind": metaphors of psychiatric medication', *Culture, Medicine and Psychiatry* 8: 49–70.

Richards, M.P.M. (1974) *The Integration of the Child into a Social World*, Cambridge: Cambridge University Press.

Riedel, M. and Zahn, M.S. (1982) *The Nature and Patterns of American Homicide: An Annotated Biblioghraphy*, Washington, DC: National Institute of Justice.

Rieker, P.P. and Carmen (Hilberman), E. (1984) *The Gender Gap in Psychotherapy: Social Realities and Psychological Processes*, New York: Plenum Press.

Robert, L. (1964) in N. Firatli and L. Robert, *Les stèles funeraires de Byzance greco-romaine*, Paris: Adrien Maisonneuve.

Roberts, H. (ed.) (1981) *Doing Feminist Research*, London: Routledge & Kegan Paul.

Roberts, S. (1983) 'Oppressed group behaviour: implications for nursing', *Advances in Nursing Science* 5 (7): 21–30.

Robinson, D. (1971) *The Process of Becoming Ill*, London: Routledge & Kegan Paul.

Robinson, O. (1984) 'Part-time employment and industrial relations development in the EEC', *Industrial Relations Journal* 15.

Robinson, O. and Wallace, J. (1981) 'Relative pay and part-time employment in Great Britain', *Oxford Bulletin of Economics and Statistics* 43: 149–74.

Robinson, V. (1946) *White Caps: the Story of Nursing*, Philadelphia, PA: Lippincott.

Rosenberg, C. (1979) 'Florence Nightingale on contagion: the hospital as a moral universe', in C. Rosenberg, (ed.) *Healing and History*, New York: Dawson.

Rosenberg, M.L. and Mercer, J.A. (1985) 'Homicide and assaultive violence', background paper submitted to Surgeon General's Workshop on Violence and Public Health, Leesburg, VA, October.

Ruddick, S. (1989) *Maternal Thinking: Toward a Politics of Peace*, Boston: Beacon Press.

Russell, D.E.H. (1982) *Rape in Marriage*, New York: Collier Books.

Russell, D.E.H. (1986) *The Secret Trauma: Incest in the Lives of Girls and Women*, New York: Basic Books.

Ryan, W. (1970) *Blaming the Victim*, New York: Vintage Books.

Salvage, J. (1985) *The Politics of Nursing*, London: Heinemann.

Sandford, R.A. (1975) 'Tolerance of debility in elderly dependants by supporters at home – its significance for hospital practice', *British Medical Journal* 3: 471–3.

Scambler, G. (1988) 'Habermas and the power of medical expertise', in G. Scamber, (ed.) *Sociological Theory and Medical Sociology*, London: Tavistock.

Schechter, S. (1982) *Women and Male Violence*, Boston: South End Press.

Schuster, I. (1981) 'Perspectives on development: the problem of nurses and nursing in Zambia', in N. Nelson, (ed.) *African Women in the Development Process*, London: Frank Cass.

Searle-Chatterjee, M. (1979) 'The polluted identity of work: a study of Benares sweepers', in S. Wallman, (ed.) *The Social Anthropology of Work*, ASA Monograph 19, London: Academic Press.

Seymer, L.R. (1932) *A General History of Nursing*, New York: Macmillan.

Sharma, P. (1981) *Caraka-Samhita, Agnivesa's treatise refined and annotated by Caraka and redacted by Drdhabala (Text with English translation)*, vol.I *Sutrasthana to Indriyasthana*, Varanasi: Chaukhamba Orientalia.

Sheldon, F.A. (1925) 'Nurses and the development of nursing at Guy's Hospital, 1725–1925', *Guy's Hospital Gazette*, Bicentenary Issue.

Sherman, L.W. and Berk, R.A. (1984) 'The specific deterrent effects of arrest for domestic assault', *American Sociological Review* 49 (4): 261–72.

Shotter, J. (1974) 'The development of personal powers', in Richards, M.P.M. (ed.) *The Integration of the Child into a Social World*, Cambridge: Cambridge University Press.

Simnet, A. (1986) 'The pursuit of respectability: women and the nursing profession 1860–1900', in R. White, (ed.) *Political Issues in Nursing*, Chichester: Wiley (quoting *The Englishwoman*, 1913, 53).

Singhal, G.D., Tripathi, S.N., and Chaturvedi, G.N. (1981) *Fundamental and Plastic Surgery Considerations in Ancient Indian Surgery, based on chapters 1–27 of Sutra-sthana of Susruta Samhita*, Varanasi: Singhal Publications.

Sister Grace (1898) 'Practical aspects of a nurse's life: Xlll-sisters', *The Hospital* 8 January: 127.

Smith, R. and Wiswell, O. (1982) *The Women of Suye Mura*, Chicago: University of Chicago Press.

Smith, W.D. (1979) *The Hippocratic Tradition*, Ithaca, NY: Cornell University Press.

Sneddon, I.B. (1983) 'Simulated disease', *Journal of the Royal College of Physicians* 17: 199–205.

Somjee, A.H. and Somjee, G. (1976) 'Co-operative dairying and the profiles of social change in India', *Economic Development and Cultural Change*, Chicago: Chicago University Press.

Spender, D. (1982) *Women of Ideas and What Men Have Done To Them*, London: Routledge & Kegan Paul.

Stanko, E.A. and Rafter, N.H. (1982) *Judge, Lawyer, Victim, Thief: Women, Gender Role and Criminal Justice*, Boston: Northeastern University Press.

Stark, E. (1984) *The Battering Syndrome: Social Knowledge, Social Therapy and the Abuse of Women*, PhD dissertation, Binghamton: SUNY.

Stark, E., Flitcraft, A., and Frazier, W. (1979) 'Medicine and patriarchal violence: the social construction of a "private" event', *International Journal of Health Services* 9: 461–93.

Stark, E. and Flitcraft, A.H. (1985) 'Spouse abuse', background paper submitted to Surgeon General's Workshop on Violence and Public Health, Leesburg, VA, October.

Stein, H.F. (1986) '"Sick People" and "Trolls": a contribution to the understanding of the dynamics of physician explanatory models', *Culture, Medicine and Psychiatry*, 10: 221–9.

Stephen, P.J. (1987) 'Career patterns of women medical graduates 1974–1984', *Medical Education* 21: 255–9.

Strachey, L. (1918) *Eminent Victorians*, London: Folio edition, 1967.

Straus, M.A., Gelles, R.J., and Steinmetz, S.K. (1980) *Behind Closed Doors: Violence in the American Family*, New York: Anchor Books.

Summers, A. (1983) 'Pride and prejudice: ladies and nurses in the Crimean War', *History Workshop* 16.

Surgeon General's Workshop on Violence and Public Health (1986) *Final Report*, Leesburg, VA, October.

Susruta, *Susrutasamhita: Susrutasamhita, Dalhanacaryaviracitaya Nibandha samgrahakhyavyakhyaya samullasita*, Nirnayasagara Press, Bombay *sake* 1837 (= AD 1951).

Taplin, J.R. (1971) 'Crisis theory: critique and reformulation', *Community Mental Health Journal* 7: 13–23.

The Runnymede Trust/The Radical Statistics Group (1981) 'A profile of black employment', in P. Braham, E. Rhodes, and M. Pearn, (eds) *Discrimination and Disadvantage in Employment: The Experience of Black Workers*, London: Harper & Row.

The Runnymede Trust/The Radical Statistics Group (1981) *Britain's Black Population*, London: Heinemann Education Books.

Tooley, S.A. (1906) *A History of Nursing in the British Empire*, London.

Torkington, P. (1984) 'The racial politics of health', in J. Larbie, and M. Clarke, (eds) *Black Health Workers*, Health Education Council/National Extension College for Training in Health and Race, London.

Trujillo, P. (1985) 'Understanding the experiences and perceptions of women who have stayed in a battered women's shelter', Master's thesis, Portland: University of Southern Maine.

Turner, B. (1984) *The Body and Society*, Oxford: Blackwell.

Ueno Chizuko (1987) 'The position of Japanese women reconsidered', *Current Anthropology* 28: 4 (Supplement), 85–8.

217

United Kingdom Central Council (1986) *Project 2000*, London.

Van Brock, N. (1961) *Recherches sur le vocabulaire medical du grec ancien: soins et guérison*, Paris: Klincksieck.

Vial, C. (1985) 'La femme athenienne vue par les orateurs', in A.M. Verilhac, (ed.) *La femme dans le mode méditerranéen*, vol. I, *Antiquité*, Lyon: Travaux de la Maison de l'Orient 10, pp. 47–60.

Venkatratnam, R. (1979) *Medical Sociology in an Indian Setting*, Delhi: The Macmillan Co.

Vygotsky, L.S. (1962) *Thought and Language*, MIT Cambridge, Mass.

Wajcman, J. (1983) *Women in Control: Dilemmas of Workers' Co-operatives*, Milton Keynes: Open University Press.

Walker, L.E. (1979) *The Battered Women*, New York: Harper Colophon Books.

Warshaw, R. (1988) *I Never Called It Rape*, New York: Harper & Row.

Weisman, C.S. and Teitelbaum, M.A. (1985) 'Physician gender and the physician–patient relationship', *Social Science and Medicine* 20: 119–27.

Welch, J. (1941) *Nursing Education Related to the Cultural Background in East and Southeast African Colonies*, New York: Columbia University Press.

Welshwoman (1908) 'Nurses and operations', letter, *Nursing Mirror* 18 January: 248–9.

Westwood, S. (1984) *All Day, Every Day: Factory and Family in the Making of Women's Lives*, London: Pluto Press.

Wilkinson, A. (1958) *A Brief History of Nursing in India and Pakistan*, Madras: The Trained Nurses Association of India.

Williams, B. (1969) 'The idea of equality', in P. Laslett and W.G. Runciman, (eds) *Philosophy, Politics and Society*. Oxford: Blackwell.

Williams, K. (1980) 'From Sarah Gamp to Florence Nightingale: a critical study of hospital nursing systems from 1840–1897', in C. Davies, (ed.) *Rewriting Nursing History*, London: Croom Helm, pp. 410–75.

Willis, R.S. (1978) 'Magic and medicine in Ufipa', in P. Morley and P. Wallis, (eds) *Culture and Curing*, King's Lynn: Daedalus.

Winternitz, M. (1972) *History of Indian Literature*, 3 vols, 2nd edition, New Delhi: Motilal Banarsidass.

Withington, E.T. (1928) *Hippocrates*, Vol. 3, London: Lock Classical Library, Heinemann.

Wolfgang, M.E. (1986) 'Interpersonal violence and public heath care: new directions, new challenges', in *Surgeon General's Workshop on Violence and Public Health: Report*, Washington, DC: Health Resource and Services Administration.

Woman Practitioner (1912) 'Hypodermic medication by nurses', letter, *British Medical Journal*, 6 April: 809.

Worcester, A. (1905) 'Nursing as a profession for college women', *Nursing Times*, 23 September: 403–4.

Yeandle, S. (1984) *Women's Working Lives: Patterns and Strategies*, London: Tavistock.

Young, A. (1976) 'Some implications of medical beliefs and practices for social anthropology', *American Anthropologist* 78: 5–24.

Young, A. (1981) 'When rational men fall sick – an inquiry into some assumptions made by medical anthropologists', *Culture, Medicine and Psychiatry* 5: 317–36.

NAME INDEX

Abel-Smith, B. 69, 80, 106, 111
Aber, S.M. 159
Adams, D. 142
Adams, R.N. 134
Aeschylus 8–9
Agnivesa 26
Ahrens, L. 145, 146
American Nurses Association 136, 144
Ardener, S. 183, 200
Aristophanes 16
Aristotle 16, 20, 21
Armstrong, D. 155
Ashley, J. 137, 143
Attorney General's Task Force on
    Family Violence 146

Baldwin, B.A. 142
Barrett, M. 138
Barrow, J. 90
Barry, K. 141
Beale, L.S. 115, 123–4
Beard, A.W. 163, 164
Beardwell, I. 87
Bellaby, P. 106
Berk, R.A. 142
Beveridge Report 151
Bogard, M. 139
Bolton, G. 70
Boston Police Department 131
Braxton-Hicks, J. 112
Breines, W. 133
British Medical Journal 113, 118,
    122–3, 124, 157–8, 163
British Medical Sociology Bulletin 171
Broverman, I.K. 138, 151
Browne, A. 132, 141
Brownmiller, S. 132, 140
Bruner, J.S. 172
Bullogh, B. 12, 18

Bullogh, V. 12, 18
Burgess, A.W. 140, 142

Cakrapanidatta 25, 26
Campbell, J. 142
Campbell-Heider, N. 173
Caraka 25–8, 29
Carmen, E.H. 141
Carpenter, M. 156, 157
Cassell, J. 154, 155
Chaney, J. 89, 94, 108
Chesler, P. 151
Chiaromonte, N. 130, 144
Chodoff, P. 164
Chodorow, N. 138
Chopoorian, T. 144
Cicourel, A.V. 134
Cloward, R.A. 138
Cohen, G. 105
Cole, T. 9
Comaroff, J. 149
Connor Versluysen, M. 14
Corea, G. 137, 138
Coyle, A. 87, 88, 107
Crateuas 16
Cunnison, S. 85

Dale, A.J. 106
Daley, M. 87, 93
Dalhana 28
Davidson, T. 132, 139
Davies, C. 7, 19
Davies, D.S. 117
Dean, M. 70
Delamont, S. 124
Delougbery, G. 11
Demosthenes 13
Department of Health and Social
    Security 170

220

Dex, S. 89
Dexter, L.A. 138
Diers, D. 36
Dobash, R.E. 141
Dobash, R.P. 141
Dock, L.L. 12
Dolan, J.A. 11, 12
Dommen, T.K. 39
Donzelot, J. 151
Douglas, M. 104, 171, 176
Doyal, L. 87, 91
Drdhabala 25–6
Driver, G. 90
Dubos, R. 135
Duffin, L. 124
Dunlop, M.J. 177
Durkheim, E. 171
Dutoit, B.M. 134

Edelstein, L. 7, 9, 10, 11, 15, 19
Ehrenreich, B. 136
Elias, P. 89
Ellenberger, H.F. 164
Engel, G.L. 135
English, D. 136
Englishwoman, The 154
Entralgo, P.L. 149

Fagin, C. 36
Ferrari, G.A. 9
Fidell, L. 157
Filliozat, J. 25, 26
Finkelhor, D. 131
Finseninstitutet 199
Fitzpatrick, M.L. 19
Flitcraft, A.H. 131, 141
Flynn, J.M. 136
Foucault, M. 19–20. 114, 119, 182, 197
Fox, M.E. 125–6
Freire, P. 144
Freud, S. 171

Galen 22
Gamarnikow, E. 19, 110, 128
Gaze, H. 153, 154
Gelles, R.J. 133, 138
Gergen, K.J. 134
Gil, D.G. 140
Gilligan, C. 138
Ginsberg, G.P. 158
Givner, D. 174
Good, B.J. 150, 180–1
Good, M.J.D. 150
Goodnow, M. 11
Goody, J. 153
Gordon, L. 133

Gould, Miss 125
Grace, Sister 127
Gullestad, M. 103
Guthrie, D. 12

Harrisson, S. 97, 107
Hedin, B. 144
Heelas, P. 173, 174
Heffron, P.B. 136
Helfer, R.E. 135
Henderson, V. 155, 170
Herfst, P. 10
Herman, J. 140, 141
Higgins, P.M. 159
Hilberman, E. 140–1
Hillband, J.H. 151
Hoekelman, R.A. 19
Hoff, L.A. 134, 139, 142, 143, 145, 146
Holmstrom, L.L. 140
Homer 13
Horwitz, A. 151
Hospital, The 118, 127
Humphreys, J. 142
Hutt, R. 154

Illich, I. 136
Ingleby, D. 151
Isocrates 13, 18

Jaeger, W. 20
James, C.W.B. 152
Jensen, D.M. 11, 191
Joly, R. 8, 11
Jones, A. 141
Jones, W.H.S. 9, 10, 11, 12, 14, 15–16,
  17, 18, 20
Jordanova, L.J. 152
Joshel, S.R. 10, 22
Jouanna, J. 9

Kakar, D.N. 50
Kangle, R.P. 29
Kempe, C.H. 135, 139
King, H. 17
Kleinman, A. 192
Kodama, K. 60, 61, 64, 65
Kolowski, B. 172
Kuper, H. 67, 76, 80

La Fontaine, J.S. 150, 171
Labour Research Department 87, 88
Lady Grigg Welfare League 71, 73
Lancet 113, 115, 116, 121, 124, 163
Le Bon, G. 164
Levitt, R. 99
Lewin, E. 110

Lienhardt, G. 180
Lipsedge, M. 151, 152, 157, 158
Littlewood, J. 170, 175, 177
Littlewood, R. 149, 151, 152, 157, 158,
    163, 164, 171
Littré, E. 9–10, 16, 17, 18, 21
Lloyd, G.E.R. 8, 9, 10, 11, 16
Lock, A. 173, 174
Lock, M. 58, 59, 64, 174
Lonie, I.M. 9
Lonsdale, S. 88
Loudon, J. 173
Lupton, T. 85
Lyons, H. 164

McBride, A. 137, 138
McEvedy, C.P. 163, 164
McIntosh, M. 138
Macleod, M.F. 106, 107
Macleod, R.B. 173
Maggs, C. 156
Mailly, R. 86
Main, B. 89
Mama, A. 91
Manpower Studies Unit 87, 91
Mansfield, J. 11
Maranhão, T. 149
Markham, J. 106
Martin, D. 140
Mauss, M. 171
Meadows, R. 162
Medical Times and Gazette 115, 119,
    123–4
Mercer, J.A. 132, 146
Miller, J.B. 138
Miller, N. 145
Mills, C.W. 130
Mitchell, J. 177
Moore, N. 111
Murphy, R.F. 132
Murphy, Y. 132

Nagarjuna 28, 174
Newberger, E.H. 140
Nightingale, F. 112, 116, 117, 118,
    120–1, 137
NOVA-NIMH 142
Nursing Mirror 117–18, 126, 127, 128
Nursing Times 117, 119, 120, 124, 125,
    153, 154
Nutton, V. 22

Oakley, A. 134, 177
O'Brien, J.E. 132
Odlum, D.M. 36
Ohnuki-Tierney, E. 57, 62, 65

Okely, J. 105
Oppert, F. 106
Oribabor, P. 106
Ortner, S.B. 150
Overseas Nursing Association 71

Pahl, R.E. 89
Parsons, T. 150
Pavey, A.E. 12, 32
Perkins, T. 88
Phillips, D.L. 151
Phizacklea, A. 90
Pillemer, K. 131
Piven, F.F. 138
Plato 11
Platt, S. 171
Pollock, D. 173
Pope, C.R. 151
Prather, J. 157
President's Task Force on Victims of
    Crime 146
Pyle, F. 35

Rafter, N.H. 141
Ramon, S. 158
Ray, P.C. 25
Reinach, S. 10, 22
Reinharz, S. 134
Reiter, R.R. 132
Reverby, S.M. 137
Rhodes, L.A. 181
Richards, M.P.M. 172
Riedel, M. 145
Rieker, P.P. 141
Robert, L. 21
Roberts, H. 134
Roberts, S. 144
Robinson, O. 88–9
Robinson, V. 12, 18
Rosenberg, C. 70
Rosenberg, M.L. 132, 146
Ruddick, S. 138
Runnymeade, Trust/Radical Statistics
    Group 90
Russell, D.E.H. 141
Ryan, W. 141

Salvage, J. 170
Schechter, S. 141
Schuster, I. 76
Searle-Chatterjee, M. 104
Segal, B. 151
Seymer, L.R. 13
Sheldon, F.A. 111
Sherman, L.W. 142
Shotter, J. 172

Simnet, A. 154
Smith, R. 60
Smith, W.D. 11
Sneddon, I.B. 162
Somjee, A.H. 48
Somjee, G. 48
Spender, D. 137
Stanko, E.A. 141
Stark, E. 131, 141
Stephen, P.J. 152
Stewart, I.M. 12
Straus, M.A. 132, 133
Summers, A. 69
Surgeon General's Workshop on
    Violence and Public Health 146
Susruta 28–9, 32

Tacitus 13
Taplin, J.R. 139
Thucydides 13
Times, The 148
Tooley, S.A. 68
Tribhuvandas Foundation 50
Trujillo, P. 142
Turner, B. 151–2, 171

United Kingdom Central Council 107

Van Brock, N. 8, 17, 21
Vegetti, M. 9
Venkatratnam, R. 43
Vygotsky, L.S. 172

Wajcman, J. 92
Walker, A. 147
Walker, L.E. 144
Wall, A. 99
Wallace, J. 88
Warshaw, R. 141
Welch, J. 71–2, 75
Wilkinson, A. 32
Williams, B. 143
Williams, K. 7
Winternitz, M. 25
Wiswell, O. 60
Withington, E.T. 9, 16
Wolfgang, M.E. 132
Worcester, A. 117, 120, 124

Xenophon 12

Yeandle, S. 92, 98–9
Young, A. 149, 182, 192

Zahn, M.S. 145

SUBJECT INDEX

abuse *see* violence
Africa: colonial nursing in 67–77;
    community health in 71–2; *see also*
    Uganda
Afro-Caribbean women, work patterns
    of 89–91
age: of hospital domestics 92–4; and
    work patterns 89
Agnivesa 26
alternative medicine: and cancer
    195–7; in Japan 58–9, 64; and
    nurses 135, 136; *see also* holism
ambiguity: management of 170–85;
    and nurses' role 190–201
animal health care 48
anthropology: of Ancient Greece 7–23;
    and gender 110–29, 148–65; and
    hospital domestics 84–108; and
    illness 190–201; in India 25–9,
    31–54; in Japan 56–65; and nurses'
    role 170–85; in Uganda 67–82; and
    violence 130–47
army: damages Ugandan hospital
    77–8; medical staff in 29, 34–5
Arthasastra 29
Asklepios, temple medicine of 11
assistants, medical: in Ancient Greece
    10–15, 17–19, 22–3; in Ancient
    India 26–9
Atreya 26
auxiliary, nursing 99
Ayurveda 32
ayurvedic medical system 25, 37

battered wives 131–2, 140–1, 143, 144,
    145
behaviour, social, and bodily functions
    171–7, 181–2
Bhore Committee Report (1946) 35

biomedicine: and cancer 190–1, 192,
    194, 195–8, 200, 201; and health
    134–6
bowel control *see* excretion
Burgess, Ann 140, 142

cancer: and alternative medicine
    195–7; and biomedicine 190–1,
    192, 194, 195–8, 200, 201;
    patients' attitudes to 192–4;
    psycho-social factors 192–5, 196–7,
    198, 199–200, 201
Carakasamhita 25–8
caste system: of dais 51–2; and doctors
    38, 43; and nurses 29, 32–3, 35,
    37–43, 53–4
Charaka 32
childbirth *see* obstetrics
children: and excretion 172–3; and
    factitious illness 162; and violence
    139–40; and work patterns 89
Civil Rights movement 133
class, social 125; in colonies 69–70,
    73–4; in India 40–3, 53–4; in Japan
    60, 61
cleaners *see* domestics
COHSE 87
colonies: attractions 73; history 68–77;
    recruitment for 34–5, 52, 69–70,
    73–4; training 70–2, 74–6;
    uniforms 70, 76, 78, 82; working
    conditions 74–7
communication, hidden 180–4
community health service: in Africa
    71–2; in India 35, 47–52
contract cleaning 85–6, 87, 107
control: of bodily functions 171–7; and
    gender in Ancient Greece 19–23;
    of nursing departments 111–12;

and order in Uganda 80–2; of work 104

dais (midwives) 29, 33, 36; in rural India 50–2, 53
death and hospital domestics 100–1
Denmark: cancer hospitals 190–201; Cancer Society 191
Descartes, René 135
deviance and disability 176
diagnosis: and prescription 117–23; theory of 180–1
dirt *see* pollution
disability, social reaction to 176–7
disease *see* biomedicine; illness
doctors: in Ancient Greece 8–10, 14–23; attitudes to illness 134–6, 190–1, 192, 194–8, 199; and caste system 38, 43; and communication 181; and drug overdose 157–8; and factitious illness 159, 162, 163, 164, 165; female 152, 163–4; in India 26–9, 33–4; in Japan 63; and male role 148–52, 154–6; and nursing 111–29, 153–6, 192–201; and patients 149, 150, 184; power of 115–16, 123–9, 197–8; psychopathologies 158; sexuality 155–6; in Uganda 78; and violence 134–6, 139–47
domestics, hospital 84–108; attitudes to work 85–6, 92–4; boundary with nursing 98–100, 105–7, 177–8; and contract cleaning 85–6, 87, 107; and death 100–1; hours of work 87–92, 107–8; identity 102–5; networks 93–4, 108; and nurses 101–2; and patient contact 95–102; pollution beliefs 103–5; salary 86–92, 106–7; social differentiation 88–94, 107–8; status 85, 93–4, 102–3, 107; work conditions 85–8; work organisation 95–100
drama, and medicine 8–10
drugs: in Ancient World 13–14; and nursing techniques 43–4; overdose 157–8; psychotropic 157–8; *see also* prescription

economics *see* salaries
education, general 43, 74–6; see also training
environment, and disease 135–6, 144
ethnicity, and work patterns 89–91
excretion, bodily 170–85; and communication 180–4; control of, 171–7; incontinence 174–7; and nurses, 177–84; and pollution 173, 176–7; social code 171–80

family care for patients: Ancient Greece 12–13, 17–18; India 33; Japan 58–9, 62; Uganda 80–1
female *see* women
femininity *see* gender
feminism 143; and violence 133–4, 140–1
Finseninstitutet 191, 199
Freud, Sigmund 140, 155–6

Ganser psychosis 159
gender: in Ancient Greece 10–15, 17–23; female doctors 152, 163–4; female role of nurse 110–11, 123–9, 137, 148–9, 153–65, 201; female role of patient 148–52; in Japan 63; male nurses 153; male role of doctor 148–9, 152, 155; *see also* power; status
generational shifts 43–7
Goldmark Report (1923) 137
Greece, Ancient 7–23; gender and control 19–23; healers 8–10, 14–23; illness 20–2; medical assistants 10–15, 17–19, 22–3; medicine as craft 8–10; midwives 21, 22; nursing role 10–19; women's role 10–11, 12–15, 17–23
gynaecology: in Ancient Greece 21–2; and female doctors 152
gypsies, pollution beliefs of 104–5

healers 26–9; *see also iatroi*
health: and Ancient Greeks 20; and Japanese 56–60; social factors 135–6; *see also* illness
health service: African 71–2; Indian 31, 32, 33, 34; rural 35, 47–52, 71–2; and violence 132–47; *see also* hospitals
Hippocratic: medicine 8–23; texts 9–10, 14–18, 20, 21, 26
holism: and cancer 192–4, 195, 196–7, 198, 199–200, 201; and health 135–6, 144–5; in Japan 58–9, 64
hospitals: 'addiction syndrome' 161–2; cancer 190–201; contract cleaning 85–6, 87, 107; domestic work 84–108; and families 58–9, 62, 80–1; hierarchy 111–12, 113–14, 125–9, 197–8; Indian 32, 33, 34; Japanese 58–9; social code in

178–80; Ugandan 77–82; ward organisation 177–80
hostels 74–5, 156–7
hygiene: in colonies 70; and excreta 173, 176; and hospital domestics 103–5; in Japan 56–8; in Uganda 81–2
hysteria 159, 163–5

iatroi (healers) 8–10, 14–23; assistants 10–15, 17–19, 22–3; duties 14–15; power of 19–23; training 18–19
illness: in Ancient Greece 20–2; biomedical factors 134–6, 190–1, 192, 194, 195–8, 200, 201; cancer 190–201; factitious 158–65; in Japan 56–60; of nurses 158–65; patients' attitudes to 192–4; psychosocial factors 190–1, 192, 194–201; social responses 149–50; *see also* health; patients
incontinence 174–7
India 31–54; Ancient 25–9; caste system 32–3, 35, 37–43, 53–4; colonial 34–5, 52; community health 35, 47–52; gender roles 29, 33–4, 39, 53; generational shifts 43–7; history 32–6; marriage 39–43, 53; medical assistants 26–9; midwives 29, 33, 36, 50–3; nurses' image 36–47, 52–4; salaries 39–43, 44–6, 53; training 28, 34–5, 40–3
Industrial Revolution 151

Japan 56–65; alternative medicine in 58–9, 64; attitudes to illness 56–60; family care for patients 58–9, 62; gender roles 63; midwives 59–60; nurses' image 62–5; pollution beliefs 56–8, 62, 65; status 60, 61, 62, 65; training 60–2, 64–5; Western medicine in 56, 58, 60–1

Karamsad school of nursing 41, 42

labour *see* work
language, function of 174, 180–1
Loin Pain Haematuria 159–61
Low Pay Unit 86

male *see* men, gender
malingering 159–62
manipulation 126–8, 154, 157–8
marriage: in India 39–43, 53; in Japan 63
matron, duties 111, 112

mediators 63, 177–85, 190–201
medical: gaze 119, 197–8, 200; staff *see* assistants, auxiliary, doctors, healers, midwives, nurses
medicine: as craft 8–10; preventive 72–3; *see also* drugs
men: in nursing 153; victims of violence 141–2; violent 142, 145; and wives' work 91–2
midwives: in Ancient Greece 21, 22; in India 29, 33, 36, 50–2, 53; in Japan 59–60; *see also* obstetrics
military *see* army
missions 35, 52, 71
morality: of Ancient Greeks 19–20; and colonial nurses 69–70, 75; in India 39
mothering role 173, 182; absence in India 36, 37
Mudaliar Committee Report (1961) 35
Mulago Hospital 67, 77–82
Munchasen's Syndrome by Proxy 161–2

Nalanda 32
Nightingale, Florence 34, 64, 68, 110–14, 136–7
normative theory 138–9
NUPE 86, 87
nurses and nursing: children's 10, 22; concepts of 170–85, 190–201; and doctors 111–29, 153–6, 192–201; gender roles 110–29, 148–65; and hospital domestics 98–100, 101–2, 105–7; and illness 148–65, 190–201; image 36–47, 52–4, 62–5, 153–4; male 153; and patients 157–8, 177–85, 190–7, 198–201; psychopathologies 158–65; reform 110–29; role 10–19, 78–82, 170–85, 190–201; sexuality 75, 153, 156–7; status 60–2, 65, 76, 82, 110–29, 197–8; student 156–7; and violence 142–5, 147; wet 10, 29; *see also* Ancient Greece, hospitals, India, Japan, midwives, training, Uganda

observation and reporting 63–4, 118–23
obstetrics: in Ancient Greece 18, 21, 22; and female doctors 152; in India 29, 33, 36, 50–1; in Japan 59–60
Overseas Nursing Association 68, 69–70, 71

patients: in Ancient Greece 15–17, 20–2; attitudes to illness 192–4; and bowel control 178–85; cancer 190–7; and doctors 149, 150, 184; female 21–2, 33–4; female role of 148–52; and hidden texts 180–4; and hospital domestics 95–102; Indian 29, 36–7; Japanese 58–9, 62; and nursing role 157–8, 177–85, 190–7, 198–201; and social code 178–80; troublesome 199; Ugandan 80–1

politics and Ugandan hospital 77–8

pollution beliefs: and excreta 173, 176–7; and gypsies 104–5; and hospital domestics 103–5; in India 31, 32–3, 35, 38, 53; in Japan 56–8, 62, 65; and nurses 177–80

power: in Ancient Greece 19–23; of doctors 115–16, 123–9, 197–8; in society 150–1; see also status

pregnancy 75

prescription, drug 117–18, 119–23

privatisation of hospital cleaning 85–6, 107

psychology 193, 194–5, 196–7, 198, 199–200, 201

psychopathology 158–65; of doctors 158; of nurses and violence 144–6

psychosocial aspects of illness 192–5, 196–7, 198, 199–200, 201

purity 177; in Japan 57

quacks in Ancient Greece 9–10, 11

race and recruitment 34–5

radiation levels 96

rape 140

recruitment: of colonial nurses 34–5, 52, 69–70, 73–4; of doctors in Ancient India 28; of domestic staff 91, 93–4

reform 110–29; ambivalence to 114–15; and diagnosis 117–23; and doctors 111–29; and gender 110–11, 123–9; hierarchy 111–12, 113–14; subordination 115–16, 123–9; training 112–14, 137; work division 116–20

relatives see family

religion: and health 135; in India 38–9, 41, 42–3; missions 35, 52, 71; see also caste

role 170–85, 190–201; in Ancient Greece 10–19; in India 36–47,

52–4; in Japan 62–5; in Uganda 78–82; of women 137, 150–2

Royal Free Disease 163–4

rural health service see community

salaries: of hospital domestics 86–92, 106–7; in India 39–43, 44–6, 53; in Uganda 78, 79

Savage, Wendy 152

self, sense of 173–7, 182–3

sexuality 75, 153, 156–7; and doctors 155–6

shame, and bowel control 174–7

sisters, duties of 111–12

social conditions: and health 135–6; and violence 144–7 socialization 74–6, 156–7

Srivastava Committee Report (1975) 35

status 110–29, 197–8; of doctors 171; of health workers 49, 51–52; of hospital domestics 85, 93–4, 102–3, 107; in Japan 60, 61, 62, 65; in Uganda 76, 82; of women 137, 150–2

Sunyavada 174

superstition: in Ancient Greece 11; in Japan 57, 59

Surgeon General's Workshop on Violence and Public Health (1985) 142–3, 144, 146

Susruta 32

Susrutasamhità 28–9

systems theory 138–9

Taxila 26, 32

techne (craft) 8–10

time and identity 182–3

training: in Africa 71–2; of health workers 50–1, 52; in India 28, 34–5, 40–3; in Japan 60–2, 64–5; after reform 112–14, 137; schools 40–3; and segregation 74–6, 156–7; in Uganda 70–2, 74–6

transference and doctors 155–6

Tribhuvandas Foundation 47–52

Trivandrum nursing school 41–2

Uganda 67–82: colonial 68–77; control and order 80–2; crisis in 77–82; family care for patients 80–1; native culture 72, 74–6, 80–1; nurses' role 78–82; salary 78, 79; status 76, 82; training 70–2, 74–6; uniforms 70, 76, 78, 82; working conditions 77–82

uniforms 70, 76, 78, 82

United States, violence in 130–47
Usui, Hiroko 64

Vietnam War Veterans 141
violence 130–47; and children 139–40;
    and feminism 133–4, 140–1; and
    helping agencies 132–47; and
    nurses 142–5, 147; programmes
    for victims 139–42; social factors
    135–6, 138–9, 144–7; statistics
    131–2; theories 133–4; and women
    131–2, 138, 140–1, 143, 144, 145
voluntary organisations 35

West Indies see Afro-Caribbean
women: in Ancient Greece 10–11,
    12–15, 17–23; doctors 152, 163–4;
    healers 21–2, 23; in India 33–5; in
    Japan 63; patients 21–2, 33–4;
    status 137, 150–2; and violence
    131–2, 138, 140–1, 143, 144, 145;
    see also domestics; feminism;
    gender; nurses
work: conditions 45–7, 77–82;
    demarcation 98–100, 105–7,
    117–23, 151, 153, 177–8; see also
    domestics